Holding the Line on the River of Death

Other Books by Eric J. Wittenberg

We Have It Damned Hard Out Here:
The Civil War Letters of Sgt. Thomas W. Smith, Sixth Pennsylvania Cavalry (1999)

One of Custer's Wolverines:
The Civil War Letters of Brevet Brigadier General James H. Kidd, 6th Michigan Cavalry (2000)

Under Custer's Command: The Civil War Journal of James Henry Avery (2000)

At Custer's Side: The Civil War Writings of James Harvey Kidd (2001)

Glory Enough for All: Sheridan's Second Raid and the Battle of Trevilian Station (2001)

With Sheridan in the Final Campaign Against Lee (2002)

Little Phil:
A Reassessment of the Civil War Leadership of Gen. Philip H. Sheridan (2002)

The Union Cavalry Comes of Age: Hartwood Church to Brandy Station, 1863 (2003)

The Battle of Monroe's Crossroads and the Civil War's Final Campaign (2006)

Plenty of Blame to Go Around:
Jeb Stuart's Controversial Ride to Gettysburg (with J. David Petruzzi, 2006)

Rush's Lancers: The Sixth Pennsylvania Cavalry in the Civil War (2007)

One Continuous Fight: The Retreat from Gettysburg and the Pursuit of Lee's Army of Northern Virginia, July 4-14, 1863 (with J. David Petruzzi and Michael F. Nugent, 2008)

Like a Meteor Blazing Brightly:
The Short but Controversial Life of Colonel Ulric Dahlgren (2009)

The Battle of Brandy Station: North America's Largest Cavalry Battle (2010)

Gettysburg's Forgotten Cavalry Actions:
Farnsworth's Charge, South Cavalry Field and the Battle of Fairfield (Second Edition, 2011)

The Battle of White Sulphur Springs; Averell Fails to Secure West Virginia (2011)

Protecting the Flank at Gettysburg: The Battles for Brinkerhoff's Ridge and East Cavalry Field (Second Edition, 2013)

The Devil's to Pay: John Buford at Gettysburg: A History and Walking Tour (2014)

The Second Battle of Winchester:
The Confederate Victory That Opened the Door to Gettysburg (with Scott L. Mingus Sr., 2016)

Holding the Line on the River of Death

Union Mounted Forces at the Battle of Chickamauga, September 18, 1863

Eric J. Wittenberg

SB

Savas Beatie
California

Library of Congress Cataloging-in-Publication Data

Names: Wittenberg, Eric J., 1961-author.
Title: Holding the Line on the River of Death: Union Mounted Forces at the Battle of Chickamauga, September 18, 1863 / by Eric J. Wittenberg.
Description: First edition. | El Dorado Hills, California: Savas Beatie LLC, [2018] Includes bibliographical references.
Identifiers: LCCN 2018040776| ISBN 9781611214307 (hardcover: alk. paper) | ISBN 9781611214314 (ebk)
Subjects: LCSH: Chickamauga, Battle of, Ga., 1863.
Classification: LCC E475.81 .W68 2018 | DDC 973.7/35—dc23
LC record available at https://lccn.loc.gov/2018040776

First Edition, First Printing

SB

Published by
Savas Beatie LLC
989 Governor Drive, Suite 102
El Dorado Hills, CA 95762

Phone: 916-941-6896
(web) www.savasbeatie.com
(E-mail) sales@savasbeatie.com

Our titles are available at special discounts for bulk purchases. For more details, contact us at sales@savasbeatie.com.

Proudly printed in the United States of America.

FSC www.fsc.org MIX Paper from responsible sources FSC® C011935

One must be born a light-cavalryman. No other position requires so much natural aptitude, such innate genius for war, as that of an officer of that arm. The qualities which make the superior man—*intelligence, will, force*—should be found united in him. Constantly left dependent on himself, exposed to frequent combats, responsible not only for his own command, but as well for that which he protects and guards, the employment of his physical and moral powers is continuous. The profession which he practises is a rude one, but the opportunities of distinguishing himself are presented daily—glorious compensation which the more richly rewards his labors by enabling his true worth to become the sooner known.

— Major General Antoine Fortuné De Brack, 1831

Table of Contents

Table of Contents (continued)

List of Maps

List of Illustrations

List of Illustrations (continued)

List of Illustrations (continued)

Foreword

Most students of the American Civil War have a favorite battlefield. I certainly do: Chickamauga, the first and largest of our national military parks. As readers of my own books dealing with that engagement know, my interest grew out of a project that began in 1999. I went to the battlefield to do some research. Once there, I realized just how little had been written about one of the Civil War's largest battles.

My second favorite is the war's most popular destination: Gettysburg. What a contrast. No dearth of interest there. That park teems with tourists and students of the battle for most of the year. The bookstore has shelf after shelf filled with Gettysburg-related titles.

Chickamauga didn't lack for historical attention because it lacked drama, complexity, human interest, or compelling personal stories. The Chickamauga Campaign was among the most complex military operations of the war. It involved opposed river-crossings, mountain ascensions, complicated logistical challenges, and a tremendously violent three-day contest (evening of September 18 through September 20, 1863) as scene-stealing finale. That titanic battle involved 130,000 men, more than 34,000 of whom became casualties. It was the second-bloodiest fight of the entire war. It was also one of the most confusing campaigns and battles, a back-and-forth contest conducted amidst the heavily wooded hills and valleys of North Georgia. I suspect it was this very confusion that kept historians at arms-length. It is an exceedingly difficult battle to understand, let alone interpret for the general reader.

As my interest in the battle of Chickamauga moved from casual to serious, I immediately noted a dearth of specialist studies surrounding the campaign. Not one single-day monograph of any of the three days that comprised the battle existed, nor were there any detailed cavalry or artillery studies, and very few specialized unit or leadership monographs. This last is especially surprising because Chickamauga had some of the most complicated command and leadership relationships of all Civil War battles, with more than its share of disputatious officers and highly consequential military blunders—often with dire consequences.

Even many of the participants lacked biographies. When I began my own study of the campaign, there was only one biography of Union Major General William Rosecrans and two concerning Confederate Braxton Bragg. Moreover, most of that work was quite dated. Even Major General George Thomas, who has been the subject of four books, lacked a recent biographer, with the best published work on him dating back to 1961. Any Civil War student wishing to learn more about Chickamauga had not choice but to piece together scraps of information almost entirely from primary sources. And that is the marvelous thing about exploring Chickamauga. The original participants left us a rich trove of eyewitness accounts, both published and unpublished. Fortunately, they number in the thousands—more than even I could use in my own three-volume narrative history of the battle.

I am happy to report that modern interest in Chickamauga (indeed, in the whole of the Western Theater) is on the upswing. Nothing could delight me more. When I first started visiting the park, its bookstore had only a single short shelf devoted to works on the topic. Happily, fifteen years later, published titles relating to Chickamauga take up an entire bookcase. I firmly believe that writing about civil war battles is not a zero-sum game; each new work sparks additional interest, and, in time, provokes response. More readers get drawn in, and the cycle continues.

One of the most fascinating aspects of the campaign is the role played by the Union and Confederate cavalry. Rather than launch a frontal assault against the Confederate defenses of Chattanooga, Federal commander Rosecrans adopted an operational scheme of sweeping maneuver aimed at leveraging his opponent out of the city by threatening Bragg's supply lines. Effective cavalry operations were critical to the successful execution of Rosecrans's plans, and conversely, vital to Bragg's effort to foil those plans. In 2009, I authored my own examination of the Confederate side of that equation called *Failure in the Saddle: Nathan Bedford Forrest, Joseph Wheeler, and the Confederate Cavalry in the Chickamauga Campaign* (Savas Beatie). That book only told part of the story. More remained to be done.

Eric Wittenberg is no stranger to cavalry operations. Indeed, his long list of publications that document the history of the Cavalry Corps of the Army of the Potomac have made him pre-eminent among a growing field of Civil War cavalry scholars. His deep understanding of the role played by the Union Cavalry at Gettysburg has led to some of his best work. There is no better account of the Federal horse soldiers' vital role in the fighting of July 1, 1863, than his 2014 volume *"The Devil's to Pay": John Buford at Gettysburg. A History and Walking Tour* (Savas Beatie). Buford's role in developing a more complete picture of Confederate intentions for his superiors, and in delaying the approaching Rebel troops long enough for Union infantry to reach the field, is now often recognized as a critical component of the Army of the Potomac's ultimate victory at that Pennsylvania crossroads town. The details concerning how Buford accomplished his mission, however, were frequently misunderstood in earlier works on the subject. Eric's work on Buford reveals a deep understanding of the Union cavalryman's mission and intentions. He also demonstrates not only a thorough grasp of cavalry tactics of the time, but also explains them to the reader with force and clarity.

The opening of the battle of Chickamauga, fought in a different theater of the war just three months later, contains many parallels to that initial engagement on the ridges west of Gettysburg. In North Georgia, two Federal mounted brigades confronted many times their number of Confederate troops. Once again, a thin screen of Union horsemen delayed several greatly superior enemy infantry columns, buying precious time for the Federal Army commander—Rosecrans, this time—to react. In Georgia the fight was for bridges, but the action played out very similarly to the contest in Pennsylvania. The Blue troopers gave ground grudgingly, slowing the enemy and ultimately frustrating Bragg's plans for September 18, 1863. Those Union troopers and mounted infantrymen belonged to two very interesting commands: The brigades of Cols. Robert H. G. Minty and John T. Wilder.

Minty was an émigré, born in Ireland to parents of English descent. Before coming to America he followed in his father's footsteps and gained experience in the British army. Once in the new world, Minty pursued engineering and worked for the railroads. When war arrived he returned to uniform and by September of 1863 was in command of a trio of first-rate cavalry regiments: the 4th Michigan, 7th Pennsylvania, and 4th U.S. Regulars.

A native-born young entrepreneur from Indiana, Wilder had no pre-war military experience. He learned his martial trade on the job by leading the 17th Indiana Infantry, and by the time of Chickamauga commanded a brigade of mounted infantry. In early 1863, Wilder, who had always been an innovative thinker, proposed mounting his infantrymen and arming them with Spencer repeating rifles for enhanced firepower. This idea dovetailed nicely with Rosecrans's own thoughts on the subject and Wilder was allowed to proceed. By the summer of that year, Wilder's brigade was outsized both in numbers and, thanks to the Spencers, more than a match for any similar-sized body of Confederates. Wilder proved the worth of his scheme at Hoover's Gap on June 24, 1863.

Each of these brigades operated mostly independently, detached from their usual divisions, and each commander was entrusted by Rosecrans with responsibilities well beyond their nominal rank and position. Wilder's large brigade included the 17th and 72nd Indiana, as well as the 92nd, 98th, and 123rd Illinois, though regiments were often detached or off on independent missions of their own. Both Minty and Wilder tended to be supremely confident, even a bit brash. On September 18, they each proved they could match deeds to words. When Eric mentioned to me that he wanted to visit Chickamauga, and more specifically, explore the areas where Minty and Wilder made their fights, I was delighted to help. When he revealed that he was thinking of writing on the subject, I was even more pleased and offered to lend a hand.

Holding the Line on the River of Death is exactly the sort of tactical study I wished I had available to me when I first began learning about the battle. It is also a uniquely focused monograph worthy of the subject.

David A. Powell
Chicago, Illinois

Preface

My studies of Brig. Gen. John Buford's magnificently designed and perfectly executed delaying action on the first day of the battle of Gettysburg led naturally to the equally magnificent delaying actions designed and executed by Union Cols. Robert H. G. Minty and John T. Wilder on the first day of the battle of Chickamauga, September 18, 1863. Buford's delaying action was intended to trade space for time to allow the main body of the Army of the Potomac to come up and take position so as to hold the high ground to the south of the town of Gettysburg. By contrast, the stands by Minty and Wilder were intended to hold off Gen. Braxton Bragg's Army of Tennessee long enough to allow Maj. Gen. William S. Rosecrans's Army of the Cumberland to entirely realign its position so that it would not be cut off from its base of operations at Chattanooga and to prevent Bragg from outflanking the Army of the Cumberland and defeating it in detail. Buford knew that Maj. Gen. John F. Reynolds and his 1st Corps were on their way to reinforce his cavalry if he could hold out long enough for them to get there. Minty and Wilder, by contrast, had no such expectation. They had no realistic expectation of being reinforced. They would either hold out long enough to disrupt Bragg's plans or they would fail. The fate of the Army of the Cumberland depended on their success.

With only 973 officers and men and 2 pieces of artillery, Minty delayed the advance of 8,000 Confederate infantry at Reed's Bridge across West Chickamauga Creek while a regiment and a half of Wilder's Lightning

Brigade held Alexander's Bridge, two and a half miles downstream, against a like number of enemy infantry. Minty's soldiers opened the battle of Chickamauga that morning, and they held for more than six hours against vast odds until they were finally flanked out of their position at Reed's Bridge by Confederate infantry fording the Chickamauga downstream. Wilder's men held on for about two hours until their stout resistance compelled Maj. Gen. William H. T. Walker to abandon further direct assaults on Alexander's Bridge and to instead find a ford to flank both Wilder and Minty out of their positions. In the process, they used up an entire day and forced an extremely frustrated Bragg to alter dramatically his well-laid plan for the coming battle. That delay also bought sufficient time for Rosecrans to recognize the exposed and dangerous position his army was in and to begin the process of completely realigning the Army of the Cumberland to prevent it from being cut off from its base of supply and operations at Chattanooga.

After nightfall, the brigades of Minty and Wilder, reinforced by two regiments of infantry, fell back to a position on the Viniard farmstead, where they repulsed a determined nighttime attack by Bragg's infantry that was intended to reach and hold the La Fayette Road, which was the main and direct route to Chattanooga used by Rosecrans's army. Had the Union troops failed to repulse those attacks on the Viniard farm, the Army of Tennessee would have interdicted the La Fayette Road and would have interposed itself squarely between Rosecrans's army and its base of operations in Chattanooga, with most of Bragg's army on its flanks, in a position to destroy the Union army. Instead, Minty and Wilder held their positions, repulsed the Confederate attacks, and kept the La Fayette Road open for use by the Army of the Cumberland and permitted Rosecrans to reposition his army so that it was no longer in danger of being outflanked. This small unit action saved the Army of the Cumberland on the night of September 18, 1863.

This book addresses these actions in detail for the first time, as this is the first monograph devoted solely to the actions of September 18, 1863. It places them squarely in the context of the battle of Chickamauga as a whole and brings focus to these unheralded stands by Minty and Wilder that day. It is intended to serve as a companion volume to my 2014 book, *The Devil's to Pay: John Buford at Gettysburg: A History and Walking Tour*. In addition to addressing these actions in detail, it includes orders of battle for the actions at Reed's and Alexander's Bridges, and it also includes an appendix that defines the sort of vidette, patrol, and outpost duty performed by both Minty and Wilder at Chickamauga and by John Buford at Gettysburg in greater detail than anywhere else. Finally, it includes a detailed walking and driving tour of the pertinent portions of the great battlefield at Chickamauga addressed by these actions.

Unlike John Buford, who did not survive 1863, both Minty and Wilder lived to old age. Minty, in particular, spent decades after the war documenting his exploits and those of the men who followed his guidon into battle. Similarly, Wilder also left his own accounts of the events of September 18, 1863. By contrast, Buford died before he could document the events of July 1, 1863 in any fashion other than his after-action report of the battle of Gettysburg, which made it more difficult to document those events. The existence and accessibility of the accounts by Minty and Wilder made it easier to describe these events in full detail for the first time.

When you have finished reading this narrative, I hope you will have gained an appreciation for the sacrifices of Minty, Wilder, and their commands as they bought time to save the Army of the Cumberland from the trap laid for it by a wily Braxton Bragg that day.

A brief note about sources: Thanks to the largesse of Dave Powell, I was able to review several hundred primary sources that deal with the battle of Chickamauga before beginning to write. If I were so inclined to do so, I could fill 20 or 30 pages of bibliography listing them all. Rather than cluttering up the bibliography with a long list of sources that were simply glanced at but played no particular role in the construction of this narrative, I have instead limited the entries in the bibliography to those sources that are actually cited in the footnotes or in the main text itself. This means that the bibliography represents only a fraction of the sources I actually reviewed in writing this book.

As with every project of this nature, I owe a great debt of gratitude to a number of people without whose assistance this project would not have been possible. First and foremost, I am incredibly grateful to my good friend David A. Powell, who is the author of the definitive study of the battle of Chickamauga. Dave has spent years gathering information and insight on the Chickamauga campaign. This book has its roots in a weekend spent on the battlefield with Dave and several late-night conversations that persuaded me to proceed. Dave then saved me several years' worth of research by sharing the fruits of his labors. His generosity in providing me with a treasure trove of material made this project possible. He then assisted me in laying out the walking and driving tour at the end of the book, reviewed the manuscript for accuracy, and wrote the excellent foreword that follows.

National Park Service historians Jim Ogden and Lee White also provided valuable material. Rand Bitter, who has documented the life and work of Robert H. G. Minty, also provided invaluable material and some of the photographic images that grace this work. Larry Fryer, the authority on the 7th Pennsylvania Cavalry, gave me some of his large trove of information on the Saber Regiment to use in this project. Ken Turner gave me an image of Capt. Charles C. Davis of the 7th Pennsylvania to use here.

I am also grateful to my two tour assistants, Mike Peters and Tim Maurice, who rendered a great deal of assistance in putting together the walking-driving tour found at the end of this book. My cousin David Wittenberg also assisted with the process of laying out the tour. I appreciate the roles played by all of them.

The excellent maps of master cartographer Mark Anderson Moore grace this volume. I am honored to have them grace the pages of this book.

This is now the seventh book I have done with the good folks at Savas Beatie. I greatly appreciate Theodore P. Savas's support of my work and the freedom he gives me in choosing the topics I research and write about. Ted and his excellent staff design and make a handsome book, and they know how to market and sell those books. I value this close working relationship that I have with the folks at Savas Beatie, and I look forward to continuing it into the future.

Finally, as always, I owe the largest debt of all to my much-loved and long-suffering wife, travel companion, photographer, and battlefield tour assistant, Susan Skilken Wittenberg. None of what I do in this field of endeavor would be possible without Susan's support and endless patience, and I am deeply grateful to her for all of it.

Eric J. Wittenberg
Columbus, Ohio

Chapter One

The Union Forces

In order to appreciate the defensive stands conducted by Robert H. G. Minty's troopers at Reed's Bridge and John T. Wilder's Lightning Brigade at Alexander's Bridge, we need to get a sense of who the Union troopers were and how they ended up being the right men in the right place. Neither commander was a professional soldier, and neither had West Point training. Both, however, performed magnificently at Chickamauga, and both played critical roles in the drama that played out there. Their actions helped save the Army of the Cumberland from destruction.

Colonel Robert H. G. Minty and his Saber Brigade

Robert Horatio George Minty was born in Westport, County Mayo, Ireland, on December 4, 1831. His father was born in Scotland and his mother was born in Ireland. His father was a respected officer in the British Army, serving in the 1st West India Regiment of Foot, a black regiment with white officers. After his father died of a tropical fever in 1848, the 17-year-old Minty entered the British Army as an ensign and served five years in the West Indies, Honduras, and along the west coast of Africa. After contracting a severe attack of inflammation of the liver while serving in Sierra Leone in September 1853, Minty sold his

Col. Robert H. G. Minty as a British soldier in the 1850's. *Judith Minty*

commission and migrated to Ontario, Canada.[1]

Once settled, Minty took up railroading as a profession. He worked on the Great Western Railroad Company, which ran trains across Ontario Niagara Falls on the American side and Sarnia and Windsor, Ontario, on the Canadian side. On November 5, 1857, he married Grace Ann Abbott of London, Ontario, Canada, in London's St. Paul's Cathedral. Observers described the newlyweds as "a brilliant match . . . a handsome couple, well to-do, socially prominent, traveled, proud, and secure."[2] Their first child, Anna Rebecca Grace "Nan" Minty, was born on September 29, 1858. After Nan's birth, the family moved to Detroit, Michigan, so Robert could accept employment with the Detroit and Milwaukee Railway. He was working there as a freight agent when the storm clouds of war began gathering in the spring of 1861.[3]

Possessing some prior military experience, Minty was commissioned a major in the 2nd Michigan Cavalry in 1861, the lieutenant colonel of the 3rd Michigan Cavalry a few weeks afterward, and was appointed colonel of the 4th Michigan Cavalry on July 31, 1862. He commanded the brigade that included the 4th Michigan for most of its service in the field. Minty, an Irish-born soldier of fortune, was one of a kind, having

1 John Fitch, *Annals of the Army of the Cumberland: Biographies, Descriptions of Departments, Accounts of Expeditions, Skirmishes, and Battles* (Philadelphia: J. B. Lippincott, 1864), 205.

2 Rand K. Bitter, *Minty and His Cavalry: A History of the Saber Brigade and Its Commander* (N.p.: Privately published, 2006), 10.

3 William H. Powell, ed., *Officers of the Army and Navy (Volunteer) Who Served in the Civil War* (Philadelphia: L. R. Hamersly & Co., 1893), 313.

A previously unpublished image of Col. Robert H. G. Minty early in the war, probably in 1862. Note the outsized shoulder straps. *May Revell*

developed a fondness for the saber while fighting for the queen in the Caribbean islands and western Africa.

The diminutive Minty had a wild mane of light brown hair and a thick beard. He stood five feet seven inches tall and had hazel eyes. He also possessed a "clear and ringing voice."[4] The "natty, fair-haired, and debonair" Minty was a devout Episcopalian who loved music but was also known as a teetotaler who did not use profanity. A Confederate officer paid him the highest possible compliment: "Col. Minty is one of the most gallant and dashing officers in the Federal army, and those who 'scare him up' may count on having to fight."[5]

His last commander, Maj. Gen. James H. Wilson, left perhaps the most detailed description of Minty the soldier, calling him "an educated soldier of great intelligence and enterprise . . . [who] had gained the esteem of all who had served with him. Long before the close of the war his regiment had justly come to be regarded as one of the very best in the army. Young, natty, fair-haired, and debonair, Minty was a dandy cavalryman, or many hard knocks and not a few vicissitudes. As a man of military instincts and professional aptitudes, he naturally had his own ideas, and it was not strange that they did not always receive the approval of his less enterprising and less experienced superiors." Wilson concluded, "At all events, they gave him the reputation of being

4 Bitter, *Minty and His Cavalry*, 4.

5 *Atlanta Daily Appeal*, June 25, 1864.

headstrong and bumptious, but from the time he fell under my command till the end of the war, he was in every respect a modest and obedient officer, an excellent disciplinarian, and as good a soldier as Murat himself. He needed but the continuous chances of war to become famous as the best Irish soldier of his day."[6]

The men liked him. His background and service in the British army probably made him more aware of the plight of the common soldier than most volunteer officers of the Civil War. He was "a very genial gentleman, who endeared himself to the men by his unassuming yet soldierly manners," wrote a fellow officer. "He lived in his tent in camp and could call his men by name, and was ever ready to impart any instructions or listen to any communication they might make."[7]

During the war, Minty was personally engaged in 109 skirmishes and battles, and he had five horses shot out from under him. Thirteen enemy bullets pierced his clothing, though he never received a single wound. The feisty, dynamic little Englishman, however, was neither deterred nor frightened by any of these things. Instead, he drove on, making him one of the most effective small-unit cavalry officers of the war. No unit on either side made more saber charges than did Minty's Saber Brigade, a record that the men and their commander were rightly proud of. He never received a promotion to full brigadier general during the war, but he was eventually brevetted to brigadier and later major general of volunteers after commanding a division of cavalry in Wilson's cavalry corps during the war's final days and following the capture of Confederate president Jefferson Davis by his 4th Michigan Cavalry.[8]

Minty commanded an excellent veteran brigade of horse soldiers designated as the 1st Brigade, 2nd Cavalry Division, Army of the Cumberland, a command described as a "splendid body of cavalry"

6 James H. Wilson, *Under the Old Flag: Recollections of Military Operations in the War for the Union, the Spanish War, the Boxer Rebellions, etc.*, 2 vols. (New York: D. Appleton, 1912), vol. 2, 171-72.

7 Marshall P. Thatcher, *A Hundred Battles in the West: St. Louis to Atlanta, 1861-1865, The Second Michigan Cavalry with the Armies of the Mississippi, Ohio, Kentucky and Cumberland, under Generals Halleck, Sherman, Pope, Rosecrans, Thomas and Others; with Mention of a Few of the Famous Regiments and Brigades of the West* (Detroit: L. F. Kilroy, 1884), 24.

8 "Military Record of Robert H. G. Minty, in the United States Volunteer Army of the Civil War, 1861-1865," included in the Proposed Volunteer Retired List, *Senate Documents* vol. 8, 59th Congress, 1st Session (Washington, DC: Government Printing Office, 1906), 80-81.

by a contemporary newspaper account.[9] His brigade consisted of his own 4th Michigan Cavalry, the 4th U.S. Cavalry (one of the six regular army cavalry regiments), the 7th Pennsylvania Cavalry, and a battalion of the 3rd Indiana Cavalry.[10] Minty's commands were known for their proficiency with the blade and were famous and feared for their many thunderous mounted charges. Most of the men also carried revolvers and a Sharps, Smith, or Burnside carbine—single-shot, breech-loading weapons that could lay down rapid and effective firepower, while the men of the 4th Michigan carried Colt's revolving rifles.[11]

The 4th U.S. Cavalry was originally known as the 1st U.S. Cavalry. It was organized on March 26, 1855, at Jefferson Barracks in St. Louis, Missouri, and saw its first action in Bleeding Kansas the following year. Its early officers included Col. Edwin V. Sumner, Lt. Col. Joseph E. Johnston, and Lt. Col. Robert E. Lee, and its ranks at one time included Lt. J. E. B. Stuart and Capt. George B. McClellan. With the coming of war in 1861, the U.S. Army's five mounted regiments were all reorganized and redesignated, and the 1st U.S. Cavalry was redesignated as the 4th U.S. Cavalry.[12] Two companies of the 4th U.S. briefly served in the

9 "General Burnside's East Tennessee Campaign," *Semi-Weekly Wisconsin*, September 18, 1863.

10 The final unit of Minty's brigade was a portion of the 3rd Indiana Cavalry. The 3rd Indiana was divided into two wings, the East Wing and the West Wing. The East Wing, consisting of Cos. A, B, C, D, E, and F, served with the Cavalry Corps of the Army of the Potomac, and ironically played a critical role in Brig. Gen. John Buford's legendary stand on the first day of the battle of Gettysburg. The West Wing, consisting of Cos. G, H, I, K, L, and M, was organized at Madison, Indiana, on October 1, 1861. Originally, only four companies (G, H, I, and K) were sent west, and two additional companies (L and M) were raised and then assigned to the West Wing in 1862. The West Wing was originally assigned to the Army of the Ohio and then joined the Army of the Cumberland when the Army of the Ohio was merged into the Army of the Cumberland. Lt. Col. Robert Klein commanded the West Wing of the 3rd Indiana Cavalry, having been promoted up the ranks from captain to lieutenant colonel as a consequence of solid, dependable service. His battalion joined Minty's brigade on June 3, 1863. Klein's battalion, however, was detached and serving in Chattanooga on September 18, 1863, and played no part in the drama that unfolded at Reed's Bridge. See William N. Pickerell, *History of the Third Indiana Cavalry* (Indianapolis: Aetna Printing Co., 1906), 30-52.

11 William B. Sipes, *The Saber Regiment: History of the 7th Pennsylvania Veteran Volunteer Cavalry, 1861-1865* (Pottsville, PA: Pottsville Miner's Journal, 1905), 46; Joseph G. Vale, *Minty and His Cavalry: A History of Cavalry Campaigns in the Western Armies* (Harrisburg, PA: Edwin K. Meyers, 1886), 9.

12 The other prewar regular army mounted units were the 1st Dragoons, the 2nd Dragoons, the Regiment of Mounted Rifles, and the 2nd U.S. Cavalry. The 1st Dragoons,

eastern theater of the war as headquarters escort companies to the Army of the Potomac. These two companies rejoined the regiment after the September 17, 1862, Battle of Antietam.[13]

The rest of the 4th U.S. Cavalry saw action in Missouri, Mississippi, and Kentucky during the early phases of the war and participated in the Forts Henry and Donelson campaign of 1862. On December 31, 1862, two companies of the regulars charged and routed an entire Confederate cavalry brigade during the battle of Stones River. "The 4th U.S. Cav. was as fine a regiment as was ever organized in any war," proudly claimed a veteran of the regiment. "The discipline, the gallantry, the bravery and prowess of that regiment was not excelled by any regiment in any department of the armies of the United States."[14] Captain James B. McIntyre commanded the 4th U.S. Cavalry at Chickamauga. After the Civil War, Maj. Gen. George H. Thomas gave McIntyre a glowing endorsement: "Capt. McIntyre has been an industrious and zealous officer and has performed the duties of every position he has held with ability, and with great credit to himself and to the satisfaction of his commanding officers."[15] McIntyre ably led the 711 officers and men of the 4th U.S. Cavalry during the Chickamauga campaign.[16]

---

the oldest mounted unit, became the 1st U.S. Cavalry. The 2nd Dragoons, as next oldest, became the 2nd U.S. Cavalry. The Regiment of Mounted Rifles was redesignated as the 3rd U.S. Cavalry. The 1st U.S. Cavalry became the 4th U.S. Cavalry. The 2nd U.S. Cavalry became the 5th U.S. Cavalry, and a new regiment of regulars, the 6th U.S. Cavalry, was recruited. The six regular army mounted units never served together as a single brigade or division during the Civil War. See James M. Merrill, *Spurs to Glory: The Story of the United States Cavalry* (Chicago: Rand, McNally & Co., 1966), 122-23.

13 For a good history of the prewar and Civil War service of the 4th U.S. Cavalry, see John L. Herberich, *Masters of the Field: The Fourth United States Cavalry in the Civil War* (Atglen, PA: Schiffer Publishing, 2015).

14 Will A. McTeer, "Smith's Raid," *National Tribune*, May 28, 1891.

15 Quoted in Don Caughey, "Fiddler's Green: James B. McIntyre," Regular Cavalry in the Civil War, December 17, 2014, http://regularcavalryincivilwar.wordpress.com/2014/12/17/fiddlers-green-james-b-mcintyre/.

16 Vale, *Minty and His Cavalry*, 7-29; Minty's brigade return, Army of the Cumberland, September 30, 1863, RG 94, Entry 65, Box 64, National Archives and Records Administration (hereafter cited as NARA), Washington, DC. Thirty-year-old Capt. James B. McIntyre was the only West Point-trained regimental commander in Minty's brigade. McIntyre, a member of the West Point class of 1849, was a career regular. He spent the first three years of his regular army career in the infantry and then transferred to the 1st Cavalry in March 1855. McIntyre served as regimental quartermaster for more than two years and was promoted to captain on May 3, 1861. McIntyre died in

The 7th Pennsylvania Cavalry was raised mainly in Schuylkill County, Pennsylvania, and many of its men came from Pottsville. Colonel George C. Wynkoop, a veteran of the Mexican War, was selected as the regiment's first commander when the unit mustered in during the fall of 1861. Colonel William B. Sipes succeeded Wynkoop in command of the regiment on June 25, 1863, but he was on detached duty in September 1863. The new regiment was sent to Nashville, Tennessee, where it quickly established its proficiency with the saber. It became so proficient with the blade that it soon earned the moniker "the Saber Regiment of the Army of the Cumberland" at the specific order of the army's commander, Maj. Gen. William S. Rosecrans.[17] With Sipes absent on detached duty, Lt. Col. James J. Seibert of Philadelphia commanded the 496 officers and men of the 7th Pennsylvania during the Chickamauga campaign.[18] "Without a shadow of a doubt in my mind there was no regiment of cavalry in the Army of the Cumberland that excelled [the 7th Pennsylvania]," declared an admiring Union cavalryman from Tennessee. "They were always in the forefront of the fray, always ready to carve the enemy with their bright blades."[19]

The 4th Michigan Cavalry, of which Minty was its first colonel, was organized in Detroit on August 28, 1862. It departed for duty in Louisville at the end of September and served with the Army of the Ohio until November 1862. When the Army of the Ohio was folded into the Army of the Cumberland, the 4th Michigan became part of that army's cavalry corps. In December of that year, Colonel Minty became brigade commander, so command of the regiment fell to its lieutenant colonel, Josiah B. Park.[20] With Minty as its commander, the 4th Michigan earned a

---

1867 at the very young age of 34. See George W. Cullum, *Biographical Register of the Officers and Graduates of the U.S. Military Academy at West Point, N.Y., from Its Establishment, March 16, 1802 to the Army Reorganization of 1866-1867*, 2 vols. (New York: D. Van Nostrand, 1868), vol. 2, 364-65. For a detailed sketch of McIntyre's life and service, see Caughey, "Fiddler's Green: James B. McIntyre."

17 Vale, *Minty and His Cavalry*, 135-36.

18 Ibid., 30-48; Roger D. Hunt, *Colonels in Blue: Union Army Colonels of the Civil War, The Mid-Atlantic States* (Mechanicsburg, PA: Stackpole, 2007), 151; Minty's brigade return.

19 C. B. King, "The Saber Brigade," *National Tribune*, June 1, 1893.

20 Park was 32 years old in September 1863. Born April 23, 1861, in Cheemung County, New York, Park was educated in the public schools in New York. In 1851 he moved to Michigan, where he studied surveying and engineering for several years.

solid reputation as a reliable, hard-fighting regiment and proudly claimed it was the first Union regiment to enter Murfreesboro on January 5, 1863. Early in September 1863, Minty wrote to Michigan governor Austin Blair to discuss the status of his regiment. "The 4th Michigan Cavalry has been reduced to below the minimum by hard but glorious service," he wrote. "Most of the Sergeants are deserving of promotion, and are qualified to handle and fill the position of Commissioned Officers." He threatened to resign if steps were not taken to restore the 4th Michigan to the status it achieved under him: "First among the several cavalry regiments of the Army of the Cumberland."[21] Major Horace Gray of Grosse Isle, Michigan, the senior officer then serving with the regiment, commanded the 210 officers and men of the 4th Michigan Cavalry at Chickamauga on September 18.[22]

"Never were three regiments more firmly united than the 4th Regulars, 7th P.V.C. and the 4th Michigan," declared trooper D. H. Haines of the 4th Michigan. "They were brigaded together near the commencement of the Murfreesboro campaign and remained so until nearly the close of the war. Each regiment had the utmost confidence in the others and no regiment feared to go into action when they knew that they had the support of the others." The closeness and compatibility of these three regiments made the Saber Brigade one of the most effective, efficient, and successful brigades of cavalry to serve in any theater of the Civil War.[23]

Like Brig. Gen. John Buford's epic stand on the first day of the battle of Gettysburg, Robert Minty's single brigade held off nearly 6,000

He was the founder and first settler of Ovid, Michigan, and raised a company of the 1st Michigan Cavalry. He was commissioned a captain in the 1st Michigan and served in its campaigns of the spring of 1862. On August 20, 1862, he was commissioned a major in the 4th Michigan Cavalry, served as inspector general of cavalry for the Army of the Cumberland, and then was promoted to lieutenant colonel of the 4th Michigan and assumed command of the regiment in April 1863. See "Colonel Josiah B. Park," *Illinois Central Magazine* 4, no. 12 (June 1916): 12, 13-14.

21 Minty to Austin Blair, September 7, 1863, 4th Cavalry Regimental Files, Michigan State Archives, Lansing, MI.

22 *Annual Report of the Adjutant General of the State of Michigan, for the Year 1863* (Lansing: John A. Kerr & Co., 1864), 31; Minty's brigade return. Captain Henry Potter of the 4th Michigan reported on September 19, the day after the combat that is the subject of this monograph, a battalion of 260 men under command of Maj. Frank W. Mix joined the regiment, giving it a total strength of 470 officers and men. See Henry Potter, diary, September 19, 1863, Bentley Historical Library, University of Michigan, Ann Arbor, MI (hereafter cited as BHL).

23 D. H. Haines, "Record of Fourth Michigan Cavalry," September 18, 1863, BHL.

Confederate infantry for five hours on September 18, 1863, without the benefit of Spencer repeating rifles.[24] The table below contains a breakdown of the weaponry carried by Minty's troopers:

REGIMENT	SHARPS	SMITH	BURNSIDE	COLTS
4th Michigan	0	0	0	147
4th U.S.	51	20	692	0
7th Pennsylvania	22	232	134	0

Therefore, with the notable exception of the 4th Michigan Cavalry, Minty's command was armed with single-shot breech-loading carbines.[25]

The primary weapon carried by Minty's troopers was the Burnside carbine, developed before the war by the former commander of the Army of the Potomac, Maj. Gen. Ambrose E. Burnside. These single-shot, breech-loading carbines each fired a .54 caliber lead ball (although there was some variation in the size and bore of the bullets). Unlike muzzle-loading infantry weapons, which could typically get off three rounds per minute, a proficient cavalryman could get off five to seven rounds per minute with their breechloaders. These guns traded a relatively short range of 300 yards or so for their rapid firing capabilities.

The men of the 4th Michigan Cavalry carried .56 caliber Colt revolving rifles, which were among the first repeating rifles to enter mass production. Rosecrans was a great admirer of this weapon. He spent most of the fall and winter of 1863 begging the War Department for more cavalry and better weaponry, correctly pointing out that the Confederates greatly outnumbered his army's cavalry corps. Of the Colt revolving rifle, Rosecrans declared: "If you cannot add to my numerical

24 For a detailed examination of the stand conducted by Buford's troopers at Gettysburg on July 1, 1863, see Eric J. Wittenberg, *The Devil's to Pay: John Buford at Gettysburg, A History and Walking Tour* (El Dorado Hills, CA: Savas-Beatie, 2014).

25 Quarterly Statements of Ordnance in Cavalry, 1862-1864, Statement for September 30, 1863, RG 156, Records of the Chief of Ordnance, NARA. The return for the 4th Michigan Cavalry is incomplete, as Companies B, D, E, F, and I did not report on September 30, 1863. The battalion of the 3rd Indiana Cavalry that normally served with Minty's brigade was on detached duty in Chattanooga and was not present for the battle of Chickamauga. Consequently, its arms have not been included here. The entire brigade was armed with Spencer repeating carbines in early 1864. In an account published in the *National Tribune*, Minty erroneously claimed that his men had Spencers at Reed's Bridge, but they did not.

strength, please made a great effort to send me 5,000 revolving rifles. Each rifle will add a man to my strength, and for the service for which I wish them they will add two men for each gun."[26]

"These weapons were basically a larger version of Colt's world-famous handguns and were loaded in the same manner—cartridges (or loose powder and balls) were inserted one at a time into the revolving chambers and then the corresponding nipples were capped with standard pistol percussion caps," noted Civil War weapons expert Dean S. Thomas.[27] The War Department purchased less than 5,000 of these rifles during the war, in part because they required special ammunition and cartridges. They had a longer range than the carbines used by the rest of Minty's brigade, and they were fairly accurate (they were the standard weapon carried by Berdan's Sharpshooters early in the war), but they also had a lot of problems that caused them to become largely obsolete after Spencer and Henry rifles went into mass production. The Colt revolving rifle could lay down a great deal of firepower, but it also took a long time to reload due to the cumbersome revolver mechanism involved.[28]

While these breech-loading weapons had a much faster rate of fire, they also ate ammunition at a frightening pace. A report by Lt. Col. George A. Purington of the 2nd Ohio Cavalry from 1864 emphasizes this problem: "Allow me to call your attention to the necessity of having some organized system of ordnance sergeants or men detailed,

26 U.S. War Department, *The War of the Rebellion: A Compilation of the Official Records of the Union and Confederate Armies*, 128 vols., 3 series (Washington, DC: Government Printing Office, 1889), vol. 20, pt. 2, 330. (Hereafter abbreviated as *OR*. All further references are to Series 1 unless otherwise noted.) In February 1863 Rosecrans said in a letter to Halleck, "If one regiment can be made equal to two by revolving rifles, no other one thing is so worth of your attention as this, by which you increase the power and effectiveness of your armies, without adding to their members, by a small permanent outlay" (Idem, 23, pt. 2, 62).

27 Dean S. Thomas, *Round Ball to Rimfire: A History of Civil War Small Arms Ammunition,* Part 2: *Federal Breechloading Carbines & Rifles* (Gettysburg, PA: Thomas Publications, 2002), 43-44.

28 Joseph G. Bilby, *A Revolution in Arms: A History of the First Repeating Rifles* (Yardley, PA: Westholme, 2006), 44-48. One major problem was noted by the historian of the 9th Illinois Cavalry: "The Colt's revolving rifle was an excellent arm, and had served us well on many an occasion; but there was serious objection to them; when being discharged they would shoot splinters of lead into the wrist and hand of the man firing" (Ken Bauman, *Arming the Suckers, 1861-1865: A Compilation of Illinois Civil War Weapons* [Dayton, OH: Morningside, 1989], 53).

whose duty it shall be to keep cavalry commands well supplied with ammunition during engagements. Men armed with the breech-loading weapon will necessarily fire a greater number of rounds than those armed with a muzzle-loading piece, and it is utterly impossible for a cavalry man to carry more than from 60 to 80 rounds upon his person, and when dismounted and away from his horse this supply can be easily exhausted in a few hours' firing. In this case my regiment expended its ammunition in the battle of May 31." Thus, keeping his troopers supplied with ammunition was a constant struggle for Minty and the other Union cavalry commanders.[29]

Finally, Minty's troopers also carried the standard complement of other weapons usually carried by Union cavalrymen of the Civil War—sabers and revolvers. The pistols had a very short effective range and were only useful in hand-to-hand combat. The sabers were intended for use in hand-to-hand combat. The sort of tactics that Minty designed and implemented on September 18, 1863, rendered these weapons useless, and they played no role in the tough fighting at Reed's Bridge.

In addition, Minty also had one section of Capt. James H. Stokes's Chicago Board of Trade Battery with him on September 18.[30] This battery, raised and funded by the Chicago Board of Trade, in response to Abraham Lincoln's call for 300,000 volunteers in the summer of 1862, served with distinction during the battle of Stones River. It was converted to horse artillery just before the Tullahoma campaign began in June 1863 and was attached to the Army of the Cumberland's 2nd Cavalry Division, which included Minty's brigade. "The Board of Trade Battery was composed of well drilled artillerists and it had fine guns too," recalled a sergeant of the 4th U.S. Cavalry. "It was a militia organization of the State of Illinois and was equal in every respect to the best drilled battery in the regular army and rendered Minty's brigade great assistance in many tight

29 Alonzo Gray, *Cavalry Tactics as Illustrated by the War of the Rebellion Together with Many Interesting Facts Important for Cavalry to Know*, 2 parts (Fort Leavenworth: U.S. Cavalry Association, 1910), pt. 1, 154.

30 Stokes was a member of the West Point class of 1835 and had served in the regular artillery service from 1835 to 1843 and would have been approximately 53 years old in 1863. Prior to returning to the army, he had served as the auditor and treasurer of the Illinois Central Railroad. He did good service in the Civil War. See Cullum, *Biographical Register*, vol. 1, 471.

Col. Robert H. G. Minty in 1863, a few months prior to the Battle of Chickamauga.
Judith Minty

places."[31] Minty had Lt. Trumbull D. Griffin's second section of two three-inch ordnance rifles with him on September 18, 1863, and those guns played a critical role in the defense of Reed's Bridge.[32]

In December 1862, Minty became commander of the brigade when its regular leader, Col. Edward M. McCook, who had led the 2nd Indiana Cavalry before he was promoted to brigade command and who had been

31 James Larson, ed., *Sergeant Larson, 4th Cav.* (San Antonio, TX: Southern Literary Institute, 1935), 179.

32 Chicago Board of Trade Battery, *Historical Sketch of the Chicago Board of Trade Battery, Horse Artillery Illinois Volunteers* (Chicago: Henneberry Co., 1902), 24, 45. Trumbull Durrance Griffin, born on October 11, 1835, was a native of Clinton, New York. He enlisted in the Chicago Board of Trade Battery as a second lieutenant on July 31, 1862. He was promoted to first lieutenant on August 22, 1864. He mustered out on June 30, 1865. After the war he settled in St. Louis, where he founded the *St. Louis Market Reporter* newspaper. He died in St. Louis on February 21, 1912, and was buried in Bellefontaine Cemetery, not far from the final resting place of Gen. William T. Sherman. See www.wc.rootsweb.ancestry.com/cgi-bin/igm.cgi?&db=mbwheeler&id=1,040,772.

in charge of the brigade at Perryville, was injured after a fall from his horse and had to go on medical leave. Minty led the brigade for the rest of the war.[33] Although he had only been in command of the brigade for a few weeks when the battle of Stones River commenced on December 31, 1862, after a fierce three-hour fight, Minty's brigade made a determined saber charge against Maj. Gen. Joseph Wheeler's Cavalry Corps on the Shelbyville Pike that drove Wheeler's troopers from the field in a wild rout.[34] Minty prevailed that day, even though the Confederates had two and a half times as many cavalrymen.[35]

The Army of the Cumberland severely lacked cavalry, which prevented Rosecrans from advancing until late spring. He had been complaining about it to anyone who would listen since the battle of Stones River. He kept asking for more horses, more saddles, and better weaponry. Confederate cavalry under Joseph Wheeler, John Hunt Morgan, Earl Van Dorn, and Nathan Bedford Forrest buzzed around the edges of his army like angry bees. These Southern horsemen constantly harassed Rosecrans's army and endangered his lines of supply and communication. As early as January, Rosecrans began pleading for horses to mount his infantry because he had insufficient cavalry to do the job. Halleck resisted the idea. "Mounted infantry are neither good infantry nor good cavalry," sniffed the general in chief.[36]

"I must have cavalry or mounted infantry," Rosecrans declared in a January 1863 letter to Halleck. "With mounted infantry, I can drive the rebel cavalry to the wall, and keep the roads open to my rear. Not so now," he wrote.[37] In a February letter to Secretary of War Edwin M. Stanton, he stated: "One rebel cavalryman takes, on an average, three

33 Sipes, *The Saber Regiment*, 46.

34 Vale, *Minty and His Cavalry*, 117.

35 Fitch, *Annals of the Army of the Cumberland*, 207.

36 *OR* 23, pt. 2, 155. This dialog between Rosecrans and Halleck began not long after the end of the Confederate invasion of Kentucky in October 1862 and continued for nearly seven months. Rosecrans constantly hectored the War Department seeking more cavalry and more cavalry weapons to the point that Halleck's frustration became palpable and could readily be detected in his responses to Rosecrans. It is no wonder the commander of the Army of the Cumberland was not popular with the Union high command. His constant carping did nothing to improve his standing with the War Department.

37 Ibid., 20, pt. 2, 328.

of our infantry to watch our communications, while our progress is made slow and cautious, and we command the forage of the country only sending large train guards. It is a prime necessity, in every point of view, to master their cavalry."[38] Minty and his brigade played a major role in mastering the Confederate cavalry.

On March 4, 1863, Rosecrans ordered a general reconnaissance to try to determine the strength of the enemy forces in his front. Major General Philip H. Sheridan, with four brigades of infantry and Minty's horsemen, moved from the Army of the Cumberland's camps around Murfreesboro toward Rover. Finding enemy cavalry in his front, Minty led a saber charge that drove a brigade of Confederate cavalry from the field and then charged into Lt. Gen. Leonidas Polk's infantry near Shelbyville, taking a number of prisoners to boot. It was a remarkable charge. Rosecrans noted: "They drove the rebel cavalry wherever they met them, captured one of their camps, 17 wagons, 42 mules, and 64 prisoners. The brave Colonel Minty used sabers where carbines would delay."[39] As a result, Rosecrans issued an order declaring, "In recognition of the dash and gallantry displayed by this brigade on all occasions, it shall hereafter be known in this department as 'The Saber Brigade of the Army of the Cumberland.'"[40]

Minty's men were veterans, and they were not afraid to go boot-to-boot, saber-to-saber with the best the Confederate cavalry had to offer in the western theater. Minty's troopers made one of the most remarkable and determined saber charges of the war at Shelbyville, Tennessee, on June 27, 1863, during the Tullahoma campaign. Minty's single brigade shattered and routed two divisions of Maj. Gen. Joseph Wheeler's cavalry corps, sending them flying from the battlefield and capturing Wheeler's guns. Wheeler was nearly captured himself and suffered the indignity of plunging headlong into the Duck River to escape. "I cannot refrain from expressing . . . my admiration of the conduct of Colonel Minty and his brigade," wrote Brig. Gen. Robert M. Mitchell, who commanded one of Rosecrans's cavalry divisions. "Though not under my command, they came under my immediate observation. Before the gallantry and skill

38 Ibid., 23, pt. 2, 34.

39 Ibid., pt. 1, 127.

40 "Military Record of Robert H. G. Minty," 79.

Col. John T. Wilder, commander of the Lightning Brigade. *Library of Congress*

of this commander and the dashing bravery and skill of his troops, all efforts of the rebels to withstand his advance were ineffectual."[41] They made perhaps the most remarkable saber charge of the entire Civil War against immense odds and carried the day. These veteran horse soldiers knew their business and knew it well. They proved to be the right men in the right place at Reed's Bridge.

During the coming months, Minty's brigade was seldom separated from the mounted infantry brigade of Col. John T. Wilder. These two brigades were usually deployed together, always relied upon each other, and shared success and glory together.

Colonel John T. Wilder and His Lightning Brigade

Hoosier John T. Wilder commanded a unique brigade. Originally constituted as infantry, Wilder armed his men with seven-shot Spencer rifles and mounted them on horses. His Lightning Brigade, as it became known, was famous for rapid movement and severe firepower. These men played a major role in the Army of the Cumberland's 1863 campaigns. They often worked in concert with Minty's cavalry brigade, and the two brigades made a stout stand, holding the two main bridges across Chickamauga Creek for the better part of a full day on September 18, 1863.

John T. Wilder was born on January 31, 1830, in Hunter Village, Greene County, New York. His grandfather and great-grandfather were

41 *OR* 23, part 1, 545. Captain Charles C. Davis of the 7th Pennsylvania was awarded the Medal of Honor for his role in the charge. His Medal of Honor citation reads, "Led one of the most desperate and successful charges of the war." For a discussion of the battle of Shelbyville, see Stephen Z. Starr, *The Union Cavalry in the Civil War*, 3 vols. (Baton Rouge: Louisiana State University Press, 1979-1985), vol. 3, 243-48. No good monograph on the battle of Shelbyville exists.

both veterans of the Revolutionary War (when his great-grandfather lost a leg at the battle of Bunker Hill, his 16-year-old son took his place in the line of battle), and his father was a veteran of the War of 1812. With that sort of pedigree, Wilder was destined to become a soldier. He attended local schools in Hunter, New York, until he reached the age of 14, and he did well there. He "was a handsome young man, of fine physique, mentally alert, fond of research [and possessed a] genial and hospitable nature."[42]

In 1849, at the young age of 19, and contrary to the wishes of his parents, Wilder left the family home in the lovely Catskill Mountains and traveled to Columbus, Ohio, where he apprenticed himself as a draftsman, pattern maker, and millwright in a foundry for a period of seven years, learning the industry as he did.[43] In 1857, he moved to Greensburg, Indiana, and established his own foundry there. By 1861, Wilder was half owner of the largest operation of its type in the Midwest, had mills in six different states, and his business was booming. Wilder became an authority on hydraulics (he held patents on a number of inventions, including a unique waterwheel), and the 31-year-old industrialist grew quite wealthy. He married the former Mary Jane Stewart and was the father of two little girls.[44]

With the outbreak of war in 1861, Wilder enlisted as a private in the 1st Independent Battery of Artillery. He equipped the new battery with two cannons cast in one of his mills. The unit was not mustered as artillery but was instead designated as Company A of the 17th Indiana Volunteer Infantry. Wilder was unanimously elected the new company's captain. In June 1861, after refusing a commission as colonel because he did not believe he was qualified for the position, he accepted promotion to lieutenant colonel. The green regiment fought in western Virginia at Cheat Mountain and in the Greenbrier Valley. In one of those skirmishes, John A. Washington, a nephew of Robert E. Lee, was mortally wounded. Wilder lifted the dying young man in his arms, gave him a drink of

42 Richard A. Baumgartner, *Blue Lightning: Wilder's Mounted Infantry Brigade in the Battle of Chickamauga* (Huntington, WV: Blue Acorn Press, 2007), 20.

43 Will T. Hale and Dixon L. Merritt, *A History of Tennessee and Tennesseans: The Leaders and Representative Men in Commerce, Industry and Modern Activities*, 8 vols. (Chicago: Lewis Publishing Co., 1913), vol. 6, 1609.

44 Baumgartner, *Blue Lightning*, 20.

water, and held him as he died. Wilder then delivered the body to Lee under a flag of truce, earning the personal thanks of the Confederate chieftain.[45] In November the 17th Indiana was assigned to the Army of the Ohio and sent to the western theater of operations.

On March 12, 1862, Wilder was promoted to colonel of the 17th Indiana, which did not make it to the battlefield in time to participate in the battle of Shiloh. The 17th Indiana participated in the advance on Corinth. Shortly after Corinth fell to the besieging Union forces on May 30, 1862, Wilder contracted typhoid fever, a bacterial disease spread by drinking contaminated water. Typhoid is often fatal, and it nearly claimed Wilder's life.[46] After being absent on medical leave for nearly three months, he eventually regained his health sufficiently to return to duty. He, however, suffered from regular, debilitating bouts of diarrhea that made it difficult for him to be in the field for extended campaigning. After he returned to duty, Wilder's command helped to defend against Gen. Braxton Bragg's invasion of Kentucky in the fall of 1862. Outnumbered six-to-one, Wilder, now in command of a brigade, was left with no alternative but to surrender to Bragg at Fort Craig during the battle of Munfordville in Kentucky on September 17, 1862. Wilder and his men were paroled and marched to Louisville.[47]

Wilder was exchanged two months later, and he assumed command of a brigade in the 5th Division of the 14th Corps, which was part of the Army of the Cumberland. The brigade included his old command, the 17th Indiana (now commanded by 27-year-old Lt. Col. Henry Jordan, a tanner from Corydon, Indiana), and three green regiments: the 72nd Indiana, the 75th Indiana, and the 98th Illinois. Thirty-six-year-old physician Col. Abram O. Miller commanded the 72nd Indiana. Like Wilder, he began the war as a captain and made his way up the ranks to colonel. He was the most experienced of Wilder's regimental commanders. Miller was an Ohio-born farmer and had been reluctant to take command of the regiment.[48] Twenty-seven-year-old Col. John J. Funkhouser of Effingham,

45 Hale and Merritt, *A History of Tennessee*, vol. 6, 1609.

46 As just one example, John Buford died of typhoid fever on December 16, 1863, just five months after his magnificent stand at Gettysburg.

47 Baumgartner, *Blue Lightning*, 23-24.

48 Roger D. Hunt and Jack R. Brown, *Brevet Brigadier Generals in Blue* (Gaithersburg, MD: Olde Soldier Books, 1997), 414.

Capt. Eli Lilly, commander of the 18th Indiana Battery, also known as Lilly's Battery.
Eli S. Lilly & Co. company archives

Illinois, the son of U.S. Senator Presley Funkhouser, commanded the 98th Illinois. Funkhouser had little prior experience, having briefly served as a company commander in the 26th Illinois. This unit from south-central Illinois had seen no action at all when it joined Wilder's new brigade. The 75th Indiana, commanded by 31-year-old Col. Milton S. Robinson, a lawyer from Versailles, Indiana, had seen some service during the invasion of Kentucky but was also an inexperienced regiment.[49]

Finally, twenty-five-year-old Capt. Eli Lilly's 18th Indiana Battery was assigned to serve with Wilder's brigade. Lilly, a pharmacist from Greencastle, Indiana, who went on to found one of the largest and most successful drug companies in the world, was armed with six Rodman guns, also known as three-inch ordnance rifles. The three-inch ordnance rifle was particularly well-suited to mounted operations because it was accurate and durable but could be moved quickly and easily due to its light weight.[50] The 18th Indiana Battery also had four mountain howitzers attached to it, meaning that, with ten guns, this battery was the largest battery in Union service in 1863.[51] "Lilly's gunners, when they knew the

49 Baumgartner, *Blue Lighting*, 26-28; Hunt and Brown, *Brevet Brigadier Generals in Blue*, 513. Robinson had previously served as lieutenant colonel of the 47th Indiana Infantry and served in Congress from 1875 to 1879.

50 For a good history of Lilly's battery, see John W. Rowell, *Yankee Artillerymen: Through the Civil War with Eli Lilly's Indiana Battery* (Knoxville: University of Tennessee Press, 1975).

51 The Model 1841 mountain howitzer, also known as a "bull pup," was a bronze smoothbore cannon that fired a twelve-pound ball and had a maximum range of about 1,000 yards. They were designed to be light and mobile and were especially well-

distance and elevation, could hit the mark with the first shot two miles away," recalled one of Wilder's men. These artillerists became famous for the accuracy of their fire.[52]

During the winter of 1862-63, Wilder was given the task of trying to run down a cavalry raid led by Brig. Gen. John Hunt Morgan. Wilder improvised by mounting his command on mules, but the stubborn beasts could not catch up to Morgan's well-mounted men, meaning that Wilder and his brigade missed the battle of Stones River. Frustrated by his inability to catch Morgan, Wilder sought permission to mount his entire brigade on horses, which would be impressed from the countryside. His men would use the horses to move quickly from place to place, dismount, and fight as infantry. Rosecrans, who was terribly short on cavalry, embraced the idea and approved Wilder's request. Wilder, however, did not want to force this radical new idea on his command, so he put the idea to a vote. Three of his four regiments voted to approve the proposal to mount them. The 75th Indiana, however, did not, and it was removed from the brigade so it could remain an infantry regiment. The 123rd Illinois wanted to be mounted, so it was transferred in to take the place of the 75th Indiana.[53]

The 123rd Illinois was from central Illinois and had been mustered in at Mattoon under the command of 33-year-old Col. James Monroe, the former mayor of Mattoon. Monroe was a veteran of the early battles under Maj. Gen. Ulysses S. Grant at Belmont, Fort Donelson, and Shiloh.[54]

---

suited to fighting against Indians and in mountainous country. Because of their limited range, however, they were not well-suited to counterbattery fire. See James C. Hazlett, Edwin Olmstead, and M. Hume Parks, *Field Artillery Weapons of the Civil War*, 2nd ed. (Bloomington: University of Illinois Press, 2004), 133-37.

52 Lawson S. Kilborn, *Dedication of the Wilder Brigade Monument on Chickamauga Battlefield on the Thirty-Sixth Anniversary of the Battle, September 20, 1899* (Marshall, IL: Herald Press, 1900), 25.

53 David B. Floyd, *History of the Seventy-Fifth Regiment of Indiana Volunteers, Its Organization, Campaigns, and Battles (1862-65)* (Philadelphia: Lutheran Publication Society, 1893), 82.

54 Monroe was born January 4, 1832, in Green County, Kentucky. The family relocated to Illinois in 1835. He was a successful dry goods merchant and served as the first Mattoon Township supervisor in 1860. He was then elected mayor of Mattoon in 1861. He resigned his position as mayor to become a captain in the 7th Illinois Infantry. He was later promoted to major and was then commissioned colonel of the 123rd Illinois when it mustered into service on September 5, 1862. See Col. James Monroe, Find a Grave Memorial 70110968, May 20, 2011, https://www.findagrave.com/memorial/70110968/james-monroe.

Col. James Monroe, commander of the 123rd Illinois Mounted Infantry of the Lightning Brigade. *Abraham Lincoln Presidential Library*

The regiment mustered in on September 6, 1862, and was assigned to the Army of the Ohio. A month later, with almost no training and no combat experience, the 123rd Illinois fought at Perryville. The regiment's brigade and division commanders were killed in the savage fighting at Perryville, and the green Illinois soldiers lost 36 men killed and 180 wounded that long day. These veterans were a good addition to a largely inexperienced brigade.[55] Colonel Smith D. Atkins's 92nd Illinois Infantry also joined the brigade in 1863, as a result of Atkins's desire for his regiment to be part of a fighting brigade.[56] The 92nd Illinois however, was on detached duty on September 18, 1863, and played no part in the events that are addressed in this monograph.

Once the final makeup of the brigade was set, it took about a month for Wilder to mount his command, including Lilly's battery.[57] "Many expeditions were made, sometimes by the whole Brigade and again by parts of it, and soon nearly the entire number of horses necessary for the mount were brought in, together with a sufficient number of mules for the Brigade wagon train and some to spare for other commands," one officer of Wilder's brigade remembered. "Whenever animals were taken, the owners, if loyal to the government, were given vouchers for the same that enabled them to get compensation from the government." Of course, those taken from families that supported the Confederacy received no such vouchers.[58]

55 Glenn W. Sunderland, *Wilder's Lightning Brigade and Its Spencer Repeaters* (Washington, IL: Book Works, 1984), 18.

56 Baumgartner, *Blue Lightning*, 104.

57 Ibid., 37-39.

58 Kilborn, *Dedication of the Wilder Brigade Monument*, 37.

George S. Wilson, a noncommissioned officer of the 17th Indiana, left a detailed account of the brigade's foraging for horses, the scope of which was previously unheard of during the first half of the Civil War. "Our operations in this enterprise extended east to the base of the Cumberland range of mountains, from McMinnville north to the Cumberland River, and back to Lebanon and the Hermitage. Besides overrunning this country, we made two or three excursions to the southwest. All this extensive and rich section we stripped of horses and mules, and by the middle of April the entire brigade was mounted on serviceable animals. Up to this period of the war our forces had, as a rule, respected the property rights of citizens. Now a new policy had come into operation, and we were its pioneers—the first of all the Army of the Cumberland to commence a system to forcing the disloyal inhabitants of the South to contribute to the support of the army."[59]

Consequently, the command rode a hodgepodge of mounts that ran the gamut of thoroughbred racehorses, plow horses, old nags, brood mares, stallions, ponies, and mules. Functionality mattered, not appearance. So as long as a horse had a saddle, it was fair game and was probably good enough. Of course, this practice did little to endear Wilder's soldiers to the local citizenry.[60]

Colonel Wilder "was not a starched, prim, polished commander—not a MADE commander, but a born one, and all through his career with his Brigade, he showed the grain, tenacity, the elasticity, the supreme handiwork of unspoiled Nature," as a comrade remembered him. "He won the entire confidence of his Brigade without an effort and the men knew they could do whatever Wilder ordered. And his modesty equaled his merit. He never boasted; he was willing to be judged 'by his chips.' He was active; he hated the monotony of the camp and his Brigade was early imbued with the same idea."[61]

Like nearly all other Union infantry commands, Wilder's brigade was originally armed with Springfield and Enfield muzzle-loading rifles, and the innovative colonel was bothered by the inefficiency of these weapons. Instead, Wilder armed his entire brigade with Spencer rifles and hatchets

59 George S. Wilson, "Wilder's Brigade of Mounted Infantry in the Tullahoma-Chickamauga Campaigns," *National Tribune*, October 12, 1893.

60 Kilborn, *Dedication of the Wilder Brigade Monument*, 48-49.

61 Ibid., 14.

instead of sabers (although the hatchets disappeared before the newly mounted brigade's first campaign). They did not carry pistols, because they were mounted infantry and not cavalry. Developed by Christopher Spencer, the Spencer rifle was a long-barreled breech-loading weapon that could fire seven shots before it needed to be reloaded. Spencers used a rimfire bullet that was loaded into a tube. When the seven shots were fired, the soldier could either reload the tube or replace the tube from a ready supply of already-loaded tubes. The Spencer rifle enabled Wilder's men to lay down a tremendous amount of fire that could be delivered at a high rate of speed.[62]

Wilder expressed his opinion clearly: "The Spencer magazine rifle . . . was a most formidable weapon. I believe them to be the best arm for army use that I have seen. No line of men, who came within fifty yards of another force armed with the Spencer Repeating Rifles, can either get away alive, or reach them with a charge, as in either case they are certain to be destroyed by the terrible fire poured into their ranks by cool men thus armed. If the government would expend the large sums now used to induce men to enlist, in arming the men now in the field with this kind of weapon, the rebellion would be, in my opinion, speedily crushed."[63]

Wilder, however, was unable to get the army to commit to purchasing Spencer rifles for his brigade, so he went to his hometown bank and borrowed the funds to purchase them using his own credit.[64] After they were persuaded of the efficacy of the new rifles, the men of Wilder's brigade voted to reimburse their brigade commander for the weapons if that was what it took to keep them. The cost of the guns was to be deducted from their pay, but by the time the first payments were supposed to be made, the men of the brigade had already proven the worth of the guns, and the government assumed responsibility for paying for them and reimbursed Wilder and his men.[65]

The problem, however, was that his brigade was unique. As one of his officers put it: "This was the original and only Brigade of mounted

62 For a detailed discussion of the history of the Spencer repeating rifle, see Bilby, *A Revolution in Arms*, 68-80.

63 John T. Wilder to the Spencer Repeating Rifle Co., November 28, 1863, in John T. Wilder Papers, Indiana State Library, Indianapolis, IN.

64 Starr, *The Union Cavalry in the Civil War*, vol. 3, 212.

65 Kilborn, *Dedication of the Wilder Brigade Monument*, 36.

infantry." Wilder had invented the concept of a mounted infantry brigade, and he had to develop his own tactics for it. The brigade fought in a single rank on foot. He drilled his troops by the same commands whether mounted or dismounted. He invented an entirely new concept for use of his brigade as well as the tactics to make it happen.[66]

Years later Wilder left behind a detailed description of the unique tactics he developed for his unique brigade:

> My brigade, composed of the 17th and 72d Indiana Infantry and the 92d, 98th and 123rd Illinois Infantry and the 18th Indiana Battery, were mounted in February 1863. They were all pretty well drilled under Hardee's tactics, and as we nearly always fought dismounted, we simply kept that manner of movement, except that we made a single line with the men at intervals of six feet, as we had Spencer rifles, a magazine gun with seven rounds in the magazine, and could use a single round without drawing on the magazine, which was kept full for fighting at short range. The caliber was 52 and carried an ounce bullet, and had a range of one mile. We always tried to get close to our opponents, as we then got the benefit of rapid fire, which was very effective then. I trained my command to hold their rapid fire until our opponents were within 300 yards, when our rapid fire with aim never failed to break their charge, and if it was desirable to advance, we did so at once, and in that way lost less men than we otherwise might have done.
>
> Magazine guns are most effective at close range. I do not believe in long range fighting, as my most effective work was done at short ranges.
>
> My command had little time for drill, as we were kept close to the enemy and our movements were mostly in firing range of our opponents, and that I found to be the most useful drill we could have. My lines *were never broken*, as we had so many shots at close quarter no troops, however capable, could withstand the fire we could give, and I always tried to compel our opponents to charge us and then our plan of action was most effective.
>
> I tried to keep our men down under cover or lying down until attacked, and then orders were to fire and load at will, always taking aim.
>
> Volley fire was mostly a waste of ammunition, and I hardly ever practiced it.
>
> My usual artillery ammunition was 80% canister and 20% percussion shells and we always exhausted the canister first.[67]

The contributions of this untrained soldier cannot be overstated.

66 Ibid., 24.

67 Undated letter by John T. Wilder, quoted in George H. Morgan, "Cavalry in the Eastern Theatre, 1862," Thesis, U.S. Army War College, 1913-14.

Armed with these formidable weapons, Wilder and his Lightning Brigade were poised to help change the face of Civil War tactics. Often fighting alongside Minty's cavalrymen, the men of the Lightning Brigade left their mark on many a battlefield across Tennessee and Georgia in the coming months. They made their most famous contribution on June 24, 1863, when Wilder's men and Lilly's artillerists stole a march on Bragg's army, dashed through and captured the critical seven-mile-long Hoover's Gap opening through the Highland Rim of Middle Tennessee. Wilder's men then entrenched on the hills at the southern entrance to Hoover's Gap and defended their position against Brig. Gen. William B. Bate's and Brig. Gen. Bushrod R. Johnson's brigades of Maj. Gen. Alexander P. Stewart's division until reinforcements from the Army of the Cumberland's 14th Corps arrived.[68]

Wilder's cost for taking and holding Hoover's Gap was one officer killed (Chaplain John R. Eddy of the 72nd Indiana, who had only joined the regiment on June 17 and who had just preached his first sermon the day before, was killed by an overshot of the Confederate artillery aimed at Lilly's guns that fell in the road and exploded), one officer mortally wounded (Lt. James T. Moreland of the 17th Indiana), and 12 enlisted men killed and 47 wounded, for a total of 61 casualties. "The conduct of both officers and men was all that the most sanguine could ask," proudly proclaimed Colonel Wilder. "Each officer seemed to appreciate the importance of taking and holding the very strong position of Hoover's Gap, and the men were eager to obey and sustain their officers. Their conduct was the same whether driving in rebel outposts or defending their position against fearful odds, or when lying in support of our battery, exposed to a terrible cross fire of shot and shell, or when advancing against the rebel columns; always earnest, cool, determined, ready, and brave, seeming best pleased when necessarily in greatest danger."[69]

On June 25, Rosecrans had a special order read to every regiment in Thomas's 14th Corps that described the Hoover's Gap attack, declaring that "the conduct of [Wilder's] brigade should be emulated by all." It also "directed that the command should thereafter be known as Wilder's Lightning Brigade," a moniker that the men of the brigade wore with

68 For the best treatment of these events, see Glenn W. Sunderland, *Lightning at Hoover's Gap: Wilder's Brigade in the Civil War* (New York: Thomas Yoseloff, 1969), 36-50.

69 *OR* 23, part 1, 459.

great honor for the rest of the war.[70] After learning of the Lightning Brigade's heroics, Rosecrans recommended that Wilder be promoted to brigadier general in recognition of his feat at Hoover's Gap.[71]

A member of the 17th Indiana noted, "This engagement thoroughly tested the power of the Spencer rifles and proved their great superiority to the muzzleloader. For us it did more; it inspired us with a confidence in ourselves which of itself was worth double our numbers. Ever after the brigade would cheerfully have fought ten times its own strength."[72] George S. Wilson said, "Our Spencer Rifles work like a charm, and had we not been armed with them, nothing could have prevented our being captured."[73] While the Lightning Brigade was badly outnumbered at Hoover's Gap, the immense firepower of the Spencer rifles evened the odds. "One half of our boys emptied the chambers of their guns seven shots in half a minute," noted a member of the 98th Illinois. "The Rebs couldn't stand it, but supposed the woods were full of Feds."[74] It was a remarkable stand against long odds and established the Lightning Brigade as a force to be reckoned with. The Confederates would soon learn just how formidable the Lightning Brigade could be.

At Chickamauga, Wilder and his 1,900 officers and men left their mark on the battlefield, seemingly fighting everywhere, and inflicting heavy losses on the Army of Tennessee with the massed firepower of their Spencer rifles.[75] Along with the stands by Minty and the two guns

70 John T. Wilder, "The Battle of Hoover's Gap," *Sketches of War History, 1861-1865*, vol. 6, Ohio Commandery, Military Order of the Loyal Legion of the United States (Cincinnati: Monfort, 1908), 172.

71 Ibid. That promotion never came through. Wilder received a brevet to brigadier general of volunteers on August 7, 1864, but illness forced him to resign his commission in October of that year. Wilder's official rank at the end of the war remained colonel.

72 Wilson, "Wilder's Brigade of Mounted Infantry in the Tullahoma-Chickamauga Campaigns," *National Tribune*, October 12, 1893.

73 "Harry," "Letter from the 17th Indiana Regiment," *Weekly Wabash Express*, July 22, 1863.

74 Edward Kitchell, diary, June 24, 1863, Illinois State Historical Library, Springfield, IL, 1.

75 The reported strengths of Wilder's regiments on September 18, 1863, are as follows: the 98th Illinois had 485 officers and men, the 123rd Illinois had 422 officers and men, the 17th Indiana had 513 officers and men, and the 72nd Indiana had 480 officers and men. See September 30 brigade return for Wilder's Lightning Brigade, RG 94, Entry 65, Box 28, NARA. According to historian Richard Baumgartner, the 92nd

of the Chicago Board of Trade Battery at Reed's Bridge, the stand by a regiment and a half of the Lightning Brigade at Alexander's Bridge on September 18 forced Bragg to change his entire plan of battle for what became the battle of Chickamauga. Their work that day was nothing short of remarkable.

The Tullahoma campaign marked the declarations by Minty (at Shelbyville on June 27) and Wilder (at Hoover's Gap on June 24) that they were forces to be reckoned with. They proved it beyond dispute at Chickamauga. These two talented amateur soldiers and the men they commanded found themselves in the right places at the right times on September 18, 1863. Their stout stands that day forced Braxton Bragg to completely overhaul his plan of attack and probably saved Rosecrans's army from destruction.

Illinois, which was on detached duty and did not serve with the rest of the brigade on September 18, 1863, had eight companies present, numbering 383 officers and men. These men are not counted in the strength of Wilder's brigade on September 18, 1863. See Baumgartner, *Blue Lightning*, 152.

Chapter Two

Opening Moves: August 14-September 17, 1863

On June 24, 1863, Maj. Gen. William S. Rosecrans, the commander of the Army of the Cumberland, commenced a spectacular campaign of maneuver designed to flank Gen. Braxton Bragg's Army of Tennessee out of Middle Tennessee. With Wilder's Lightning Brigade leading the way, the Union army successfully drove Bragg's army from Middle Tennessee while incurring less than 600 casualties in the process. The Army of Tennessee retreated all the way to Chattanooga, leaving Rosecrans to seize the initiative.[1] Rosecrans—brilliant, eccentric, and mercurial—had designed and delivered a masterstroke that was overshadowed by the critical twin Union victories at Gettysburg and Vicksburg during the first week of July. Gettysburg, in particular, was a bloodletting of nearly unprecedented magnitude where the Army of the Potomac defeated Gen. Robert E. Lee's vaunted Army of Northern Virginia north of the Mason-Dixon Line and blunted its bid to achieve a great victory on Northern soil. The fall of the Confederate bastion at Vicksburg meant the Mississippi River was now entirely under Union control and the Confederacy had been split in twain. Consequently, Rosecrans's spectacular but nearly bloodless success during the Tullahoma campaign was almost completely overlooked.[2]

1 There is no satisfactory monograph on the Tullahoma campaign. For the most detailed treatment of these events, see Michael R. Bradley, *Tullahoma: The 1863 Campaign for the Control of Middle Tennessee* (Shippensburg, PA: White Mane, 1999).

2 Forty-four-year-old Maj. Gen. William S. Rosecrans was born in Delaware County, Ohio. He had little formal education as a boy but had an active and eager intelligence.

Maj. Gen. William S. Rosecrans, commander of the Army of the Cumberland. *Library of Congress*

He graduated fifth in the West Point class of 1842 and was commissioned into the Corps of Engineers. He resigned his commission in 1854. In 1861, he was appointed colonel of the 23rd Ohio Infantry as well as a brigadier general in the regular army. He fought well in West Virginia in 1861 and commanded the left wing of Maj. Gen. John Pope's Army of the Mississippi in 1862 and succeeded Pope in command when Pope went east to assume command of the new Army of Virginia. He was promoted to major general in September 1862 and assumed command of the Army of the Cumberland that

In the wake of the three major successes that summer, Union general in chief Maj. Gen. Henry W. Halleck and President Lincoln were determined to press their advantage. They insisted that Rosecrans move quickly to seize the vital rail hub city of Chattanooga in southeastern Tennessee. Doing so would secure the railheads needed to advance on Atlanta and would interdict the Confederate lines of supply going north toward Nashville and Knoxville and south toward Atlanta. Chattanooga was also an important manufacturing center with a large, busy ironworks on the Tennessee River, which was also a critical route of commerce. Situated at the base of Lookout Mountain, which extended from Chattanooga to northern Alabama, Chattanooga held the key to unlocking the Deep South for the Union.

Bragg's beaten Army of Tennessee retreated across the Cumberland Mountains, crossed the Tennessee River at Bridgeport, and then fell back to Chattanooga, where the Confederates began digging in along the mountain passes above and below the important railroad and river town. Rosecrans pursued and took up a line from McMinnville to Winchester, with advances to Pelham and Stevenson. The Army of the Cumberland then moved to Bridgeport in time to save a major sawmill from destruction but not the important railroad bridge across the Tennessee, which is both broad and deep (about 2,700 feet wide at Bridgeport alone). One of Rosecrans's men described the Tennessee River as "the most serious natural obstacle which the Union army had encountered since it left the Ohio River."[3]

Because of the damage done to the railroad, it took Rosecrans time to resupply his army. The Army of the Cumberland finally moved out on August 14, 1863. The movement over the mountains began on August 16, and by August 20 the entire army had reached the banks of the

fall. Rosecrans had converted to Catholicism in his youth and was a devout follower. Brilliant, mercurial, restless, and high-strung, Rosecrans was a strategic genius. See Ezra J. Warner, *Generals in Blue: Lives of the Union Commanders* (Baton Rouge: Louisiana State University Press, 1964), 410-11. For the best full-length biography of Rosecrans, who is probably the most misunderstood and most unappreciated Union army commander of the Civil War, see William M. Lamers, *The Edge of Glory: A Biography of General William S. Rosecrans, U.S.A.* (Baton Rouge: Louisiana State University Press, 1961). While quite dated, this book gives the best overview of Rosecrans's remarkable life and accomplishments.

3 Commissioners for the Chickamauga and Chattanooga National Park, *Indiana at Chickamauga 1863-1900: Report of the Indiana Commissioners Chickamauga National Military Park* (Indianapolis: William D. Burford, 1901), 38.

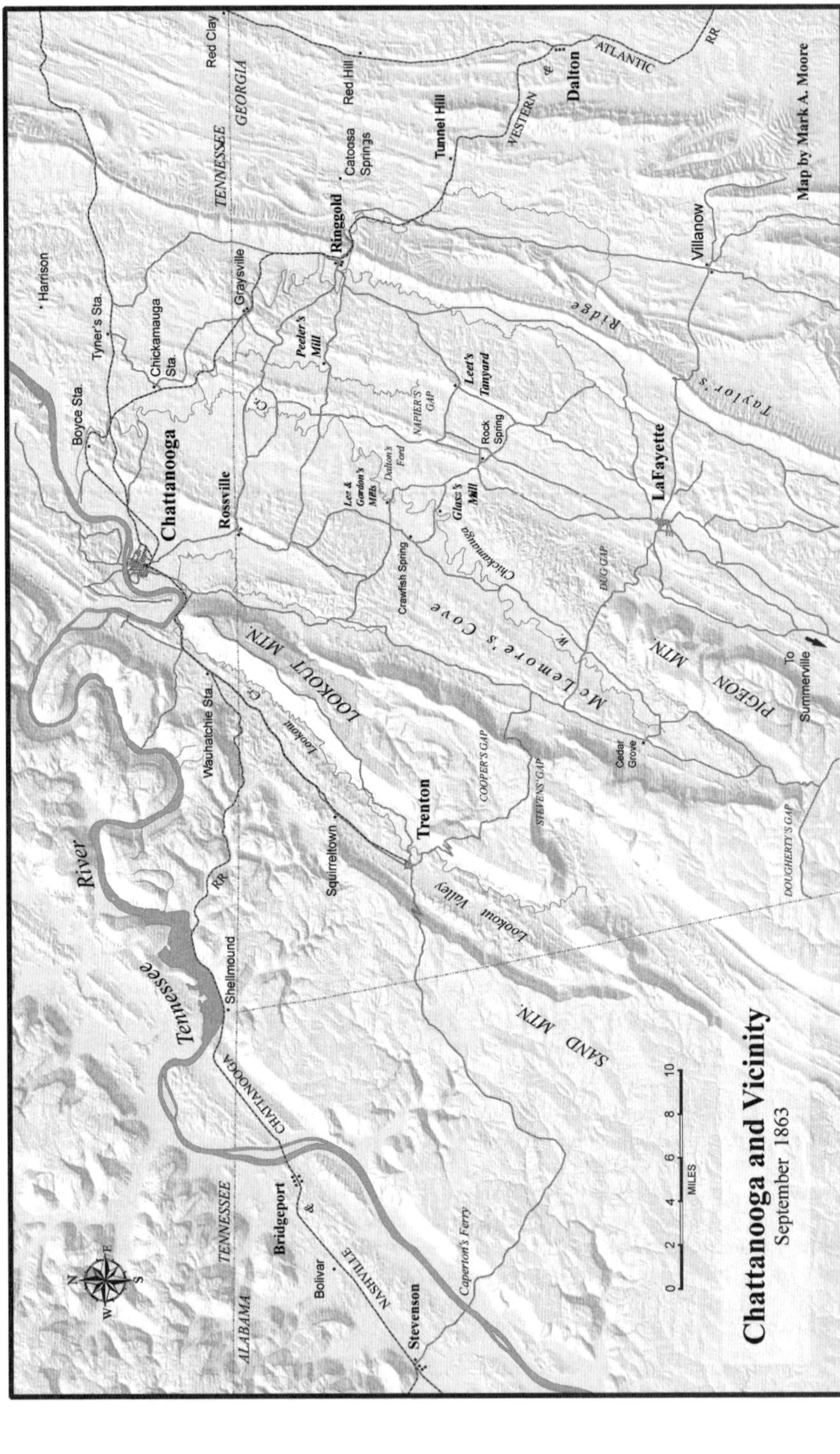

Chattanooga and its environs, September 1863.

Maj. Gen. Thomas Crittenden, commander of the Army of the Cumberland's 21st Corps. *Library of Congress*

Tennessee River above Stevenson, Alabama.[4] Because Confederate cavalry commander Maj. Gen. Joseph Wheeler failed to adequately picket the river crossings, Rosecrans was able to lay a pontoon bridge across the Tennessee on August 29. The Army of the Cumberland began crossing that day, and by September 4 the entire army had made its way across the river and was in position to begin its movement on Bragg's positions in and around Chattanooga.[5]

Major General Thomas L. Crittenden commanded the Army of the Cumberland's 21st Corps.[6] His corps was to cross the river at

4 A detailed discussion of the opening phases of the Chickamauga campaign and the initial movements of the Army of the Cumberland strays far beyond the scope of this study. For the best account of these events yet published, see David A. Powell's indispensable *The Chickamauga Campaign: A Mad Irregular Battle, From the Crossing of Tennessee River Through the Second Day, August 22-September 19, 1863* (El Dorado Hills, CA: Savas-Beatie, 2014).

5 Powell has also done an outstanding job of documenting the wretched performances by Confederate cavalry commanders Joseph Wheeler and Nathan Bedford Forrest during the Chickamauga campaign, including a detailed discussion of Wheeler's failure to picket the Tennessee River at Stevenson and its implications for Bragg's army. See David A. Powell, *Failure in the Saddle: Nathan Bedford Forrest, Joe Wheeler, and the Confederate Cavalry in the Chickamauga Campaign* (El Dorado Hills, CA: Savas-Beatie, 2010).

6 Major General Thomas L. Crittenden was the son of U.S. Senator John J. Crittenden of Kentucky. His older brother, Maj. Gen. George B. Crittenden, commanded a division in the Confederate army, demonstrating the deep schisms in Kentucky society over secession. Crittenden was born in Russellville, Kentucky, on May 15, 1819. He was admitted to the bar in 1840 and elected commonwealth attorney for his district. He served as colonel of the 3rd Kentucky Infantry during the Mexican War. In 1849, President John Tyler appointed him consul to Liverpool, England. In 1853, he relocated to Frankfort and then Louisville, Kentucky. He was appointed commander of those

Bridgeport, Shellmound, and Battle Creek and advance toward the foot of Lookout Mountain, take post at Wauhatchie, and threaten Chattanooga. Along with two brigades of infantry, Minty's cavalry brigade and Wilder's Lightning Brigade were left behind to cover Crittenden's rear and to annoy the enemy. By September 6, Crittenden had completed this movement. Minty, Wilder, and Brig. Gen. William Hazen's infantry brigades then joined Crittenden there. Major General George H. Thomas's 14th Corps took the same route and completed its movement by September 8. The march was long and difficult. A severe drought had reduced the creeks to trickles or dry beds, and thick, stifling dust infiltrated everything. Billowing dust clouds suffocated men and animals.

Bragg's army occupied the brow of Lookout Mountain and the city of Chattanooga below. Rosecrans realized he would have to dislodge these troops if he was to capture Chattanooga. Bragg, however, realized that if he continued to hold Chattanooga, the Army of the Cumberland would trap his army there, so he withdrew his troops from the city. Rosecrans put his army in motion on September 8-9, and probing attacks by Crittenden's troops discovered that Bragg had withdrawn from the city all the way to La Fayette, Georgia, behind Pigeon Mountain. With Wilder's Lightning Brigade leading the way, the Army of the Cumberland then occupied Chattanooga on September 9 without incident or bloodshed, setting the stage for the great battle along West Chickamauga Creek that would soon follow. Once more Rosecrans had maneuvered Bragg and his army out of a strong position without fighting a significant battle. It seemed Bragg had no intention to stand and fight or to resist Rosecrans's advance. Bragg, however, had other plans. He was actively searching for an opportunity to pounce upon Rosecrans's scattered army and defeat it in detail.

Tasked with covering the Tennessee River crossings and concerned that Forrest's command now numbered three full brigades, Robert Minty worried about the relative weakness of his command. "I am momentarily expecting Colonel Klein with the battalion of the 3rd Indiana and my supply train, from McMinnville," he wrote on September 8. "I shouldvvery

Kentucky forces that remained loyal to the Union and was commissioned a brigadier general in September 1861. After the battle of Shiloh, he became a division commander. He was commissioned a major general on July 17, 1862, and then became a corps commander just before the Tullahoma campaign. Although an amateur, Crittenden was a capable corps commander. See Warner, *Generals in Blue*, 100.

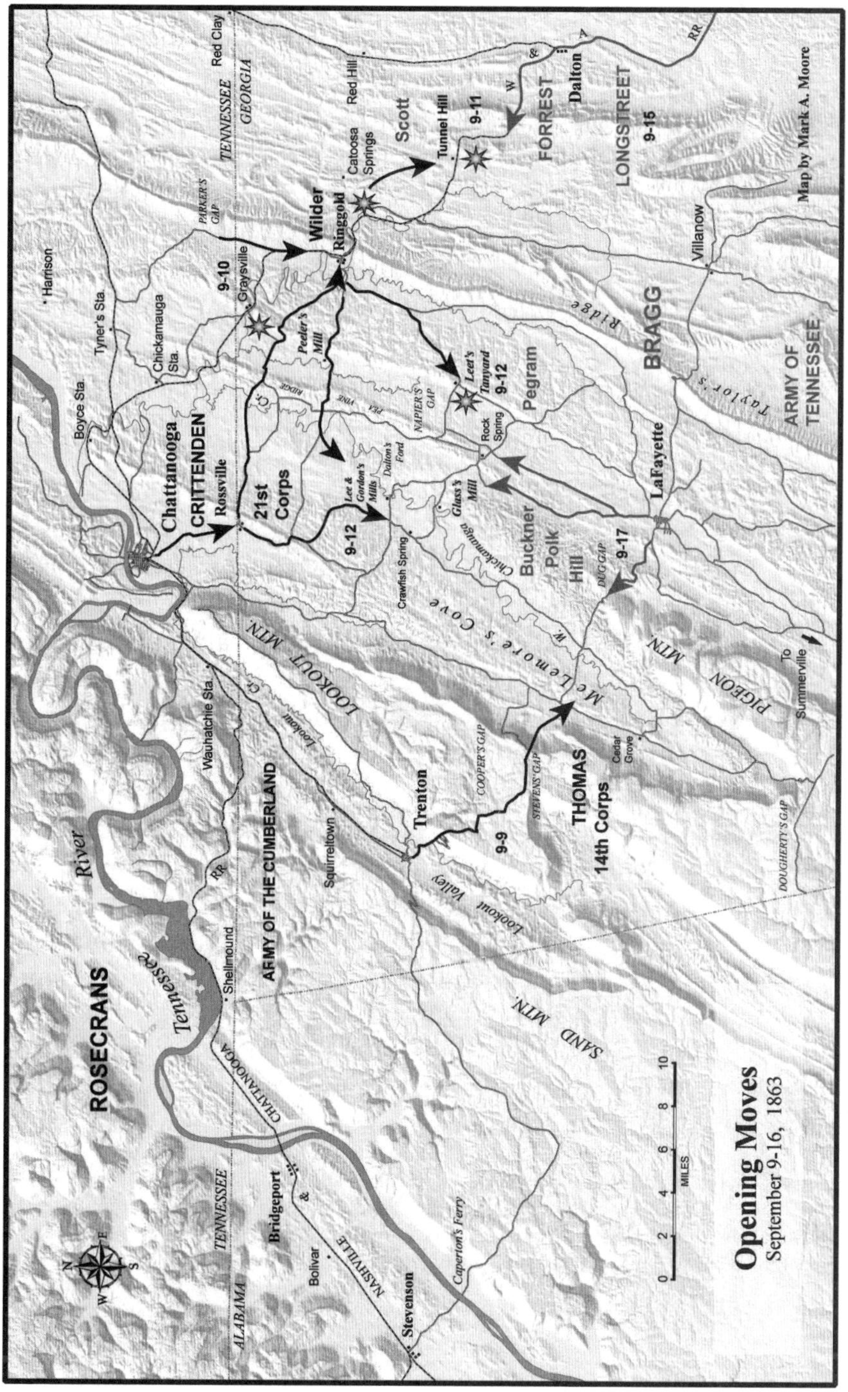

Opening moves, September 9-16, 1863.

Maj. Gen. Alexander McCook, commander of the Army of the Cumberland's 20th Corps. *Library of Congress*

much like to form a junction with him before moving. It will give me 200 more men." The request to have Klein's Hoosiers join him was denied. Minty would have to make do without them.[7]

Rosecrans's army was scattered and vulnerable. Major General Alexander M. McCook's 20th Corps was nearly 40 miles south of Chattanooga at the base of Lookout Mountain, widely separated from the rest of the army, which was strung out between Valley Head and Chattanooga. Thomas's 14th Corps was at Trenton, while Crittenden's 21st Corps held Chattanooga. By being so spread out, the Army of the Cumberland was badly exposed and could be defeated in detail if Bragg could develop an appropriate plan to do so.

Bragg intended to concentrate his army between Lee and Gordon's Mill, which is 15 miles south of Chattanooga, and La Fayette.[8] He was receiving massive reinforcements from the forces that tried to defend Vicksburg, and he would soon get reinforcements from Lt. Gen. James Longstreet's First Corps of the Army of Northern Virginia, which was being sent to him by a long, roundabout railroad route. Before long,

7 *OR* 30, pt. 3, 461.

8 In 1836, Gwinnett County, Georgia, native James Gordon established a plantation at Crawfish Springs, as the town of Chickamauga was known in those days. He built a gristmill on Chickamauga Creek two miles east of town. The mill was near a blacksmith shop and a stagecoach stop and included the area's first general store. In 1857, James Gordon passed the management of the mill on to his son-in-law, James Lee, who changed the name of the company. The mill was a prominent landmark and an important part of the local economy. Gordon and Lee both were wealthy men. See James Sartain, *History of Walker County Georgia* (Dalton, GA: A. J. Showalter Co., 1932), 215.

Gen. Braxton Bragg, the commander of the dysfunctional Army of Tennessee. *Museum of the Confederacy*

and for one of the few times during the Civil War, Bragg would enjoy a numeric advantage over his foe, Rosecrans.[9]

Bragg promoted Brig. Gen. Nathan Bedford Forrest to corps command and gave him orders to "picket the river, bring up the rear . . . so as to cover all."[10] Forrest faced a stern test that he was not well suited to perform. A talented raider and intuitive fighter, Forrest had no particular talent for the traditional roles of cavalry: scouting, screening, and reconnaissance. He had a long front to cover and only half of his inexperienced men to do it with. He left the division of Brig. Gen. John Pegram behind to perform this critical duty. Pegram had little experience commanding cavalry, and he had a difficult relationship with one of his brigade commanders, Col. John Scott of the 1st Louisiana Cavalry.[11] As a result, Forrest repeatedly failed throughout the campaign.

9 At 46 years of age, Gen. Braxton Bragg was at the apex of his military career. Born in Warrenton, North Carolina, on March 22, 1817, Bragg graduated fifth in the West Point class of 1837 and was commissioned a second lieutenant of artillery on July 1, 1837. He served in the First and Second Seminole Wars and then served in Maj. Gen. Zachary Taylor's army during the Mexican War, where he earned a brevet promotion to captain for his defense of Fort Brown, Texas, in May 1846. He was promoted to captain just a few weeks later. He earned a brevet to major for his performance at the battle of Monterey on September 23 and then distinguished himself during the battle of Buena Vista on February 23, 1847, when his artillery filled the gaps in the American line and largely repulsed the numerically superior Mexican army, earning a brevet to lieutenant colonel and a lifelong friendship with Col. Jefferson Davis of Mississippi. Bragg had a "disputatious" personality (to use Ulysses S. Grant's adjective) and had real problems getting along with any superior or subordinate officer. He resigned his commission in 1856 in a dispute over how to use horse artillery and settled in Louisiana, where he became a sugar planter. He also helped to found the State Military School (now Louisiana State University) in 1860. He was appointed to command a 5,000-man army in Louisiana and captured the Baton Rouge arsenal. He was commissioned a brigadier general in the Confederate army on March 7, 1861, and commanded a portion of the Gulf Coast. He was promoted to major general on September 12, 1861. He helped Gen. Albert S. Johnston form the Army of Tennessee and served as its chief of staff and then as a corps commander. He performed well at Shiloh and was promoted to full general on April 12, 1862. In that capacity, he led his Army of Tennessee into Kentucky in the fall of 1862 and at Stones River at the end of the year. Just as he was difficult, dyspeptic, and unpopular with his subordinates and the men in the ranks and unable to get along with anyone, his Army of Tennessee was dysfunctional and had major command problems. His close relationship with Jefferson Davis probably kept him in command of the Army of Tennessee much longer than he otherwise might have retained the command. See William C. Davis and Julie Hoffman, eds., *The Confederate General*, 6 vols. (Harrisburg, PA: National Historical Society, 1991), vol. 1, 113-14.

10 *OR* 30, pt. 4, 611.

11 Brigadier General John Pegram, born on January 24, 1832, in Petersburg, Virginia, was a member of the West Point class of 1854 (he graduated 10th in a class of 46). After graduation, he was commissioned into the 2nd Dragoons and served with his

Maj. Gen. Nathan B. Forrest, commander of one of the two cavalry corps assigned to Bragg's army. *Alabama Dept. of Archives and History*

company until he was ordered to report to West Point as an instructor of cavalry in January 1857. In September 1857, he was ordered to report back to his regiment, and he served in the Utah Expedition of 1857-58. He was given a leave of absence to go to Europe to observe the Papal War of 1859 and returned to active duty after doing so. He resigned his commission on May 10, 1861, earning the distinction of being the first former U.S. officer to offer his services to Virginia. He was commissioned a lieutenant

On the morning of September 9, Rosecrans ordered the Army of the Cumberland to pursue Bragg's retreating army. The 14th Corps was to move east "as rapidly as possible to La Fayette and make every exertion to strike the enemy in flank." Without waiting for his supply trains, McCook's 20th Corps was to go to Alpine and Summerville to attack Bragg whenever he could reach him with reasonable success. Rosecrans's Cavalry Corps was to cover the army's right flank and to head for Bragg's supply depot at Rome, Georgia.[12] With both Rosecrans and Bragg jockeying for position in an effort to find an opportunity to attack each other, something had to give.

Major General James S. Negley's 14th Corps division concentrated at the foot of Stevens's Gap through Lookout Mountain on the night of September 9. Thomas ordered Negley to march for La Fayette the next morning; other elements of Thomas's corps were to follow them a day or two later.[13] Negley found himself isolated, nearly ten miles from La Fayette in a narrow V-shaped valley called McLemore's Cove, with Pigeon Mountain between him and his objective at La Fayette. Nervous of being trapped, Thomas ordered the rest of his corps to concentrate in McLemore's Cove so as to be able to launch an assault on La Fayette if necessary.[14] The next morning, Thomas complained: "I very much regret not having Wilder's brigade, as I believe if I had it I could have seized Dug and Catlett's Gaps before the enemy could have reached those places. The want of cavalry has prevented me from communicating with General McCook also."[15]

---

colonel of the 10th Virginia Infantry and was captured at the battle of Rich Mountain on July 11, 1861. He was exchanged and returned to duty on the staff of Gen. P. G. T. Beauregard and then served as chief of staff to Maj. Gen. Edmund Kirby-Smith. He was promoted to brigadier general on November 10, 1862, and assumed command of a brigade of cavalry in the Army of Tennessee. He was promoted to division command in Forrest's corps just before the battle of Chickamauga. He was the older brother of Col. William "Willie" Pegram, the supremely gifted artillerist who was killed during the battle of Five Forks on April 1, 1865. See Davis and Hoffman, *The Confederate General*, vol. 5, 5-6.

12 *OR* 30, pt. 3, 483, 488-89, 500.

13 Ibid., 485.

14 Ibid.

15 Ibid., 511.

Lt. Gen. Leonidas Polk, an Episcopal bishop who was a confidante of Confederate Pres. Jefferson Davis. Polk and Bragg did not get along. *Museum of the Confederacy*

Thomas had good reason to be nervous. Bragg had detected the presence of the Union infantry in McLemore's Cove, and he had his entire army nearby to assault the federal troops there. Bragg decided to attack with two divisions of two different corps of his army: Maj. Gen. Thomas C. Hindman's division of Lt. Gen. Leonidas Polk's Corps and Maj. Gen. Patrick Cleburne's hard-fighting division of Lt. Gen. D. H. Hill's Corps. Cleburne's troops were already picketing the passes through Pigeon Mountain and were nearby. The fact that these two divisions were from two different corps created command, control, and coordination problems for two units that were not accustomed to working together. The combined force of about 12,000 Confederates was ordered to pounce on the Union troops in the cove.[16]

However well planned this movement might be, it did not go off as scheduled. Word reached Hindman that more Union troops had moved into the area, and timing issues also intervened. Finally, the selection of two divisions from two different corps meant there was friction over who was to be in overall command, causing delays. Negley learned the entire Confederate army was concentrated at La Fayette, so he immediately called for reinforcements. Bragg would soon be able to spring his attack on the Union infantry in McLemore's Cove.[17]

On September 10, Wilder's brigade advanced toward Ringgold. The 72nd Indiana arrived there that night and reported there were no enemy troops in the town, which was supposed to be defended by Col. John S.

16 Ibid., pt. 2, 28.

17 Powell, *The Chickamauga Campaign*, 118-25.

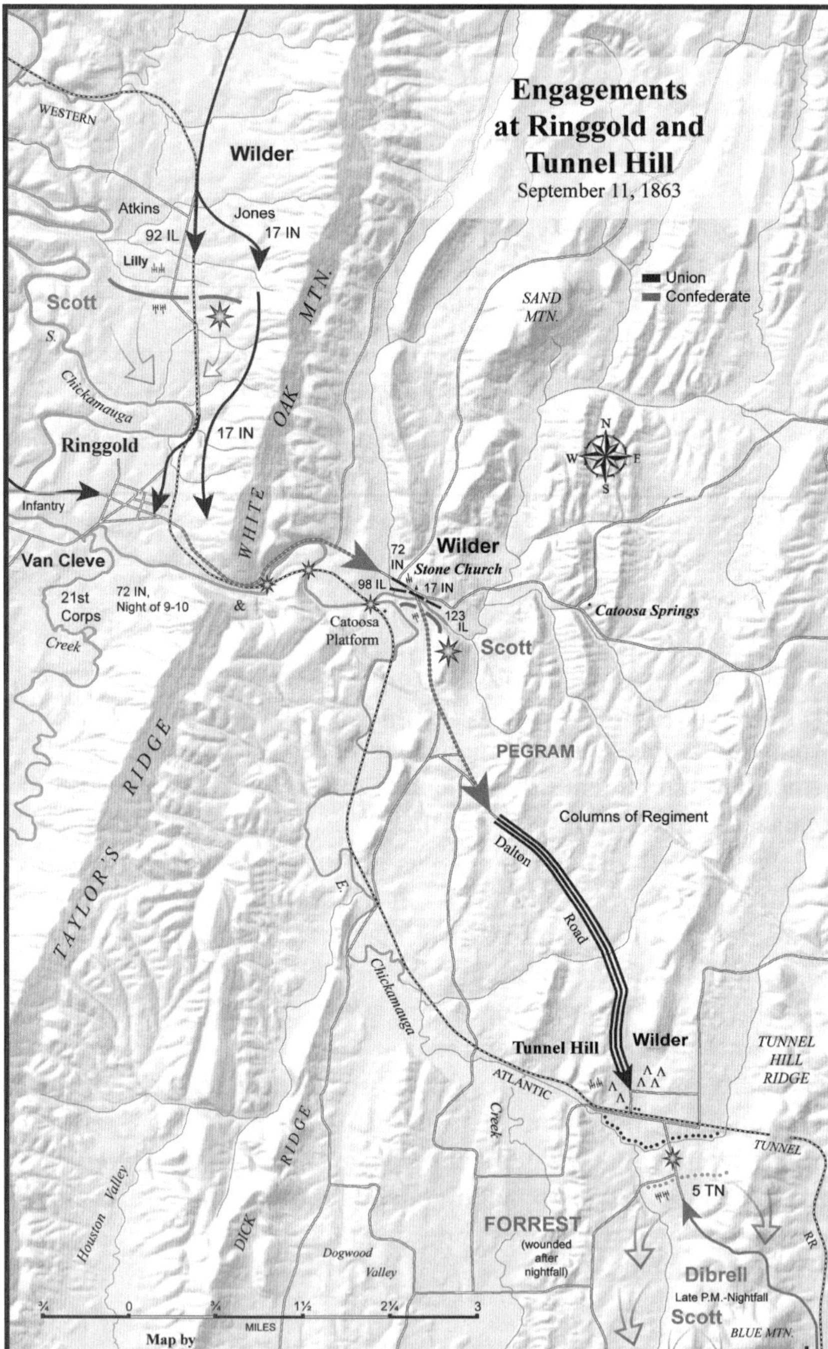

Engagements at Ringgold and Tunnel Hill, September 11, 1863.

Col. John S. Scott of the 1st Louisiana Cavalry commanded a brigade of cavalry in Pegram's Division. *National Archives*

Scott's 900-man brigade of Pegram's cavalry division.[18] The next morning the 92nd Illinois of Wilder's brigade found Scott's troopers a mile or so north of Ringgold. The Illini repulsed two mounted charges by Scott's troopers, prompting Wilder to bring up two guns of Lilly's battery and the 17th Indiana to support the 92nd Illinois. "Wilder ordered the [92nd Illinois] forward and forward it went, Wilder himself in the middle of the road, on the skirmish line, revolver in hand, and telling the boys on both sides of the road: 'Dress on me, boys.'"[19]

Although some of Scott's troopers attempted to resist, they were outflanked and outgunned. Scott's cavalrymen fell back about two and a half miles, leaving 13 of their own dead on the field, pursued by the rest of the 92nd Illinois. Pvt. Frederick Petermier of Company F of the 92nd Illinois had his horse shot out from under him, the butt of his rifle shot away, and his pants, coat flap, and coat collar torn by bullets. Nonplussed, Petermier declared, "Now, I am tired to death running after them."[20] As they retreated, the sound of artillery fire from the southeast announced

18 John Sims Scott was born on September 21, 1826, in Wilkinson County, Mississippi. He was a wealthy planter in Louisiana and a Mexican War veteran. He was commissioned colonel of the 1st Louisiana Cavalry on May 4, 1861, and led his regiment and often a brigade in Tennessee and Kentucky in 1862. He was court-martialed for insubordination and reprimanded on March 16, 1863. General Albert S. Johnston called Scott "the best cavalry officer I know of in the Confederate army." Others, however, found him "dangerous" and "headstrong." By the end of the war, he was the most senior colonel serving in the Confederate cavalry, but personality clashes with his superiors prevented him from being promoted beyond the rank of colonel. See Bruce S. Allardice, *Confederate Colonels: A Biographical Register* (Columbia: University of Missouri Press, 2008), 335.

19 Ninety-Second Illinois Infantry, *Ninety-Second Illinois Volunteers* (Freeport, IL: Journal Steam Publishing House and Bookbindery, 1875), 103.

20 *OR* 30, pt. 1, 446, 454.

the arrival of a brigade of infantry from the 21st Corps on Scott's flank. With a force of unknown strength on his flank, Scott ordered his brigade to abandon the town of Ringgold. The grayclad horsemen fell back to a position about two and a half miles south of the town, planted a section of artillery, and waited for Wilder to arrive. A section of Lilly's battery deployed and opened fire, and a determined attack by the Lightning Brigade compelled Scott to withdraw again, this time for almost seven miles to a position south of Tunnel Hill, leaving possession of Ringgold to the Union forces.

Once the advancing infantry of Brig. Gen. Horatio Van Cleve's 21st Corps division secured Ringgold, Wilder split his command. He detached the 92nd Illinois to report to Thomas's 14th Corps, while his other four regiments pushed as far as Tunnel Hill, a station on the Western and Atlantic Railroad, which connected Atlanta and Chattanooga, about ten miles south of Ringgold. The 92nd Illinois did not return to serve with the rest of the Lightning Brigade until September 20 and played no part in the stand at Alexander's Brigade on September 18.

Forrest decided to make a stand at Tunnel Hill, so he deployed his horsemen and two artillery pieces and waited for the Lightning Brigade to arrive. The 72nd Indiana led Wilder's advance. As the head of Wilder's column appeared, Forrest ordered a charge and also ordered his artillery to open. Lieutenant Colonel Samuel Kirkpatrick of the 72nd Indiana shouted: "Company A, they are charging us! Dismount and give 'em hell!" The Hoosiers dismounted as Kirkpatrick cried: "Damn 'em—damn 'em—shoot 'em in the guts! Go for 'em!" The combined firepower of the 72nd Indiana's Spencer rifles checked the charge, and the Confederates wheeled and dashed away. After going another mile or so the column halted, and the entire brigade dismounted and formed a line of battle, preparing to fight on foot. "Between our line and that tunnel there were thousands of rebels," recalled Sgt. Benjamin Magee of the 72nd Indiana. "It was near sun down and our only safety lay in keeping up a bold front. It seems that the enemy had purposely been drawing us on, and were now waiting for us to charge them, with the expectation that they would take us all in. We did not charge, but held them in check until after dark."[21] Lilly deployed a section of his battery

21 Benjamin F. Magee, *History of the 72nd Indiana Volunteer Infantry of the Mounted Lighting Brigade* (Lafayette, IN: S. Vater and Co., 1882), 155.

on a hill, and a sharp artillery duel opened that lasted for the better part of an hour, until Forrest finally withdrew.[22]

Forrest's failure to drive Wilder's men from Tunnel Hill meant that significant forces of Union troops now sat athwart Bragg's main line of supply now much closer to Dalton than Bragg's own main body at La Fayette. These Union threats to his logistics meant that Bragg would have to act soon.[23] Wilder's tired soldiers spent the night bivouacked in line of battle near the mouth of the tunnel, fully expecting the fight to resume the next day. They were ordered not to unsaddle or to light fires.[24] It was a long and unpleasant night for Wilder's weary soldiers. Forrest's troopers were "swarming around us all night," said Maj. James Connolly of the 123rd Illinois.[25] Wilder was worried. At 3:00 a.m., he sent a note to Van Cleve: "From all appearance we may have a pretty sharp fight here this morning. I desire to know whether your command will come forward to my support, and if so at what time?"[26]

On September 11, Bragg's forces finally moved on McLemore's Cove, but an overly cautious Thomas C. Hindman did not move with alacrity, meaning that only a portion of the planned attack would advance.[27] Although Bragg had ordered an immediate attack on the isolated Union forces, confusing orders and a lack of aggressiveness by Hindman ultimately caused Hindman to decide to retreat rather than to attack. Further, the Union forces in the cove recognized their precarious position and also began retreating as well. Hence the two forces repelled from each

22 *OR* 30, pt. 1, 450.

23 Powell, *The Chickamauga Campaign*, 131. Reinforced by the cavalry brigade of Col. George Dibrell, Forrest led a reconnaissance toward Tunnel Hill, which was held by Wilder's Lightning Brigade. A Spencer volley wounded Forrest, who, "faint from pain and loss of blood . . . took a drink of whiskey at the surgeon's urging but did not leave the field." See Jack D. Welsh, *Medical Histories of Confederate Generals* (Kent, OH: Kent State University Press, 1995), 71. How this wound affected Forrest's lackluster performance on September 18, 1863, is unknown, but it would not be unreasonable to assume that it did factor into his stamina and effectiveness that critical day.

24 Commissioners for the Chickamauga and Chattanooga National Park, *Indiana at Chickamauga*, 204.

25 James A. Connolly, *Three Years in the Army of the Cumberland* (Bloomington: Indiana University Press, 1987), 280.

26 *OR* 30, pt. 3, 586.

27 Hindman's hesitation persisted even after Bragg reinforced him with Buckner's whole corps, another 9,500 men, doubling the attack force.

Brig. Gen. Thomas J. Wood, commander of the First Division of Crittenden's 21st Corps. *Library of Congress*

other rather than coming together. To Bragg's eternal frustration, the opportunity to destroy a significant portion of Thomas's 14th Corps in McLemore's Cove slipped away, upsetting the North Carolinian's plans to defeat Rosecrans in detail.[28]

Finally alerted to the exposed position of his army and the narrow escape at McLemore's Cove and that Bragg was not retreating after all, William S. Rosecrans began taking steps to concentrate the far-flung elements of his army. That night he directed Crittenden to pull his 21st Corps back toward La Fayette and to connect with Brig. Gen. Thomas Wood's division at Lee and Gordon's Mill, meaning that Crittenden could then defend the direct route to Chattanooga if Bragg decided to move that way or support Thomas if the 14th Corps moved to attack La Fayette.[29] In the meantime, Wilder's men were recalled from their distant outpost on Tunnel Hill and ordered to ride down the Ringgold-La Fayette Road via Leet's Tanyard. They were "to attack boldly, and report often."[30]

Rosecrans sent all of his available cavalry but Minty and Wilder to McCook on the southern flank, leaving only these two brigades. Thomas, still smarting from the near-disaster at McLemore's Cove, wrote: "I am

28 For a detailed discussion of the Confederate failure at McLemore's Cove, which is well beyond the scope of this study, see Powell, *The Chickamauga Campaign*, 138-60.

29 *OR* 30, part 4, 546.

30 Ibid., 574.

greatly in want of cavalry, and would respectfully ask that if Wilder's brigade . . . is not on special duty, to have it sent to me at once. . . . The information I desire, and which is all important, is beyond my reach."[31] Further, Minty's brigade was still on the north side of the Tennessee River, upstream from Chattanooga, trying to maintain communication with Maj. Gen. Ambrose E. Burnside's army in Eastern Tennessee near Knoxville. On September 11, Rosecrans recalled Minty and sent Wilder to Thomas once Minty joined Crittenden's command in and around Chattanooga. His troopers spent September 12 crossing the Tennessee River with orders to join Crittenden. They did not do so until the next day. Until Minty arrived, Wilder's Lightning Brigade had to suffice to screen Crittenden.[32]

When the time came for Minty's troopers to cross, they did not have an easy time of it. Private Thomas Dornblaser, in the 7th Pennsylvania Cavalry, wrote: "While I was trying to keep my legs out of the water by folding them over the pommel of the saddle, admiring the scene and wishing for a Raphael to reproduce it on canvas, my clumsy sorrel stumbled over a rock, plunging forward with his nose to the bottom. The strain bursted the saddle girth, and both rider and saddle toppled over into the flowing stream." Desperate, Dornblaser managed to raise his head above the water and also catch his saddle before the swift current carried it away. "A comrade brought my horse to me, and with herculean efforts I remounted and rode to shore," he recalled. "A good ducking on that cool September morning was more than I had bargained for, but the sun shone brightly, and in a few hours, I was quite comfortable." The swift current swept several troopers of the 7th Pennsylvania downstream, and they were never heard from again. "So I felt quite lucky," concluded Dornblaser.[33]

31 Ibid., 564.

32 Ibid., pt. 1, 925.

33 Thomas Franklin Dornblaser, *My Life-Story for Young and Old* (Philadelphia: Privately published, 1930), 58-59. In addition to serving as the historian for his regiment, Dornblaser became a prominent Lutheran minister in Kansas in the years after the Civil War. He not only published a well-regarded history of the 7th Pennsylvania Cavalry but also an autobiography. Dornblaser needn't have feared his drowning, as he lived to be over 100 years old, passing away on December 21, 1941, two weeks after the attack on Pearl Harbor.

Maj. James A. Connolly of the 123rd Illinois Mounted Infantry. *Abraham Lincoln Presidential Library*

Crittenden concentrated his entire corps around Lee and Gordon's Mill on September 12 after some skirmishing between Wood's division and some of Forrest's troopers. In the meantime, Wilder pulled out of Tunnel Hill before dawn that morning, leaving a part of the 123rd Illinois as a rear guard. Major James Connolly commanded the three companies of the rear guard, which engaged in active skirmishing with Scott's and Dibrell's troopers. Connolly "had to cover the retreat of the brigade," he wrote, "for some six hours before we got to a safe place." Connolly noted that although his command suffered no losses during this skirmishing, "We had to run like greyhounds to prevent being surrounded and cut off."[34]

That morning Scott's advance drove in Wilder's pickets. "After a sharp engagement, Wilder withdrew and [took up] a new position," recalled Lt. William G. Allen of the 5th Tennessee Cavalry of Scott's brigade. "We followed him up at a narrow place in the valley. He posted his cannons on either side of a pine thicket and placed his guns on a hill . . . sighted the guns and had them fired." Colonel G. W. McKenzie, the commander of the 5th Tennessee, wanted to charge Wilder's columns, but Scott said no, fearing a trap.[35]

Wilder and his command arrived at Ringgold about 9:00 a.m. Wilder halted for two hours to feed the horses and issue rations to his men. He then mounted up and headed out of town, southwest toward La Fayette, in the direction of Leet's Spring at Rev. Arthur I. Leet's tannery. Wilder had no way of knowing it, but his chosen route put him on the same

34 Connolly, *Three Years in the Army of the Cumberland*, 280.

35 W. G. Allen, "Lieutenant W. G. Allen Fights Gen. J. T. Wilder's Infantry Twelve Days," *Dayton Herald*, May 18, 1911.

road being used by John Pegram's Confederate cavalry division. Given the severe drought conditions, an active spring was an attractive stop for cavalry on the march, and Pegram's troopers halted to water and feed their horses, bathe, and launder their clothing.[36] Pegram sent out a patrol of 15 troopers to scout in the direction of Ringgold "to avoid a surprise," as Capt. Gustave A. Huwald, the commander of the battery of Tennessee horse artillery assigned to Pegram's command, put it, but Wilder's command gobbled up this patrol before any warning could be sent.[37] Thus, when Pegram's command finally mounted up and headed out the Ringgold Road, they had no idea they were about to run into the Lightning Brigade.

Wilder deployed a mounted skirmish line of the 17th Indiana and 98th Illinois, looking for Pegram's troopers. "We had entered the woods not more than a hundred yards, riding in column of fours, when we were surprised to see a line of horsemen top the ridge ahead, strung across the road at about fifteen-yard intervals," recalled Pvt. John W. Minnich of the 6th Georgia Cavalry. "They stopped on site of us, and we stopped at the site of them. Neither of us knew who the other was, and though within easy rifle range they did not fire at us, and we wondered about our advance guard. They were in the deepest forest shade, and we were both so dust covered that at that distance in the shadows neither could at first sight distinguish friend from foe. After a very short minute or two, one of our boys addressed the colonel thus: 'By —! Colonel, they are Yankees! They must have caught the advance guard, or we'd have heard them.'"[38]

The rapid, heavy fire of Wilder's Spencers drove Pegram's troopers back to Leet's Tanyard. "We were surprised," admitted Captain Huwald, "and only a quick disposition of General Pegram's forces enabled him to check the enemy." Huwald deployed a 12-pound howitzer on a prominent piece of high ground, "and this piece, which received the advancing

36 John W. Minnich, "Unique Experiences in the Chickamauga Campaign," *Confederate Veteran* 35 (1927): 222.

37 Postwar account of Gustave A. Huwald, October 7, 1866, in Leroy Moncure Nutt Papers, Southern Historical Collections, Wilson Library, University of North Carolina, Chapel Hill, NC. Huwald's battery was known as Huwald's Howitzer Battery because it was armed with two mountain howitzers and two rifled guns, which made it unique by using mountain howitzers in combat.

38 Minnich, "Unique Experiences," 222.

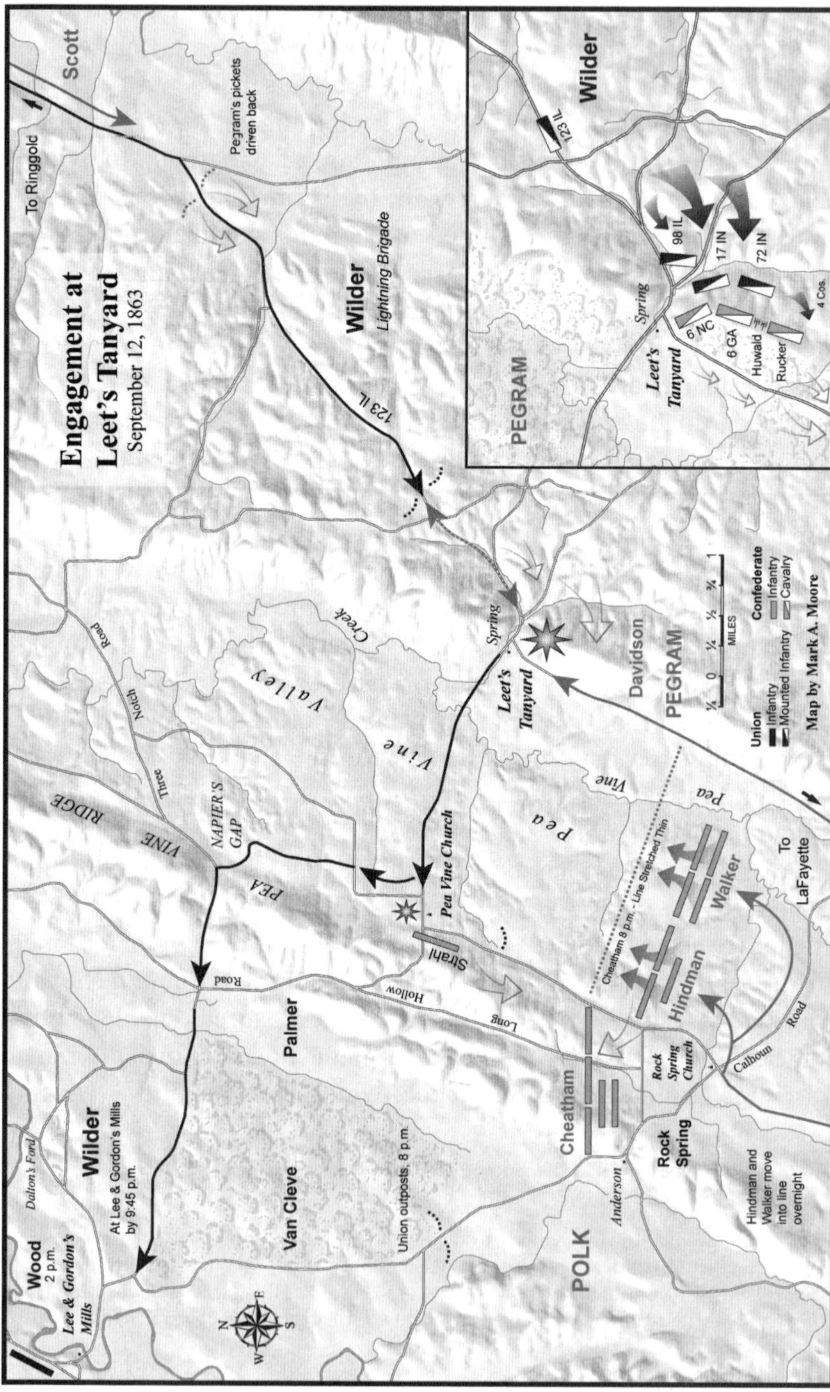

The Engagement at Leet's Tanyard, September 12, 1863.

foe with well-directed shots of shell and canister and [the 6th North Carolina Cavalry] held the enemy at bay, until another position, about three-fourths of a mile to the rear could be taken."[39]

Wilder dismounted the 17th and 72nd Indiana and ordered them to drive off the Tar Heels. A sharp skirmish broke out. Rather than make a frontal assault, four companies of the 72nd Indiana made a flanking move to the east, causing the Tar Heels to pull back half a mile to Pegram's main line of battle.[40] Wilder tried to bring Lilly's guns to bear, but Lilly "hunted all over the ground for a position for our guns but the woods were so thick that you could not load a gun without tearing away the trees," recounted one of Lilly's gunners.[41] The Lightning Brigade would have to make do without its artillery in this fight.

The 72nd Indiana swung back into line alongside the 17th Indiana and advanced, with the 98th Illinois coming up behind them in a position where the Illinoisans could support the attacks of the Hoosiers. Colonel Abram Miller of the 72nd Indiana sent the same four companies out on yet another flanking maneuver against Pegram's right. This time, though, instead of an exposed flank, they found two regiments of Confederate cavalry, the 6th Georgia and Rucker's Tennessee Legion, 785 men strong. Instead of flanking the Confederates, the Hoosiers found that the enemy line overlapped theirs, and they had to fight their way out. "The Confederates contested the ground stubbornly and poured volley after volley into the faces of our men," remembered a Hoosier, "who steadily advanced against this heavy fire until the opposing lines were within a few feet of each, when the enemy broke and fled down the other side of the ridge, leaving their dead and wounded in the field."[42]

Sergeant Benjamin Magee of the 72nd Indiana, who was hiding behind a tree, believed that "if ever there is a time when a man wishes he were as thin as a board, it is when in a place like that was. Had [Company] F wavered or faltered for one moment under this terrible fire, all would have been lost. They never stopped till in line with [Company] I, and then

39 Postwar account of Gustave A. Huwald, October 7, 1866.

40 *OR* 30, pt. 2, 528.

41 Henry Campbell, "Three Years in the Saddle," unpublished manuscript, Robert T. Ramsay Archival Center, Wabash College, Crawfordsville, IN, 94-95.

42 Commissioners for the Chickamauga and Chattanooga National Park, *Indiana at Chickamauga*, 204.

every man went to work with such earnestness and cool determination that the woods seemed a vast sheet of fire."[43] Another member of the 72nd Indiana recalled, "I thought that I was about to go up the spout when we was fighting. The rebs was concealed behind trees & bushes & I got all most on them before I knew it. We got [with]in a rod of some of them . . . and then had to fight them all most hand to hand."[44] The 72nd Indiana lost 16 killed and wounded out of 120 engaged, including the commander of Company I, Capt. William H. McMurtry, who received three different mortal wounds.[45]

Wilder pressed the attack with the rest of the 72nd Indiana and the 17th Indiana. They could hear the sounds of the heavy fighting to their right. "I never heard such firing," recounted a soldier of the 72nd Indiana. "I could hear them cheering as they advanced. . . . I never wanted to go help anybody so bad in my life. I was afraid they would all be killed or taken prisoners."[46] In the meantime, Scott's troopers were pushing the rear guard of the 123rd Illinois hard from the direction of Ringgold, meaning that Wilder could not use the same route to retreat. An officer of Scott's 5th Tennessee Cavalry called the fight "hard and hot. We drove him into the woods across Peavine Ridge to a point near Leats Springs. Here Major Rucker's Legion came in contact with Wilder's point and Capt. W. P. Darwin and his Rhea County company of the 16th Tenn. Battalion, Col. J. R. Neal, had a hard fight with Wilder's advance."[47] Wilder was almost completely surrounded, with Pegram's division to the south, Frank Armstrong's division of Forrest's corps on the left, and Brig. Gen. Otho Strahl's infantry brigade to the right, on the road to Lee and Gordon's Mills. Without the 92nd Illinois, the Lightning Brigade numbered about 1,900 men. If Forrest could link up with Pegram, he

43 Magee, *History of the Seventy-Second Indiana Infantry*, 158.

44 John M. Barnard to His Wife, September 15 and 16, 1863, in John M. Barnard Letters, Smith Library, Indiana Historical Society, Indianapolis, IN.

45 *OR* 30, pt. 1, 451; Powell, *The Chickamauga Campaign*, 172.

46 Dale Edward Linville, *Battles, Skirmishes, Events and Scenes: The Letters and Memorandum of Ambrose Remley* (Crawfordsville, IN: Montgomery County Historical Society, 1997), 81.

47 W. G. Allen, "Lieutenant W. G. Allen Fights Gen. J. T. Wilder's Infantry Twelve Days," *Dayton Herald*, May 18, 1911.

would have nearly 5,000 troopers to bring to bear on the encircled Lightning Brigade. Wilder's situation grew desperate.

The heavy fighting lasted for about two hours, prompting artillerist Huwald to describe it as a "spirited and bloody fight," while J. W. Minnick of the 6th Georgia Cavalry called it "a lively brush."[48] The 72nd Indiana fought "from tree to tree" for the entire engagement.[49] Wilder's initial assault drove Pegram's troopers far enough south to open the road leading west toward Pea Vine Church, which also led to Lee and Gordon's Mills.[50] Wilder decided to use that route to disengage, but he waited until dark to do so and use the cover of night to make his escape. Sgt. Benjamin Magee of the 72nd Indiana observed, "The longer we stayed, the more painfully apparent it became that we were in a most dangerous and exposed position, and we marveled that we had been sent out there. Rebels enough were in plain view to eat us up, and a very slight move on their part would have cut us off, and we wanted to be relieved." Magee also observed that "Col. Wilder was much confused and did not know what to do." After consulting with his regimental commanders, Wilder got his command in the saddle and moved out on the road toward Pea Vine Church. After tangling with the Lightning Brigade's Spencers, Pegram let Wilder withdraw.[51]

"We fought for two hours Wilder's Lightning Brigade of mounted infantry," reported Pegram, who called it an "unequal conflict" that was "literally hand to hand" and which cost him "about 50 killed and wounded, numbering some of my most valuable young officers."[52] The Confederate cavalry suffered heavily at the hands of the Spencer rifles. From the Union perspective, "Had it not been for our men being armed

48 Postwar account of Gustave A. Huwald, October 7, 1866; and Carolyn D. Smith, ed., "Reminiscences of J. W, Minnick, 6th Georgia Cavalry," *Northwest Georgia Historical and Genealogical Society Quarterly* 29, No. 3 (Summer 1997): 20.

49 Campbell, "Three Years in the Saddle," 95.

50 Pea Vine Church is a Baptist church organized in 1836 and is one of the oldest Baptist churches in Walker County, Georgia. It served the area between Ringgold and what became the Chickamauga battlefield. See Sartain, *History of Walker County Georgia*, 364-65.

51 Magee, *History of the 72nd Indiana Volunteer Infantry*, 159-60. According to Powell, casualties were surprisingly light on both sides: between 23 and 35 for Wilder and 50 to 82 for Pegram. See Powell, *The Chickamauga Campaign*, 174.

52 *OR* 30, pt. 2, 528.

Brig. Gen. John Pegram, a Virginian serving in the west, commanded one of Forrest's divisions. *Library of Virginia*

with the Spencer rifle, there is no doubt that the entire battalion would have been gobbled up," correctly declared Cpl. John Records of the 72nd Indiana.[53]

Wilder did not make it very far before spotting a new, more ominous threat: a large body of Confederate troops moving south, off his right flank. Wilder halted and deployed into line of battle to receive an attack from this large enemy force, but that attack never came. The threat was Maj. Gen. Benjamin F. Cheatham's large division, which had pulled back from Lee and Gordon's Mills the day before and apparently had not noticed the Lighting Brigade in its front. Worried, Wilder sought another route of escape. The 17th Indiana found a local man who was willing to guide them. Wilder had his men set up a decoy camp on a nearby hill, complete with campfires, and then he and the brigade mounted and escaped unmolested. The local guide led them across fields and farm lanes back to Lee and Gordon's Mills where, "after marching about 8 miles we reached Crittenden's Corps with greatly relieved minds," noted Sergeant Magee. It had been a close call, and Wilder was fortunate to extract his command with the minimal losses it sustained at Leet's Tanyard.[54]

Pegram reported the fight with Wilder at Leet's Tanyard to Braxton Bragg. He also reported the dispositions of the Union infantry around Lee and Gordon's Mills: "Van Cleve's division . . . said to be advancing on the Gordon Mills Road, Palmer's division on the Pea Vine Church Road, and Wood's division . . . on [the] Ringgold and Lafayette Road."[55]

53 William Records Memoir, Manuscript Section, Indiana State Library, Indianapolis, IN (hereafter cited as ISL).

54 Magee, *History of the 72nd Indiana Volunteer Infantry*, 160.

55 *OR* 30, pt. 2, 76.

Bragg realized he had another opportunity to pounce on an isolated and significant portion of the Army of the Cumberland at Lee and Gordon's Mills. The question was whether he could shake the inertia and avail himself of that opportunity, unlike the day before at McLemore's Cove.

Bragg's attack orders for dawn on September 13 were fundamentally flawed. He assumed that Polk, who often dragged his feet and bordered on insubordination, would have his troops in place to attack in a timely fashion—an assumption he should not have made. He also relied on Pegram's report of the dispositions of the Union army, which failed to inform Bragg that, instead of being strung out over 20 miles, all of Crittenden's corps had concentrated at Lee and Gordon's Mills by nightfall on September 12, meaning that Crittenden had 15,000 men in place, ready for a fight.[56]

Polk's command was not in place for a dawn attack, frustrating Bragg's plans yet again. What was supposed to be a full-on attack ended up being nothing but a reconnaissance in force by Polk, who feared being attacked by Crittenden. Crittenden ordered a series of probes, including one by the 4th U.S. Cavalry and a portion of the Chicago Board of Trade Artillery of Minty's brigade, to find out whether any Confederates had gotten between him and Thomas's 14th Corps, which was still in McLemore's Cove. The 4th U.S. and the guns came within two miles of La Fayette on their reconnaissance before finding Buckner's pickets. "Our boys captured [a picket] outpost and pickets then fell back, as we did not want to bring on an engagement" recorded Benjamin Nourse of the Chicago Board of Trade Battery. "We came back to our camp. 31 miles is good for a hot day's travel," concluded a weary Nourse.[57]

The rest of Minty's brigade enjoyed a quiet day. "Spent most of the forenoon writing letters," wrote John C. McLain of the 4th Michigan Cavalry in his diary on September 13. "Orders to move at 2 P. M. marched out 6 or 7 miles and halted. Our Company was sent on a scout to the front. Went as far as Crawfish Springs. We saw camp fires and was sure we had run on a reb camp but it was the 26th Ohio Inft. Moved back to Lee and Gordon's Mills and camped."[58]

56 Powell, *The Chickamauga Campaign*, 180.

57 Benjamin Nourse, diary, September 13, 1863, Special Collections, Duke University, Durham, NC.

58 John C. McLain, diary, September 13, 1863, Archives, State Historical Society of Iowa, Des Moines, IA.

Brig. Gen. Horatio Van Cleve, commander of the Third Division of Crittenden's 21st Corps. *USAHEC*

Brigadier General Horatio Van Cleve's division, supported by Wilder's brigade, made a reconnaissance in force down the La Fayette Road, with Wilder's men heading back toward the site of their heavy engagement at Leet's Tanyard the day before. Wilder's men "moved slowly and cautiously" because the "rebels were not far away in force."[59] Wilder reported that the enemy had fallen back toward Pea Vine Church. He also noted, "from a high hill near here I can see the entire country to Ringgold and away down toward La Fayette. No dust from moving columns in sight, except southward perhaps six miles. These do not appear to be heavy."[60]

Van Cleve's men skirmished with Confederate cavalry of Frank Armstrong's division of Forrest's corps and then with some Tennessee infantry of Brig. Gen. Otho Strahl's brigade. Having fulfilled his mission by finding the enemy, Van Cleve and Wilder then fell back to the mills. Many of the Union soldiers grew concerned. "Things begin to look dark," noted one of Lilly's artillerists. "The rebels are evidently receiving reinforcements or they wouldn't make such a stand in open country. All our officers have felt uneasy since we left Ringgold."[61]

While Van Cleve was gone, Crittenden received new orders from Rosecrans. Crittenden was to leave Wood's division to hold the mills while sending his other two divisions east to Missionary Ridge, where they were to cover several roads running north in an effort to block any attempt by Bragg to insert troops into the seam between Thomas and Crittenden. Rosecrans, however, countermanded the order when he heard about Van Cleve's dustup. He told Crittenden "to move back to Gordon's Mills . . . in case you have advanced beyond that point."[62]

Because neither the 4th U.S. Cavalry nor Wilder's probes encountered any resistance, Crittenden naively reported "there is no considerable force of [enemy] infantry near me at this time. I am satisfied they are not about to attack me . . . Indeed I think I can whip them if they do—all of them."[63] Crittenden did not realize that Polk, who had been reinforced

59 Larson, *Sergeant Larson,* 173; Richard T. Foster, diary, September 14, 1863, Archives, Ohio Historical Society, Columbus, OH.

60 *OR* 30, pt. 3, 609.

61 Quoted in Rowell, *Yankee Artillerymen*, 110.

62 *OR* 30, pt. 3, 607-8.

63 Quoted in Powell, *The Chickamauga Campaign*, 184.

by Maj. Gen. Simon B. Buckner's Corps, now had 30,000 men on hand and wanted to launch a large-scale attack. It was, however, too late in the day to stage and mount such an attack. Further, Bragg was worried that Union troops were now advancing on La Fayette from two directions, so he elected not to launch that attack.[64]

This skirmish accomplished one important thing. Bragg now had a clear understanding of the dispositions of Rosecrans's army. Frustrated once more, he called off the planned attack by Polk altogether and gave orders for his right flank to swing around toward the La Fayette Road, hoping to interpose his army between Rosecrans and Chattanooga.[65] Yet another day would go by without an attack by the Army of Tennessee. Bragg's frustration became palpable. He withdrew to La Fayette and then spent September 15 and 16 resting and refitting his command while he searched for another opportunity to attack Rosecrans and trying to understand why his orders to attack at both McLemore's Cove and then at Lee and Gordon's Mills had not been carried out. Bragg probably realized he would not have too many more similar golden opportunities to defeat his nemesis in detail such as those that had already slipped away.

Van Cleve's skirmish also convinced Rosecrans that Crittenden and Thomas needed help. Major General Gordon Granger's Reserve Corps was still at Bridgeport, guarding the lines of supply. Three of Granger's seven brigades were nearby. Granger ordered two of those brigades to march to join Rosecrans, meaning that Old Rosey would have another 6,000 men available within 24 hours. He also ordered McCook to move his 20th Corps within supporting range of Thomas's command in McLemore's Cove. Rosecrans also left his headquarters in Chattanooga and rode to join Thomas so he could be near the front and could manage things more efficiently. He spent the next two days getting his army in hand and in position to react to Bragg's threat. Finally, he also realized he had to protect the roads that would serve as his army's route of escape in case it had to retreat to Chattanooga.[66]

64 William M. Polk, *Leonidas Polk: Bishop and General*, 2 vols. (New York: Longmans, Green & Co., 1915), vol. 2, 244.

65 George W. Brent, diary, September 13, 1863, in Braxton Bragg Papers, Western Reserve Historical Society, Cleveland, OH (hereafter cited as WRHS).

66 *OR* 30, pt. 3, 570, 613.

By this time Bragg had already received heavy reinforcements from Joseph E. Johnston's army in Mississippi. More were about to come. On September 8, Longstreet and two divisions of his First Corps of the Army of Northern Virginia left their camps near Orange Court House, Virginia, and began moving toward the railheads that would take these men to Georgia to reinforce Bragg's army. Major General George E. Pickett's division, which had been battered at Gettysburg, was left to help man the defenses of Richmond, and another two brigades were sent to reinforce the defenses of Charleston, South Carolina. Brigadier General Micah Jenkins's large brigade of South Carolinians would be sent to Georgia, meaning that another 15,000 infantrymen and three battalions of artillery were coming to reinforce the Army of Tennessee. The Confederate rail system could handle only 3,000 men per day, so it would take nearly a week to move this large force to Georgia.[67]

The first of these troops, Brig. Gen. Henry Benning's brigade of Georgians, arrived in Atlanta on September 12. The next day, Brig. Gen. Jerome B. Robertson's Texas brigade arrived in Atlanta. Their division commander, Maj. Gen. John Bell Hood, was in Richmond, recuperating from a terrible wound to his arm suffered at Gettysburg. Some of his officers called on him and appealed to the Texan to return to lead them, as these men did not want Micah Jenkins—an outsider—to command them in battle. Hood agreed immediately and left Richmond on September 14. Three of Hood's brigades—Evander Law's, Henry Benning's, and Jerome Robertson's—departed Atlanta on September 14, meaning that the first 4,500 men of Longstreet's command would arrive at the front on September 15.

Because the Federals occupied Ringgold, Bragg thought that Longstreet's men would have to detrain at Resaca. Crittenden, however, was ordered to march to Lee and Gordon's Mills and abandon Ringgold, and this movement meant that Bragg could reoccupy the town. So he issued orders shifting his depot back there, "or as near thereto as possible." As near as possible proved to be an open field near Stone Church on East Chickamauga Creek, two miles south of Ringgold. Wooden walkways were constructed there that were dubbed Catoosa Platform, and they

67 Powell, *The Chickamauga Campaign*, 198. The two brigades sent to Charleston were those of Brig. Gen. George T. Anderson and Brig. Gen. William Wofford. Anderson's brigade had been mauled in the fighting around the Peach Orchard on July 2.

served as the detraining site for Longstreet's arriving host. Another 5,400 troops of Brig. Gen. Evander McNair's and Brig. Gen. John Gregg's brigades were also ordered to report to the Ringgold area, meaning that nearly 10,000 Confederate troops were converging there. For the time being, Brig. Gen. Bushrod R. Johnson would command this ragtag force until a more senior officer, such as Hood, arrived to assume command.[68]

With this huge addition to his army, Bragg would enjoy a numeric advantage over Rosecrans for one of the few times during the war. Bragg began contemplating how best to exploit this rare advantage by remaining on the offensive. On September 15, Bragg convened a council of war at his headquarters to discuss how best to do so. At least all four of his corps commanders—D. H. Hill, Polk, Buckner, and Walker—attended, along with various staff officers. Bragg was still angry with the failure to follow through with his earlier orders to attack, and the meeting was tense. Still, he had a new plan: to march directly toward Chattanooga and turn Rosecrans's left (northern) flank in doing so. This would cut him off from his supply base and trap the Army of the Cumberland in the field. Most of his commanders agreed with this plan. Thanks to the arrival of Hood's men and the shifting of the other troops to Ringgold, Bragg once again had the advantage of being closer to Chattanooga than most of Rosecrans's army. If he moved quickly, Bragg could interpose his army between Rosecrans and Chattanooga. He clearly intended to seize the initiative and take the fight to Rosecrans.[69]

On September 15, Rosecrans ordered Minty and part of his brigade to report to Crittenden to replace Wilder's Lightning Brigade, which had been ordered to report to Brig. Gen. Joseph Reynolds's division of Thomas's 14th Corps at McLemore's Cove. At the same time Crittenden sent Minty into the valley of Pea Vine Creek to cover his left flank in the direction of Ringgold.[70] Minty established his camps at Peeler's Mill, which sat on the east bank of the slow-moving tributary of West Chickamauga Creek. Minty ordered patrols toward Ringgold and Leet's

68 Powell, *The Chickamauga Campaign*, 196-204. Powell details the logistical problems posed by the movement of such a large body of men on a rail network that was already overtaxed. He also details problems caused by some of Longstreet's men during a stopover in Raleigh, North Carolina, that won them no admirers.

69 Ibid., 204.

70 *OR* 30, pt. 3, 651.

Tanyard. "Six of the enemies cavalry were seen on our right," noted an officer of the 4th Michigan in his diary. "Co. B gave chase & captured one man and 3 horses. I with 20 men of my Co. was detailed to Picket the road we came in on at the Gap."[71]

The battalion of the 3rd Indiana Cavalry assigned to Minty's brigade was serving in Chattanooga, and the 7th Pennsylvania Cavalry was at Crawfish Springs, meaning that the Englishman had a lot of ground to cover with roughly half of his brigade. Minty sent out patrols in the direction of Grayville, Ringgold, Leet's Tanyard, and Rock Springs. "I have strange reports from the citizens," he reported. "They say positively that Forrest is at Ringgold, Pegram at Leet's, Buckner at Rock Spring, Cleburne and Longstreet at Dalton."[72] Crittenden's response—"All this would indicate infantry, which the major-general commanding cannot believe"—dumbfounded Minty.[73]

With so many Confederate units in the area, Minty knew he did not have sufficient manpower to perform everything being asked of him, so he requested Crittenden send him a brigade of infantry at Reed's Bridge across the Chickamauga. "The force at Ringgold is, I believe, Scott's brigade. Pegram is at Leet's, with an outpost at Pea Vine Church. There is a good road running down the valley between Pea Vine Ridge and the Chickamauga, which exposes my rear to attack." After asking for infantry reinforcements, Minty declared: "As I am now situated I may be forced to retreat at any moment. I wish this could be avoided. If I send a patrol toward Leet's, it is liable to be cut off by an advance from Ringgold. If I move on Ringgold, I am liable to be attacked in rear from Leet's. However, if I had all of my brigade here, I could guard the road and punish the rebels if they made any demonstrations against me." He asked to have the 7th Pennsylvania and 3rd Indiana returned to him. "I am not strong enough for the position I am placed in." Minty also made sure to pass along the most current intelligence available. "I think, without doubt, that Longstreet is in this part of the country," he correctly reported. Crittenden sent the 7th Pennsylvania to Minty but not

71 Potter, diary, September 15, 1863.

72 *OR* 30, pt. 3, 651.

73 Robert H. G. Minty, "Minty's Saber Brigade: The Part They Took in the Chattanooga Campaign. Preliminary Maneuvers—Chasing Dibrell's Cavalry All Over the Country, Minty's Close Call," *National Tribune*, February 25, 1892.

the battalion of the 3rd Indiana Cavalry or any infantry reinforcements, claiming he could spare none.[74]

At 2:15 p.m., Minty sent an update. Shortly after he'd sent the first dispatch, the enemy moved against him on three different roads, including the La Fayette Road, "a narrow road on the east side of the ridge, and the road I am now on, which is on the west side of the ridge and leads from La Fayette to Harrison." He passed along Joseph Hedges's intelligence and then declared, "The intention of the enemy appears to be to gain possession of this road. This would effectually cut off all communication with you. I therefore thought it best to fall back to [Reed's Bridge], west of the ridge, but east of the river. I still picket the La Fayette road." He concluded, "The rebels have been driven on all the roads from 4 to 7 miles."[75]

According to Capt. Joseph Vale, who served as one of Minty's staff officers, "The information conveyed by Minty on the night of the 15th was the first intimation received by the army, or its commander, from any source, that Bragg was re-inforced by Longstreet's corps, from the army of Virginia, and that he had turned at bay and was threatening an advance, with a view of fighting a general battle for the possession of Chattanooga and the Tennessee river and valley." He continued, "This information, being so astonishing, and at such complete variance with all the dispatches and orders from Washington, and information up to that time had, was, as plainly stated in the extract quoted, utterly discredited; not only by General Crittenden, but by all the other corps commanders. Rosecrans, while not fully crediting the statement, took the cautionary measure of ordering an immediate concentration of his widely scattered corps." Vale correctly observed that had Minty's warnings been heeded, Rosecrans could have taken better precautions to receive the attack that Bragg was undoubtedly planning.[76]

74 *OR* 30, pt. 3, 679.

75 Ibid., 679-80.

76 Vale, *Minty and the Cavalry*, 217-18. At 4:30 on the afternoon of September 15, general in chief Henry W. Halleck telegraphed Rosecrans: "From information received here to-day it is very probable that three divisions of Lee's army have been sent to re-enforce Bragg." See OR 30, pt. 3, 644. Rosecrans certainly should have begun to understand that he was in peril.

The ongoing drought ensured the Lightning Brigade's march to join Thomas in McLemore's Cove was miserable for all involved. "The everlasting dust grows deeper and deeper every day, while our eyes grow red and swollen, as though we had all been on a week's spree while from our visages it would be difficult for our own mothers to tell whether we were Hindus, Africans or Americans," complained Alva G. Greist of Company G of the 72nd Indiana.[77]

"Our brigade properly belongs to this division," recounted William Records of the 72nd Indiana, "but this is the first time we have been together since leaving Decherd one month ago." Wilder's men were tickled to find their baggage train there. "We are occupied for a couple of days in washing and fixing up and changing our clothing, shaving, trimming hair and fixing up our equipments," continued Records. "During this time Skirmishing was going on at the front constantly. Artillery taking part but our brigade was not required to take any part."[78] More important, their horses got a break. After being on the move constantly, without good grain to eat, the brigade's mounts were in danger of breaking down, and the respite did them a world of good. Things, however, remained tense. On September 16, Greist scrawled in his diary, "We are now looking for the enemy to attack us at any time."[79] The men got little rest under such conditions.

Lieutenant Henry Potter commanded a company of the 4th Michigan Cavalry of Minty's brigade. He noted there was a disturbance in the direction of Ringgold on the night of September 15. "Our pickets in that direction were fired on, or they fired on a squad of rebels. 'To horse' sounded & every man was in his saddle. The teams were not loosened from the wagons at all thro' the night—quite an excitement this morning," he wrote in his diary on the morning of September 16. "I was ordered to go to [Reed's Bridge] & see if it was destroyed—it was safe. Our battery is planted on a hill fronting the camp & the guns masked. We are waiting—ready for anything that may turn up." Captain Potter also reported rumors of Union forces on the right linking up with

77 Alva G. Greist, journal, September 15, 1863, ISL.

78 Records Memoir. Records refered to Wilder's raid on Decherd, Tennessee at the conclusion of the Tullahoma campaign.

79 Greist, journal, September 16, 1863.

Burnside's command on the left, surrounding Bragg's army. "We will see," concluded Potter.[80]

On September 16, Confederate cavalry attacked Minty's pickets along the La Fayette and Harrison Roads, threatening his rear. "We started about 8 o'clock in the morning, and drove the pickets from the bridge back to their reserve in a sweeping gallop," recounted Lt. William G. Allen of the 5th Tennessee Cavalry of Scott's brigade. "They fired at us as we approached, but failed to hit man or horse. The road was lined with tents on both sides and as we approached they would run out to see what was the trouble but by the time they would get their guns we would be out of reach." They captured two lieutenants of the 4th Michigan Cavalry and scattered a Union wagon train.[81]

Concerned, Minty fell back to the west side of Pea Vine Ridge, covering Reed's Bridge, while still strongly picketing all of the roads in the Pea Vine Valley.[82] Minty also ordered 200 regulars under command of Lt. Joseph Hedges out to locate the enemy. Minty instructed Hedges to "press this infantry, charge into it, and bring out as many prisoners as possible." Hedges did as ordered and brought back 23 prisoners, "all infantry men with their rolled blankets over their shoulders," with the loss of one killed. Minty sent these prisoners to Crittenden's headquarters at Lee and Gordon's Mills. Unimpressed, Crittenden shot back, "It could be nothing but dismounted cavalry."[83] Flabbergasted, Minty swung into his saddle and rode off to Lee and Gordon's Mills to find Crittenden. He found the corps commander in a meeting with Rosecrans. "I did my best to convince him that Gen. Bragg was massing on his left," recounted Minty. "That he had been reinforced by Gen. Longstreet with two corps." Crittenden scoffed and said, "Longstreet is in Virginia."

"Pardon me, General, Longstreet was yesterday at Dalton, with two corps form the Army of Northern Virginia," responded the diminutive Englishman. Rosecrans indicated he believed Minty's report, prompting

80 Potter, diary, September 16, 1863.

81 William G. Allen, *Reminiscences of William G. Allen, McKenzie's 5th Tennessee Regiment* (Dayton, TN: Rhea County Historical and Genealogical Society, 2000), 34.

82 *OR* 30, pt. 1, 922.

83 R. H. G. Minty, *Remarks of Brevet Major General R. H. G. Minty Made September 18, 1895 at the Dedication of the Monument Erected to the Fourth Michigan Cavalry at Reed's Bridge, Chickamauga National Park* (Ogden, UT: Brantley Paper Co., 1896), 2-3; *OR* 30, pt. 1, 922.

Lt. Gen. James Longstreet in 1863. Longstreet, the senior subordinate in the Army of Northern Virginia, was sent west to reinforce Bragg's Army of Tennessee. *Library of Congress*

Crittenden to spring to his feet and declare, "General, I will guarantee with my corps, to whip every rebel within 20 miles of us."[84]

84 Lieutenant General D. H. Hill, who commanded one of Bragg's corps at Chickamauga, left a remarkably astute observation about Crittenden's inexplicable conduct in the days leading up to the battle. "Surely in the annals of warfare there is no parallel to

"This settled the matter," sighed a frustrated Minty. "Here was a distinguished General, commanding a magnificent corps, the left wing of the army, and I only a Colonel, commanding a little brigade of cavalry. I took my leave with a heavy heart and hastened back to my command."[85] D. H. Haines of Company L of the 4th Michigan Cavalry correctly observed, "The brigade was still alone receiving no support from the infantry at Gordon's Mills whose commanders still doubted that a large force of the enemy was near." The cavalrymen grew uneasy about being alone in such an exposed position.[86]

Despite the reports forwarded by Minty, Rosecrans nevertheless believed his army was no longer in danger and started looking for opportunities to take the offensive once more. A rude surprise awaited the Ohioan.

On September 16, Bragg issued Special Orders No. 245 to his army. Buckner's and Walker's combined corps of about 16,000 were ordered to march at dawn on September 17 for Pea Vine Church and to assume a position there facing west along Pea Vine Creek. Polk's 13,000-man corps was to follow at 8:00, allowing time for the roads to clear. Polk was to take position on Buckner's left on the banks of West Chickamauga Creek near Glass Mill. D. H. Hill's 9,000 men were to leave their positions near La Fayette and return to the gaps in Pigeon Mountain to the west of town, taking position on Polk's left. The troops concentrating near Ringgold had various assignments. Johnson's brigade would be returned to Buckner while Gregg's and McNair's brigades and Hood's three brigades were to march toward Reed's Bridge. Wheeler's cavalry would cover Polk's flank.[87]

Bragg gave the most important role to Forrest—screening Buckner's and Polk's columns as they marched north while also capturing and holding four crucial crossings over Chickamauga Creek: Dalton's Ford,

---

the coolness and nonchalance with which General Crittenden marched and countermarched for a week with a delightful unconsciousness that he was in the presence of a force of superior strength." See D. H. Hill, "Chickamauga—The Great Battle of the West," in Robert U. Johnson and Clarence C. Buel, eds., *Battles and Leaders of the Civil War*, 4 vols. (New York: Century Co., 1884-87), vol. 3, 643.

85 Minty, "Minty's Saber Brigade," February 25, 1892.

86 Haines, "Record of Fourth Michigan Cavalry."

87 *OR* 30, pt. 4, 657.

Alexander's Bridge, Byram's Ford, and Reed's Bridge.[88] Forrest had only one of his two divisions available—Pegram's—and he was being asked to perform a duty for which he had no ability. Forrest excelled as a raider and in independent command, but without any formal military training or talent for the traditional roles of cavalry—scouting, screening, and reconnaissance—he was definitely the wrong man in the wrong place being asked to seize and hold the crossings over the Chickamauga. His failure to do so nearly derailed Bragg's entire plan for the coming battle.

If this audacious plan succeeded, Bragg's entire army would be in line facing west, extending from Reed's Bridge to Dug Gap, with more than half of his command concentrated on Rosecrans's left flank to the north of Lee and Gordon's Mill. He could either try to turn Rosecrans's left or he could move to interdict the Army of the Cumberland's supply lines from Chattanooga. The plan was brilliant. A visit to Bragg's headquarters, however, by one of Longstreet's staff officers, Maj. Osmun Latrobe, caused Bragg to belay those orders, giving Rosecrans a reprieve.[89] Had Bragg unleashed the planned attack on September 17, it "must have been fatal to Rosecrans in the then huddled and confused grouping of his forces," claimed D. H. Hill years after the war.[90]

Bragg held another conference with his commanders and changed his plan, keeping Bushrod Johnson's brigade with the Ringgold contingent. Until either Longstreet or Hood arrived, Johnson, by virtue of seniority, would command what was dubbed Johnson's Provisional Division.[91]

88 Ibid.

89 Folder 10, Bragg Papers, WRHS.

90 William Glenn Robertson, "The Chickamauga Campaign: The Armies Collide," *Blue and Gray Magazine* 24, No. 3 (Fall 2007): 40.

91 Brigadier General Bushrod Johnson was a walking paradox. Born in Ohio to Quaker parents who were confirmed pacifists and devoted abolitionists, Johnson served in the Confederate army. He was born on the family farm near Morristown, Ohio, on October 17, 1817. Although he briefly worked as a schoolteacher, Johnson broke with his family's traditions and sought an appointment at West Point. He graduated 23rd in the class of 1840, along with William T. Sherman, George H. Thomas, and Richard S. Ewell. He was commissioned into the 3rd Infantry and served in Florida and in the west until the outbreak of the Mexican War. He fought with Taylor's army at Palo Alto, Resaca de la Palma, and Monterey, but harmed his career by engaging in profiteering. He was asked to resign his commission, which he did on October 21, 1847. He then worked as the superintendent of two military schools, the second of which was in Nashville. Although a Northerner by birth, he had lived in the South for years, and he cast his lot with the Confederacy. He was appointed a brigadier general in the Confederate

Brig. Gen. Bushrod R. Johnson, the Ohio-born Quaker who led a provisional division and whose men spent most of September 18 fighting for possession of Reed's Bridge. *Library of Congress*

Pursuant to new orders, Johnson's column would not leave Ringgold until the morning of September 18 in order for the rest of the army to have time to make its deployments. Wheeler was to assume the defense of the Pigeon Mountain gaps, which allowed Hill to shift his infantry as far north as Glass Mill. The entire movement was to begin on the morning of September 18.[92]

Bragg's army spent September 17 cooking rations, cleaning their weapons, loading ammunition into their cartridge boxes, writing letters, and doing the things soldiers in the field do when they know a battle is looming. Bragg issued a general order to be read to the troops: "Heretofore you have never failed to respond to your general when he asked sacrifice at your hands. Relying on your gallantry and patriotism, he asks you to add the crowning glory to the wreath you wear. Our cause is in your keeping. . . . You have but to respond to assure us a glorious victory over an insolent foe."[93]

army and helped to design and construct Fort Henry in Tennessee. He commanded a brigade at Shiloh but was wounded on the first day. He again commanded a brigade at Perryville in October 1862, having five horses shot out from under him that day. His troops broke under fire at Stones River, hurting his chances for the promotion he spent much of 1863 trying to obtain. September 18, 1863, was his first day commanding a division in battle, and his tenure in divisional command would be short-lived. See Davis and Hoffman, *The Confederate General*, vol. 3, 181-85. There is a full-length biography of Johnson for those interested in this anomalous Confederate Quaker. See Charles M. Cummings, *Yankee Quaker Confederate General: The Curious Career of Bushrod Rust Johnson* (Columbus, OH: General's Books, 1993).

92 *OR* 30, pt. 4, 660-61.

93 Quoted in Powell, *The Chickamauga Campaign*, 215.

Maj. Gen. David S. Stanley, the commander of the Army of the Cumberland's Cavalry Corps, who was ill with typhoid fever at the time of the battle. *Library of Congress*

Further complicating things for Rosecrans, his cavalry corps commander, Maj. Gen. David S. Stanley, left the army that day and was hospitalized at Stevenson, Alabama, laid "very low with fever and dysentery and unable to stand up." Stanley had been ill in bed for about a week, leaving the cavalry corps without a commander in the middle of its most important campaign yet.[94] Stanley disdained the commander of the Army of the Cumberland, whom he believed "had no idea of the use of cavalry," and he thought even less of Rosecrans's chief of staff, Brig. Gen. James A. Garfield, a future president of the United States, whom Stanley believed was a conniver and a manipulator.[95] This last-minute change in his army's command structure on the eve of battle only added more friction to an already tense situation. Stanley's replacement, Brig. Gen. Washington Elliott, had no experience in corps command. Because Elliott did not arrive at the front for some time, Brig. Gen. Robert M. Mitchell, commander of the 1st Cavalry Division, assumed temporary command of the cavalry corps.[96]

94 A Cavalry Corps staff officer noted in his diary on September 11, "Genl Stanley is quite sick & has been in bed all day." See Charles C. McCormick, diary, September 11, 1863, in Charles C. McCormick Family Papers, Pennsylvania State Archives, Harrisburg, PA.

95 David Sloan Stanley, *An American General: The Memoirs of David Sloan Stanley, ed. Samuel W. Fordyce IV.* (Santa Barbara, CA: Narrative Press, 2003), 151.

96 Elliott's most recent assignment had been to command a brigade of infantry of Maj. Gen. Robert H. Milroy at Winchester, Virginia. Like any of the survivors of Milroy's command, Elliott was fortunate to escape from Winchester and avoid being captured by the Confederate forces that captured the town and half of Milroy's garrison. For a detailed discussion of the second battle of Winchester, see Eric J. Wittenberg and Scott Mingus, *The Second Battle of Winchester: The Confederate Victory that Opened*

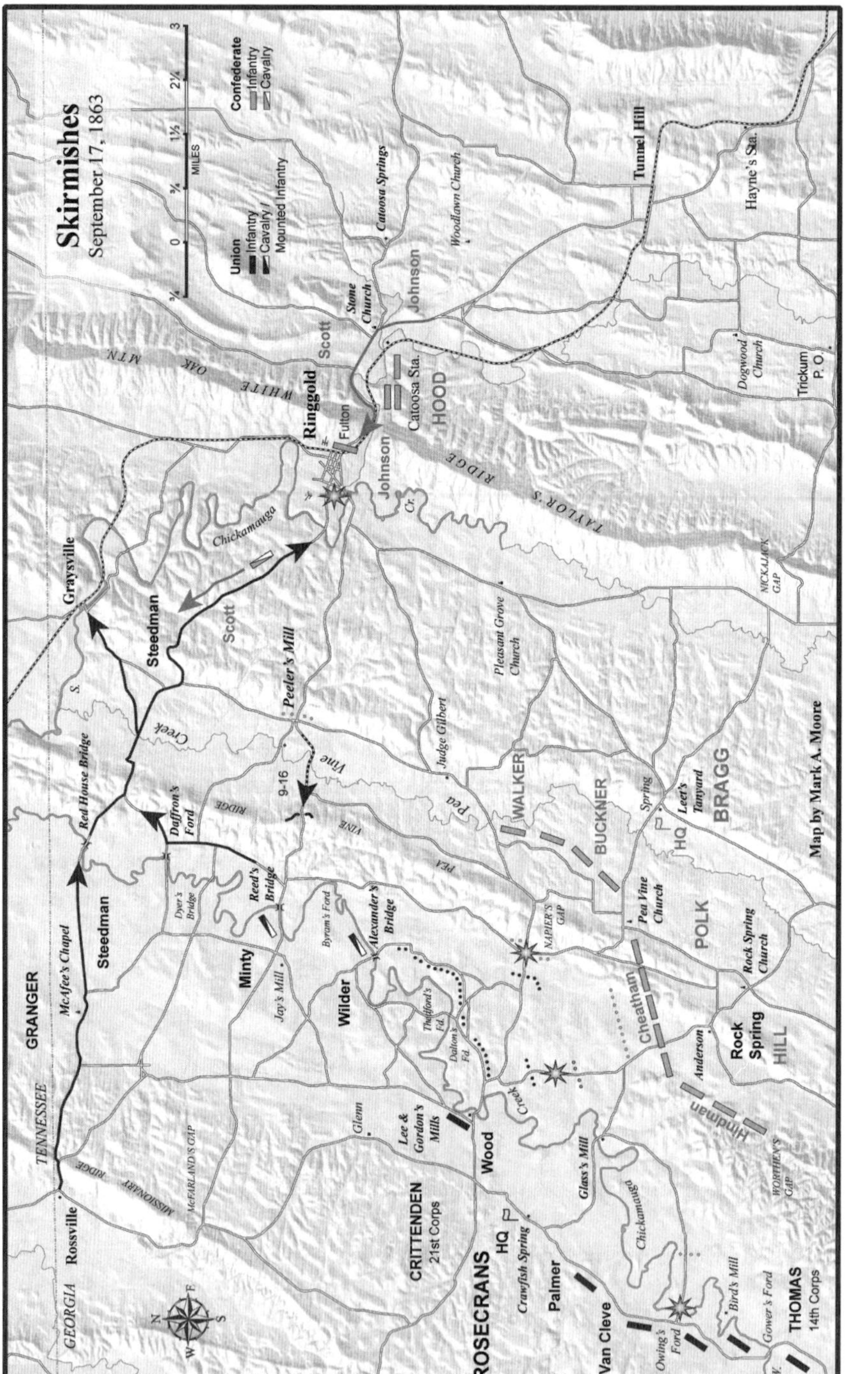

Skirmishes on September 17.

Rosecrans spent September 17 shifting his troops to meet various threats. Keeping in mind Minty's requests for reinforcements and reports of the presence of Longstreet's infantry, he grew nervous about the area around Reed's Bridge. That morning he summoned Col. John T. Wilder to his headquarters and told the colonel to shift his brigade to Alexander's Bridge—"a broken down bridge over Chickamauga Creek," which was about three miles downstream from Lee and Gordon's Mills and about a mile and a half upstream from Reed's Bridge—to help fill the gap between Minty's lone cavalry brigade and Crittenden's exposed left flank. Wilder obeyed the order promptly and got his men into position by dusk. He sent two companies of the 17th Indiana to picket the right side (west side) of the Alexander's Bridge Road along the bank of West Chickamauga Creek. The remainder of the 17th Indiana took up a position at the Alexander farm buildings, several hundred yards up the hill overlooking the bridge, supporting Lilly's battery, which "took a strong position" at the log-built Alexander farmhouse.[97] Company A of the 72nd Indiana deployed to the left side of the road in a similar manner while Company F of the 72nd was sent to Dalton's Ford, about a mile north of Alexander's Bridge.[98] The 123rd Indiana picketed between Dalton's Ford and Lee and Gordon's Mills, meaning that Wilder's men now covered all the crossings of West Chickamauga Creek between Reed's Bridge and the mills. The pieces were falling into place for the great drama that would play out the next day.[99]

John Wilder passed along whatever intelligence he could once he arrived at Alexander's Bridge and had his troops into position. He reported seeing considerable dust and hearing some gunfire from the vicinity of Napier's Gap through Pea Vine Ridge, which is about two and a half miles from the bridge and an equal distance from Lee and Gordon's Mills. Wilder sent this information to Brig. Gen. Thomas J. Wood via a courier. "It is

---

the Door to Gettysburg (El Dorado Hills, CA: Savas-Beatie, 2015). With Mitchell in temporary command of the Cavalry Corps, Col. Edward McCook assumed command of the 1st Division. Edward McCook was a first cousin of 20th Corps commander Maj. Gen. Alexander McCook.

97 *OR* 30, pt. 3, 703; W. H. H. Benefiel, *Souvenir of the Seventeenth Indiana Regiment: A History from Its Organization to the End of the War Giving Description of Battles, etc.* (Elwood, IN: Model Printing & Litho. Co., 1913).

98 W. D. Crouse, journal, September 17, 1863, Archives, Tippecanoe County Historical Society, Lafayette, IN.

99 Magee, *History of the Seventy-Second Regiment*, 167.

near this point at which the most direct [road] from here to Ringgold is crossed by the road leading from Chattanooga over Alexander's Bridge, and falling into the direct Rossville and La Fayette road near Shields' Gap." Confederate cavalry probed his outermost picket post on the La Fayette Road, leading Wood to reinforce the position. "What the meaning of the dash was, whether the precursor of a more serious attack soon or whether it was an effort to capture some of my pickets to gain information generally and specifically, I cannot give an opinion."[100] The evidence that Bragg was about to attack was there if Rosecrans wanted to see it.

Wilder's men held no illusions about what was ahead of them. "It is now evident that the enemy is moving to give us battle," noted Cpl. William Records of the 72nd Indiana. "He is reinforced by Longstreet with his veteran corps from Va. which came via R.R. and are now disembarking at Dalton." Records continued, "Gen. Rosecranes has been so over confident that McCooks corps has been detached and sent to Rome Ga. and now the great suspense is to stave off the great battle until that corps of veterans can be recalled."[101] While Records was incorrect about the whereabouts of McCook's infantry corps, he was remarkably prescient in explaining the heavy task that lay ahead of them on September 18.

Elements of Pegram's and Forrest's commands, who were reconnoitering the area, advanced on Minty's position at Peeler's Mill. Minty met their probing attack and drove them off. They launched another attack on the picket post stationed on the Harrison and Lafayette Road, which paralleled the Reed's Bridge Road. If the Confederates gained that road, they would cut Minty's brigade off from the rest of the army, but Minty successfully fended them off. A detachment of the 4th U.S. Cavalry under Lt. Joseph Rendlebock, out scouting after the repulse of this attack, ran into Buckner's infantry marching northeast toward Ringgold. Martin J. Murphy of Company G was killed when he was shot through the head and another five were wounded in the skirmishing.[102] Alarmed, Minty

100 *OR* 30, pt. 3, 711-12.

101 Records Memoir.

102 Larson, *Sergeant Larson*, 173. Rendlebock, a 41-year-old Prussian immigrant who had originally enlisted in the Regiment of Mounted Rifles as a private in 1851 and had come up through the ranks, had his name misspelled numerous ways during his military career. James Larson spelled it "Rendelbrock" in the published memoir of his service with the 4th U.S. Cavalry. According to historian Don Caughey: "Lieutenant Rendlebock distinguished himself on several occasions during the rest of the war. He was active and mentioned in reports on the battle of Stones River in January 1863.

decided to pull his camps back from Peeler's Mill to Reed's Bridge while still maintaining strong picket posts in the Pea Vine Valley. These pickets were now the only Union forces on the east side of Chickamauga Creek.[103]

"Our horses are saddled all the time and we sleep booted and spurred," observed Robert Burns of the 4th Michigan Cavalry in a letter to his brother on September 17. "Yesterday we sat for a couple of hours on horseback in line of battle, expecting the rebels, they having driven in our pickets (or attempted to). I think they are all moving South, as fast as they can, having behind a force of their cavalry to cover their movements. We expect to go forward again to see this afternoon, as a brigade of infantry has been ordered up in supporting distance." Burns concluded, "The rebels are a long time in finding their last ditch."[104] The rumor mill continued to grind away at full tilt. "Rumored that Burnside is falling back," declared Lieutenant Potter in his diary.[105]

Minty had his command awake with horses saddled at 4:00 a.m. September 17. They remained in line, ready to move for a time, and then received orders to unsaddle.[106] Some of his troopers again scouted the area assigned them on September 17. The 4th U.S. marched off toward "some high mountains far away and upon arriving at the foot of the highest one, the regiment dismounted and some of the officers took a man or two each and climbed up the mountain in different places." Sergeant James Larson of the 4th U.S. and two others climbed to a point on the

---

He was brevetted first lieutenant for gallant and meritorious service in the cavalry action at Franklin, Tennessee on May 10, 1863. Leading his company's charge, he succeeded in overrunning and capturing two guns of Freeman's Battery. Unfortunately, the guns were spiked and lost later in the battle during a counterattack by Forrest. A few months later he was brevetted captain at McMinnville, Tennessee on October 4, 1863, again for gallant and meritorious service." He was promoted to first lieutenant on December 15, 1863, and was brevetted to major in the regular army for gallant and meritorious services at the capture of Selma, Alabama, on April 2, 1865. After serving as a regimental quartermaster after the Civil War, he was promoted to captain on August 13, 1867. He retired on July 23, 1879, for a disability incurred in the line of duty and died on March 13, 1889. See Don Caughey, "Fiddler's Green: Joseph Rendlebock," Regular Cavalry in the Civil War, February 6, 2009, https://regularcavalryincivilwar.wordpress.com/2009/02/06/fiddlers-green-joseph-rendlebock/.

103 Vale, *Minty and the Cavalry*, 220.

104 Robert Burns to His Brother, September 17, 1863, in Robert Burns Letters, Archives, Minnesota Historical Society, St. Paul, MN.

105 Potter, diary, September 17, 1863.

106 McLain, diary, September 17, 1863.

Maj. Gen. Gordon Granger, commander of the Reserve Corps assigned to the Army of the Cumberland. *Library of Congress*

end of the mountain where they could see the entire valley. "It was a very fine sunny day and the roads were so dry and dusty that no body of troops or train of wagons or artillery could move without raising so much dust that it could be seen plainly from our perch on the mountain," wrote Larson. "Soon heavy clouds of dust began to rise over the tree-tops in different places far away in the valley, plainly indicating the location of the different roads and giving unmistakable evidence that large bodies of troops were moving, although the thick forest prevented us from seeing whether it was infantry or cavalry. There was no doubting the fact that the Confederate army was moving, and in heavy columns too. Not as Rosecrans supposed, retreating, but advancing on his position to give battle." When the dust clouds ceased billowing about 4:00 in the afternoon, the regulars descended from the hill, swung into their saddles, and galloped off to Minty's headquarters to report their findings.[107] The 6th Georgia Cavalry captured four members of the 4th U.S. who were on a different scouting expedition.[108]

When his scouts reported in, the colonel forwarded their intelligence to Crittenden, who dismissed them. "There is nothing but dismounted cavalry," he sniffed. When the courier returned from Crittenden's headquarters, he informed Minty that Wilder's brigade had taken position at Alexander's Bridge. "This was cheering news, for if I was in a tight place I would rather have Wilder, with his splendid brigade of mounted infantry, supporting me, than any brigade in the army," declared Minty.

107 Larson, *Sergeant Larson,* 174-75.

108 Scott, "Reminiscences of J. W. Minnick," 20.

Pvt. Thomas F. Dornblaser of the 7th Pennsylvania Cavalry became a prominent Lutheran minister in Kansas after the Civil War and penned a regimental history of the Saber Regiment. *My Life Story for Young and Old*

"We had worked and fought together, and the two brigades had full and perfect confidence in each other."[109]

Also that afternoon, a skirmish between a brigade of Maj. Gen. Gordon Granger's Reserve Corps troops and Col. John Scott's Louisiana cavalry brigade occurred near Ringgold. The Union troops nearly made their way into Ringgold undetected before Scott drove them off. Brigadier General James B. Steedman, who commanded this task force, realized Ringgold was swarming with Confederate cavalry and infantry, and he could see dust clouds billowing south of town, indicating the movement of more Confederate troops. Steedman wisely broke off and withdrew with minimal losses, but the fact that 2,500 Union soldiers with artillery had nearly made it into Ringgold undetected was alarming, and it had unexpected consequences.

Private Thomas Dornblaser of the 7th Pennsylvania Cavalry was detached from his regiment, doing courier duty at Brig. Gen. George Crook's 2nd Cavalry Division headquarters. Dornblaser accompanied Crook and Brig. Gen. William Lytle, who commanded a brigade of infantry of Maj. Gen. Philip H. Sheridan's 20th Corps division, to the highest point on Lookout Mountain for the purpose of observing the valley below and trying to ascertain the movements of the enemy. After the two generals used their field glasses, they invited the cavalryman to have a look, "supposing, no doubt, as my eyes were younger, they might discover some things that they could not see." Dornblaser swept the

109 Minty, "Minty's Saber Brigade," February 25, 1892.

valley with the field glasses. "I could see troops marching Northward, toward the Union left. We could see, to our surprise, columns of infantry and artillery with banners, indicating that they had come from Virginia to reinforce Bragg's Army. True enough, it was Longstreet's corps, with which the enemy would outnumber the Union forces." Crook and Lytle quickly composed a note to Rosecrans and ordered Dornblaser to gallop off to the army commander with it. "It was a dangerous trip of five miles or more through the enemy's country," remembered Dornblaser. "Down the mountain I galloped, and in a half hour I handed the message to General Garfield [Rosecrans's chief of staff]. He at once conferred with the commanding General Rosecrans, and in a few minutes they handed me a message for General Crook."[110] Slowly Rosecrans was becoming aware of the dire nature of the threat that faced his scattered army, which was vulnerable to being attacked and defeated in detail.

At 7:00 p.m. Minty reported to Crittenden again. He related the passage of Steedman's command and hearing slight cannonading above Ringgold and then said, "I understand that Wilder is camped near Alexander's Bridge, 2 miles below me. I have sent a party to communicate with him. Rebel pickets are 8 miles above on the La Fayette Road."[111] The flow of accurate intelligence from Minty continued. The question was what would be done with that flow of accurate intelligence.

This otherwise insignificant dustup at Ringgold caused Bragg to adjust his plans one final time. Worried about the lack of security, he ordered Scott's division commander, Pegram, to send "a sufficient force at once" to Ringgold to ensure its defense. Then, sometime after midnight on September 18, Bragg ordered Johnson's Provisional Division to head for Reed's Bridge instead of toward Leet's Tanyard, meaning that Bragg's troops would be positioned even farther up Rosecrans's flank than originally planned. He ordered Forrest to cover Johnson's "front and right flank," which proved to be a difficult task given Forrest's lack of troops for the assigned duty.[112]

110 Dornblaser, *My Life-Story,* 60-61.

111 *OR* 30, pt. 3, 709-10.

112 Bragg to Pegram, September 17, 1863, in Bragg Papers, WRHS; Bragg to Johnson and Forrest, September 18, 1863, in Bragg Papers, WRHS.

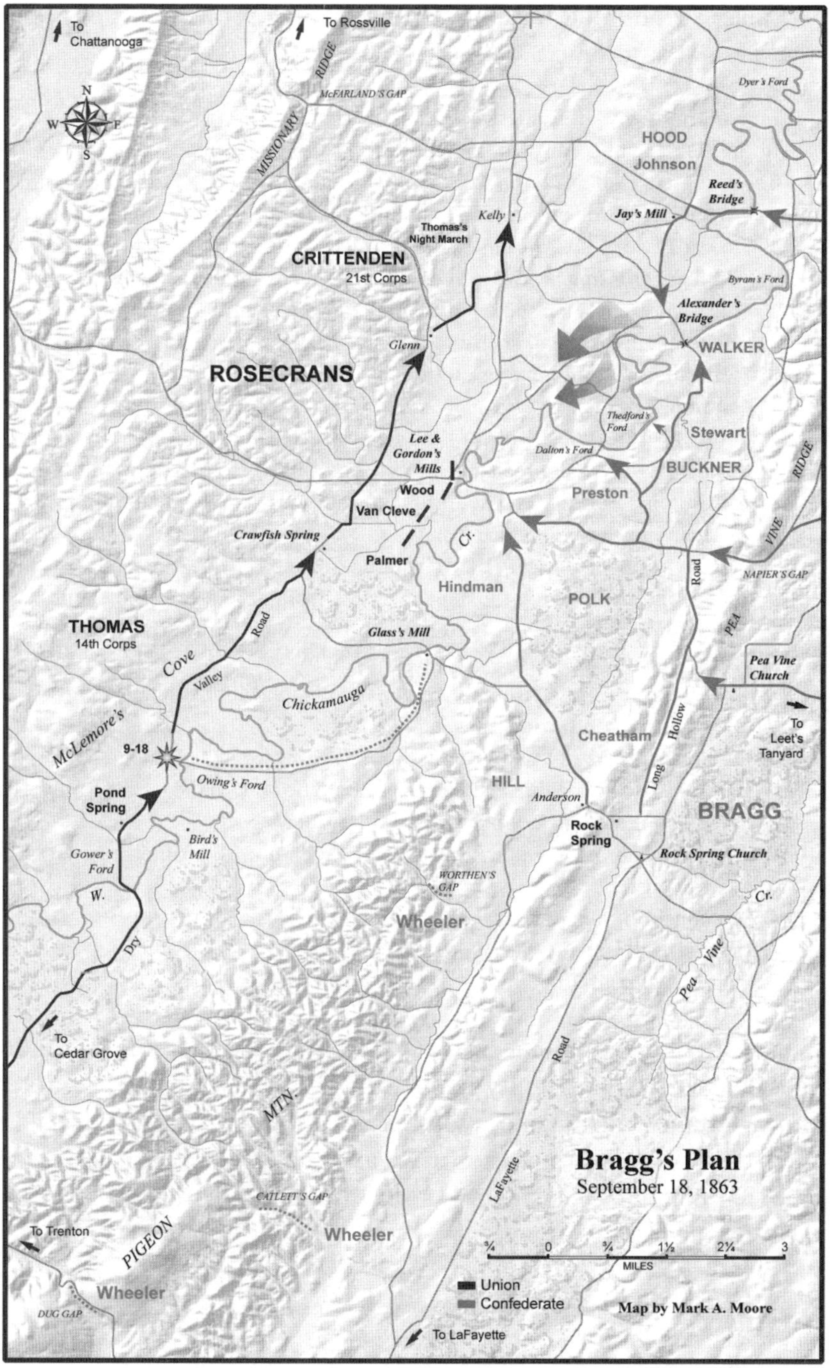

Bragg's plan for September 18.

He also issued the following circular, which set forth his entire plan for the day's operations:

> Headquarters, Army of Tennessee
> In the field, Leet's Tanyard, September 18, 1863
>
> 1. Johnson's column (Hood's) on crossing at or near Reed's Bridge, will turn to the left by the most practicable route and sweep up the Chickamauga, toward Lee and Gordon's Mills.
> 2. Walker, crossing at Alexander's Bridge, will unite in this move and push vigorously on the enemy's flank and rear in the same direction.
> 3. Buckner, crossing at Thedford's Ford, will join in this movement to the left, and press the enemy up the stream from Polk's front at Lee and Gordon's Mills.
> 4. Polk will press his forces to the front of Lee and Gordon's Mills, and if met by too much resistance to cross will bear to the right and cross at Dalton's Ford, or at Thedford's, as may be necessary, and join in the attack wherever the enemy may be.
> 5. Hill will cover our left flank from an advance of the enemy from the cove, and by pressing the cavalry in his front ascertain if the enemy is re-enforcing at Lee and Gordon's Mills, in which event he will attack them in flank.
> 6. Wheeler's cavalry will hold the gaps in Pigeon Mountain and cover our rear and left and bring up stragglers.
> 7. All teams, &c., not with troops should go toward Ringgold and Dalton, beyond Taylor's Ridge. All cooking should be done at the trains. Rations, when cooked, will be forwarded to the troops.
> 8. The above movements will be executed with utmost promptness, vigor, and persistence.
>
> By command of General Bragg:
> George Wm. Brent,
> Assistant Adjutant-General[113]

The critical places along Bragg's front were Reed's and Alexander's bridges, the very spots Minty and Wilder had been ordered to defend. "General Bragg had reckoned without considering Minty and Wilder," wrote an Indiana historian after the war, "with their splendid brigades of mounted men."[114] The stage was set for the drama that would unfold at dawn the next day.

113 *OR* 30, pt. 2, 31.

114 Commissioners for the Chickamauga and Chattanooga National Park, *Indiana at Chickamauga*, 11.

Chapter Three

The Night of September 17, 1863

Chickamauga means "River of Death" in the Cherokee language.[1] For three days—September 18, 19, and 20, 1863—it actually was a river of death. East Chickamauga Creek runs toward Ringgold and does not play a role in the events discussed here. West Chickamauga Creek—the one for which the battle was named and the one that plays a critical role in the events discussed here—is a tributary of the Tennessee River that meanders across the northwest Georgia countryside, which for purposes of clarity, will be called simply Chickamauga Creek for the rest of this narrative. It flows in a northeasterly direction through McLemore's Cove, close to the Pigeon Hills and to Lee and Gordon's Mills. It then bends sharply north, winding in a northeasterly direction and emptying into the Tennessee River about seven miles east of Chattanooga. "It is very crooked, quite deep, and dangerous to cross," declared Sgt. Benjamin Magee of the 72nd Indiana of Wilder's Brigade.[2] "The creek is a narrow—deep stream with a miry bottom and steep, high

1 Sartain, *History of Walker County Georgia*, 279. This 1932 history of Walker County states the name stems from a fatal epidemic that broke out among the Indians that resided along the stream that "virtually depopulated their settlements, very few escaping from its ravages. The early settlers of the county used to speak of the region along that stream . . . as a sickly one."

2 Magee, *History of the Seventy-Second Regiment*, 167.

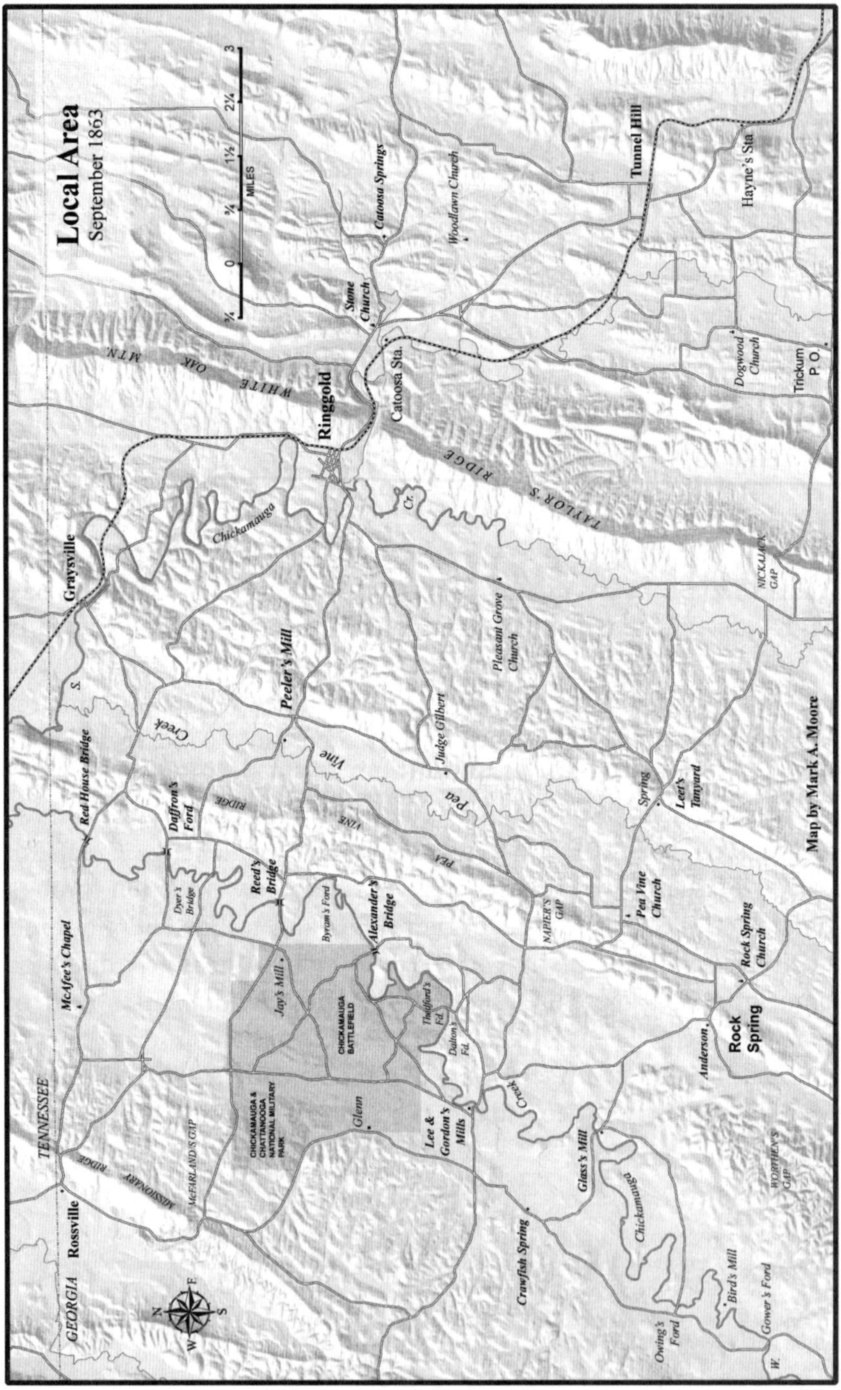

Detail of the area south of Chattanooga.

banks," as a member of Lilly's battery described it.[3] It is the predominant geographic feature in the area between Chattanooga and Ringgold. Pea Vine Ridge, a prominent ridgeline that rises to a height of several hundred feet above ground level, looms a mile and a half to the east of and parallel to Chickamauga Creek. The Chickamauga is "in general a sluggish stream, about ten feet deep . . . with either steep and rocky or low, swampy banks."[4]

East of the Chickamauga, 10 miles from Chattanooga, is Ringgold, the county seat of Catoosa County, 14 miles northeast of Lee and Gordon's Mills.[5] Ringgold is a very strategic place. Taylor Ridge passes through the town. Just east of the town, South Chickamauga Creek gouged a narrow opening between Taylor Ridge to the south and White Oak Mountain to the north. The Western and Atlantic Railroad and a major north-south thoroughfare pass through the gap. In 1849, a depot for the Western and Atlantic was constructed in the town, making the town an important railroad and road network hub—Ringgold was where the locomotive *The General* stopped on April 12, 1862, thereby ending the Great Locomotive Chase.[6] Possession of the gap and of the town controlled the Western and Atlantic, which was the means by which Longstreet's corps was being brought north from Atlanta to join Bragg's army. Consequently, Ringgold became a frequent point of contention for the opposing armies as they jockeyed for position in the days leading up to the battle of Chickamauga.[7]

3 Campbell, *Three Years in the Saddle*, 99.

4 Vale, *Minty and the Cavalry*, 223.

5 The town of Ringgold was incorporated on December 18, 1847. It was named for Maj. Samuel Ringgold of Maryland, a 50-year-old career U.S. Army artillerist who was mortally wounded on May 8, 1846, at the battle of Palo Alto, the first battle of the Mexican War, and died three days later. He was the first American officer of any rank to die in combat during the Mexican War. See City of Ringgold, Georgia, "City History," https://www.cityofringgoldga.gov/CityHistory.aspx.

6 For a detailed discussion of the Andrews Raid and the Great Locomotive Chase, see Russell S. Bonds, *Stealing The General: The Great Locomotive Chase and the First Medal of Honor* (Yardley, PA: Westholme Publishing, 2006).

7 A significant engagement occurred at Ringgold Gap on November 27, 1863, during Bragg's retreat from Chattanooga. A rear guard of 4,200 men commanded by Maj. Gen. Patrick Cleburne was left to defend Ringgold Gap against 16,000 Federals of the 11th and 12th Corps, led by the former commander of the Army of the Potomac, Maj. Gen. Joseph Hooker. After holding against overpowering odds for more than five

La Fayette, the county seat of Walker County, is 45 miles from Chattanooga and about 28 miles southwest of the mills.[8] About one and a half miles downstream from and north of the mills is Dalton's Ford. About three miles farther downstream is Alexander's Bridge. Reed's Bridge is another two miles downstream from Alexander's Bridge. Three miles north of Reed's Bridge is Dyer's Ford. Half a mile or so to the east of Pea Vine Ridge runs Pea Vine Creek, a slow-moving tributary of Chickamauga Creek that mostly flows on a north-south axis. Due to the severe drought that summer, Pea Vine Creek was "an insignificant stream which at that time a man could step across."[9]

A good road extends from the Mills to Ringgold by way of Reed's Bridge and Peeler's Mill, which sat alongside the road on the east bank of Pea Vine Creek. The stout log Reed farmhouse sat about 150 yards to the east of Reed's Bridge and served as Minty's headquarters. James Jasper "Jimmy" Reed, 34, had purchased his father's farm along the east bank of Chickamauga Creek in December 1851. He and his wife, Jemima Lambert Jay Reed, lived there with their two or three small children. Jimmy was away, serving as a private in Company D, 1st Confederate Infantry Battalion of Maj. Gen. Benjamin F. Cheatham's division of Polk's corps, leaving his 30-year-old wife Jemima in charge of the family farm operation in his absence. Jemima's family owned Jay's Steam Saw Mill, a prosperous business about half a mile to the west

---

hours, Cleburne received orders to break off and withdraw, eventually leaving the Gap to Hooker, but not before the Federals took more than 500 casualties compared to 221 for Cleburne. For a detailed discussion of the battle of Ringgold Gap, see Doyle D. Broome Jr., "Daring Rear-Guard Defense," *America's Civil War* (November 1993), vol. 6, 34-40. It was also the starting point for Maj. Gen. William T. Sherman's Atlanta campaign, which began when Sherman's grand army passed through Ringgold Gap at the beginning of May 1864.

8 Walker County was laid out and organized in 1833, meaning that at the time of the battle it had only formally existed for 30 years. The county was named for Maj. Freeman Walker, an early U.S. senator from Georgia. In 1850, the county had a population of 5,803 white males, 5,605 white females, a handful of freed blacks, and 1,664 slaves. It was largely rural and was not a wealthy area. See Sartain, *History of Walker County Georgia*, 205.

9 Joseph G. Vale, "Address of Captain Joseph G. Vale," in Pennsylvania, Chickamauga-Chattanooga Battlefields Commission, *Pennsylvania at Chickamauga and Chattanooga, Ceremonies at the Dedication of the Monuments Erected by the Commonwealth of Pennsylvania* (Harrisburg: W. S. Ray, 1901), 306 (hereafter cited as *Pennsylvania at Chickamauga*).

Reed's Bridge as it appeared in 1895. *Pennsylvania at Chickamauga and Chattanooga*

of Chickamauga Creek.[10] "She seemed to be in fair circumstances, and all her provisions, house, and premises were carefully protected during our stay," noted one of Minty's staff officers. "She was a quiet, modest lady, unobtrusive and of fair intelligence, much respected, and treated with esteem by the colonel and staff officers."[11]

The Reed's Bridge Road traverses "quite a narrow defile" through Pea Vine Ridge, meaning there was a natural choke point for Minty to take advantage of, since that road carried Bushrod Johnson's Provisional Division on the morning of September 18 on its way to attack Rosecrans's army west of Chickamauga Creek.[12] Hence, it fell upon

10 Jimmy Reed was wounded in battle at Chickamauga. Numerous accounts, including those by Minty's staff officer and brigade historian, Capt. Joseph Vale, incorrectly state that Jemima Reed was killed on September 18, but her gravestone at nearby Boynton Methodist Church indicates she lived until January 25, 1881. Once the battle began in earnest, the Reed house became the field hospital for Breckinridge's corps. President Lincoln's brother-in-law, Brig. Gen. Ben Hardin Helm, died there of his combat wound after being cared for by Jimmy Reed's mother, Sarah Lowry Reed. See Reed Family Genealogy: Reed: Descendants of Jacob R. Reed, http://www.angelfire.com/ga4/jholc/Reed.html.

11 Vale, *Minty and the Cavalry*, 233.

12 John C. West, "Fourth Texas Infantry at Chattanooga," *Houston Weekly Telegraph*, November 12, 1863.

Alexander's Bridge as it appeared in 1895. Dedication of the Chickamauga and Chattanooga National Military Park, September 18-20, 1895. *Chickamauga/Chattanooga NMP*

Robert H. G. Minty and his Saber Brigade to try to delay their advance in order to buy time and allow the main body of the army to get into position and also to keep Reed's Bridge from falling into the hands of Johnson's men. Minty had to make good use of the terrain to conduct an effective delaying action along the banks of the Chickamauga. The creek is deep at Reed's Bridge and makes a very sharp westward bend immediately to the south of the bridge. The banks of the creek are very steep and slippery, and the bridge was the only viable means of getting across the Chickamauga in that area.[13] The bridge itself was narrow and "a very frail structure." The only other place to cross was "a bad ford about three hundred yards further up the stream," recalled a trooper of the 4th Michigan Cavalry.[14]

Meanwhile, the defense of Alexander's Bridge fell to John T. Wilder and his Lightning Brigade. "The Chickamauga Creek at this point and for a considerable distance about and below is a deep and sluggish stream between precipitous banks," meaning that the bridge was the only

13 Sartain, *History of Walker County Georgia*, 205.

14 Haines, "Record of the Fourth Michigan Cavalry," September 18, 1863.

Cpl. William Records of the 72nd Indiana Mounted Infantry of Wilder's Lightning Brigade. *Indiana Historical Society*

viable way to get across the creek there.[15] "It is now evident that the enemy is moving to give us battle," noted Cpl. William Records of the 72nd Indiana.[16] Wilder knew his men would face a stern test once Bragg advanced in earnest. Due to the terrain, a well-designed and implemented defense at Alexander's Bridge, however, could choke off the Confederate advance and delay it for hours.

Minty and Wilder would have to make good use of the terrain if they were to defend their respective bridges. Minty knew the primary Confederate thrust would come in his direction and his small brigade would have its hands full against a vastly superior force. It would take all his skill to design and effectively implement a defensive scheme. Fortunately, Minty was up to the task.

In 1863 the U.S. Army published *Instructions for Officers and Non-Commissioned Officers on Outpost and Patrol Duty, and Troops in Campaign*, a field manual spelling out the army's procedures for circumstances such as those facing Minty's brigade at Reed's Bridge.[17] The manual required the officer in command to place videttes in positions where they could make a stand (always near a rock or a tree for cover) in case of attack long enough to permit the main body of the army to

15 *Souvenir of the Seventeenth Indiana Regiment. A History from Its Organization to the End of the War Giving Description of Battles, etc.* (Elwood, IN: Model Printing & Litho. Co., 1913), 12.

16 Records Memoir.

17 *U.S. War Department, Instructions for Officers and Non-Commissioned Officers on Outpost and Patrol Duty, and Troops in Campaign*, 2 parts (Washington, DC: Government Printing Office, 1863).

come up.[18] Before that placement, however, the commanding officer had to carefully reconnoiter the terrain to determine the best locations for vidette posts to be established, positions from which they could see not only what was coming in front of them but also see their fellow videttes posted on either side.[19] At night, continued the manual, videttes and the vidette reserve would move two to three miles in advance of the main body into positions on high ground with a commanding view from which they could make a firm stand in front of the main body and on its flanks, as needed. Videttes had instructions to put their ears to the ground from time to time in order to hear the movement of large bodies of men.[20] "When the videttes are posted in such a manner as to be able to overlook their front," explained the manual, "and see each other and the ground between them, so as that nothing can pass them unperceived, they are placed as they ought to be."[21]

Once posted, if the videttes spotted evidence of the enemy's approach, they were to signal the commander of the grand guard, who would report the presence of the enemy: "If obliged to retire, he must do it as slowly as possible, endeavoring to gain all the time he can, for the corps in his rear to turn out. If he had previously fixed upon places where to make a stand . . . now is the time to make use of them."[22] In other words, the whole idea was to trade time for space.[23]

The modern term to describe this scheme is a "covering force action." A recent U.S. Army manual defines a covering force action in this way:

> The covering force operates independently from the main body. The purpose of covering force operations is to develop the situation early and deceive,

18 *Vidette* is a French word, meaning "a mounted sentry in advance of the outposts of an army."

19 *U.S. War Department, Instructions for Officers*, 8-9. The picket reserve was also known as the grand guard. The grand guard was one of the posts of the second line belonging to a system of advance posts of an army. In other words, the picket reserve were reinforcements to the original line of videttes.

20 Ibid.

21 Ibid., 13.

22 Ibid., 16-18.

23 A detailed discussion of the small-unit tactics of videttes and of the implementation of the sort of delaying actions that Minty and Wilder designed is found in Appendix C to this book.

> disorganize, and destroy enemy forces. However, unlike screening and guard forces, a covering force is tactically self-contained and often seeks to become decisively engaged with the enemy. Cover operations are performed in the offense or defense and can be conducted by either the [Armored Cavalry Regiment (ACR)] or separate brigade.
>
> *There is no clear line between the covering force battle and the main battle. Covering forces continue to operate in some areas, while the main battle is pursued in others. Throughout the operation, battles shift from defensive action in one locale to offensive action.* That is why the ACR or separate brigade conducting a covering force mission must be prepared for either mission.
>
> When a covering force action begins, the main body generally is not engaged. Depending on how much warning it gets, and the mission of the main body, the covering force can be heavily augmented with engineers, [Military Intelligence (MI)], and artillery before the battle begins. With less warning, support arrives with the battle already underway. In any event, the covering force is expected to continue resistance until the corps has had time to deploy. Because it operates independently from the corps main body, the MI company must be able to move all of its personnel, systems, and equipment with its own organic assets.[24]

In other words, the idea behind a covering force action is to trade time for space, thereby allowing a detached forward unit (usually cavalry) to delay the advance of the enemy long enough to permit the main body to come up and engage. The covering force operates independently of the main body.[25]

24 Department of the Army, *Field Manual 34-35: Armored Cavalry Regiment and Separate Brigade Intelligence and Electronic Warfare Operations* (Washington, DC: Department of the Army, 1990), chapter 4 (emphasis added).

25 The definition of covering force action set forth above comes from a modern army tactics manual for armored cavalry. While horses and single-shot carbines have been traded in for tanks, Bradley armored fighting vehicles, and automatic weapons, the role and mission of cavalry remains the same. During the Cold War, before the fall of the Berlin Wall, NATO expected any potential Soviet invasion of Western Europe to pass through a narrow mountain pass in central (what was then West) Germany, to the east of Frankfurt, called Fulda Gap, which Napoleon had used to retreat after the 1813 battle of Leipzig. NATO doctrine held that armored cavalry would conduct a covering force action at Fulda Gap long enough for the main body of the allied forces to come up, engage, and halt the Soviet invasion. The NATO tactics were identical, adjusted only for advances in technology. For more on NATO doctrine and tactics during the Cold War, see Ingo Trauschweizer, *The Cold War U.S. Army: Building Deterrence for Limited War* (Lawrence: University Press of Kansas, 2008).

A further analysis of Minty's deployments reveals their classic nature. They were intended to deceive the enemy as to force type, size, disposition, intent, and dispositions and to force the Confederates to buy every foot of ground at the highest cost possible. He also intended to trade time for ground by forcing the enemy to deploy his forces, thereby identifying the type, size, disposition, intent, and location of Bushrod Johnson's division. All of this, in turn, completely disrupted Bragg's operating plans for September 18, 1863.

Minty developed his defensive scheme with the army's manual in mind. He made excellent use of the terrain available to him, and he also maximized the ability of his small brigade to hinder the advance of the numerically superior Confederate infantry. His defensive scheme extended over a distance of about three miles, from Reed's Bridge to his farthest vidette posts along Three Notch Road, which intersects with the Reed's Bridge Road about a half mile to the east of Pea Vine Creek. He extended his vidette posts almost six and a half miles to the north to Red House Bridge and south of the critical intersection of the Reed's Bridge and Three Notch Roads to where they linked up with Wilder's videttes.

Those vidette posts were spaced approximately 50 yards apart along the front. Each vidette post was manned by two to three soldiers and typically commanded by a noncommissioned officer, with a lieutenant commanding the vidette posts in a given sector.[26] Minty's network of videttes extended far enough south to link up with Wilder's vidette posts to the north of Alexander's Bridge. Minty intended to mount his primary defense at the natural choke point created by the bridge. He placed his grand guard on Pea Vine Ridge, overlooking the vidette posts in the valley below. When the Confederates drove the videttes back a mile from Pea Vine Creek, the videttes would join the grand guard on Pea Vine Ridge, where they intended to make a stand. The entire exercise was intended to buy time for Rosecrans to commit his infantry to the fight.

26 It is unclear precisely how far Minty's videttes extended to the north. Unlike the defense designed by Brig. Gen. John Buford at Gettysburg, there is little record of the precise dispositions of Minty's vidette posts. His September 10, 1863, returns indicate his brigade had approximately 1,400 men, but he indicated that he had 973 officers and men in the fight at Reed's Bridge on September 18, 1863, suggesting that some of his command was elsewhere, performing vidette duty, and was never called back to join the brigade's fight at the bridge. My description of his net of vidette posts is based on the outposting manual's requirements.

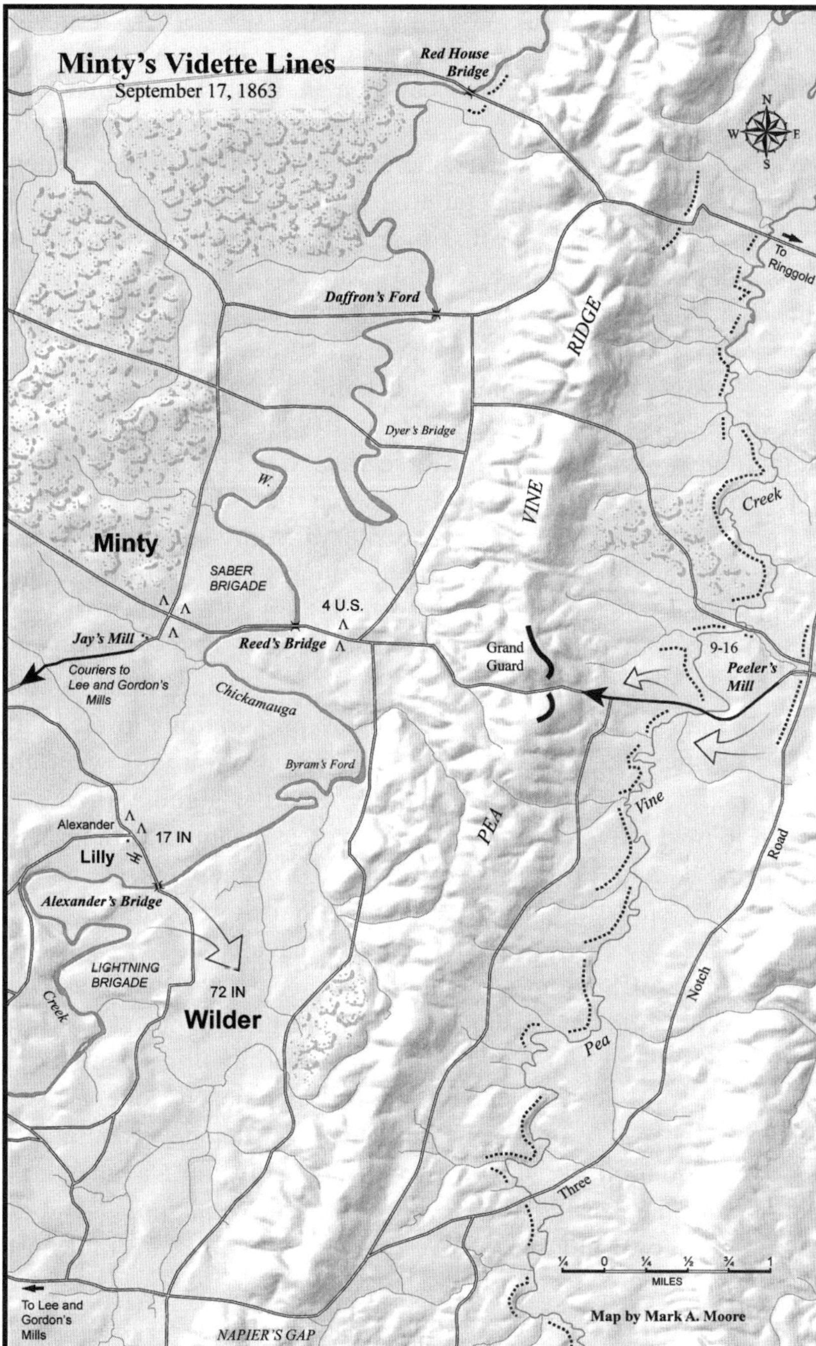

Minty's vidette lines, night of September 17.

Minty designed a delaying action that greatly resembled that used by John Buford on the first day of the battle of Gettysburg. Minty, however, had roughly one-third the number of men available to him that Buford had, meaning Minty faced an even more stern task than did Buford.

Wilder's dispositions are even more uncertain than Minty's, as neither Wilder nor his men left any detailed descriptions of those dispositions. His vidette posts extended north toward Reed's Bridge, linking up with Minty's videttes somewhere between Alexander's and Reed's Bridges. His videttes extended as far south as Glass Mill, seven and a half miles from Alexander's Bridge.[27] This far-flung network of videttes—extending for 14 miles—would provide ample prior notice to both Minty and Wilder of the advance of Bragg's army. Hopefully, they would hang on long enough to buy sufficient time for Rosecrans to get his army in hand and in place to defend its positions. At the same time, though, this 14-mile-long line of videttes meant that nearly 500 of Minty's men would not be available to defend Reed's Bridge and that almost half of Wilder's roughly 2,100 men were not readily available to defend Alexander's Bridge on September 18, 1863. The men of both brigades faced a severe test with too few of them available to accomplish the missions assigned to them.

While their brigade commanders made preparations to receive the enemy's advance the next morning, the men in the ranks went about their normal routines. Several hundred of Minty's and Wilder's men went out to man the vidette lines while the rest established their camps, tried to find something decent to eat, tended to their horses, and used the opportunity to scribble letters home to their loved ones.

The probes by Pegram's and Forrest's cavalry in the direction of Reed's Bridge on September 16 had alarmed Minty, who responded by pulling his camps back about a mile from their exposed position at Peeler's Mill on Pea Vine Creek to the area surrounding Reed's Bridge. Minty was also concerned enough about his exposed, lonely position and its lack of depth from insufficient manpower that he asked to be sent a brigade of infantry as well as the 7th Pennsylvania Cavalry and the detachment of the 3rd Indiana Cavalry to reinforce his horse soldiers.[28] Knowing that he would not receive that brigade of infantry meant that

27 We know that Wilder's vidette post at Glass Mill was relieved by the 42nd Indiana Infantry of Brig. Gen. John Beatty's 14th Corps brigade on the morning of September 18. Beyond that, we know very little about Wilder's dispositions.

28 *OR* 30, pt. 3, 679.

Minty understood he would have to make do with his brigade alone, which was missing the 159 troopers of the 3rd Indiana Cavalry, who were still in Chattanooga and would not be ordered to join the rest of its brigade in time to make a difference in the fight to hold Reed's Bridge. Minty had to do the best he could to defend with less than 1,000 troopers, not counting the nearly 500 men who were off picketing Chickamauga Creek and who could not be spared to reinforce the main body at Reed's Bridge.

The 4th U.S. Cavalry of Minty's brigade had the honor of being the easternmost regiment of the Saber Brigade to be posted along the Reed's Bridge Road. The regulars established their camp about a quarter of a mile to the east of the bridge, while the rest of the brigade set up its camps in the woods behind the west side of the bridge. "This was now the most advanced position on Rosecrans' line and in close proximity to the Confederate army," noted Sgt. James Larson of the 4th U.S. Cavalry. "And we of the 4th Cavalry knew that, as we had the pleasure of watching their movement from the top of the mountain during the afternoon." Larson and his friends went foraging and caught a fat sheep and also scavenged some sweet potatoes, cabbages, onions, and flour. They came into camp too late to cook their haul that night, so they planned on having a feast in the morning. "We, of course, had expected to hold that position until some definite move was made by the enemy."[29]

After the intense heat of the previous few days, it was unseasonably cold that night, with the temperature dropping close to freezing. A stiff wind heightened the discomfort of the soldiers as they tried to find blankets and sleep. "A sudden change, found an uncomfortably warm day on Thursday to an uncomfortably cold one on Friday, told upon us, as might have been discovered by our chattering teeth and shivering limbs," noted one of Brig. Gen. Henry Benning's Georgians. "The Autumnal Equinox was evidently heralding its advent."[30] In addition to the cold weather, many men were haunted by feelings of unease. "On both sides of the creek, soldiers could not sleep and told of strange feelings of death," noted one historian. "The very atmosphere was eerie, mysterious."[31]

29 Larson, *Sergeant Larson*, 174-75.

30 Charles Frederick Terrill to His Brother, September 22, 1863, Chickamauga and Chattanooga National Military Park, Archives, Fort Oglethorpe, GA (hereafter cited as CCNMP).

31 Louise Booth, *The Beleaguered Forty-First Tennessee* (Villa Park, CA: D. R. Booth Associates, 1996), 76.

Sergeant Larson also left a vivid description of the camps of Minty's troopers that night. "There is something very fascinating in the appearance of a temporary camp of a large body of cavalry in the woods on a pleasant summer night," he wrote. "The trees covered with foliage are lit up from under by the numerous campfires scattered here and there over hundreds of acres and the colors and shades of the leaves are changed to various hues as they are moved by the night breezes to and from the rays of light. Then the irregularity in the formation of such a camp adds another charm to the scene and gives the camp a gypsy-like appearance. There is no rule as to where the horses shall be tied or the fires built or the men spread their blankets. Hence the horses are tied promiscuously among the trees where they are munching their feed," he continued. "The campfires, in like manner, are built here and there among the trees and men are lying about on their blankets or busying themselves with cooking. In fact, the camp has all the appearance of comfort, ease and peace, and could easily be mistaken for a camp of a pleasure excursion, a picnic party in fact, if it were not for the bright sabers and carbines resting against the trees wherever a person looked."[32]

The 17th Indiana of the Lightning Brigade drew the duty of defending Alexander's Bridge. When they arrived at the bridge late on the afternoon of September 17, they established their camp on the west bank of the Chickamauga, near a large cornfield. Unfortunately, the ground was very rocky, and the Hoosiers "could scarcely find room to lie down," complained Richard T. Foster of the 17th.[33] Wilder sent Companies A and F of the 72nd Indiana to picket the creek, with Company A positioned at Alexander's Bridge and Company F a mile south at Dalton's Ford. The 123rd Illinois picketed the west bank of the Chickamauga between Dalton's Ford and Lee and Gordon's Mills. "The night was quiet, and we rested well," recalled Sergeant Magee.[34] Recognizing the possibility that the enemy's advance could come at any time, they kept their horses saddled all night.[35]

Unlike Minty's regular troopers, Capt. Elli Lilly's artillerists did not have to wait to enjoy a bounty gathered in the area. Lilly's gunners

32 Larson, *Sergeant Larson*, 173.

33 Foster, diary, September 17, 1862.

34 Magee, *History of the Seventy-Second Regiment*, 167.

35 Greist, diary, September 17, 1863.

established their camp at the Alexander house and outbuildings, about a quarter of a mile up the hill from the bridge. They found a large potato patch near their campsite. "I took a coffee sack and in company with some of the mess boys started over to gather in a harvest of potatoes," recalled gunner Henry Campbell. "While we were busily digging, the Provost Marshal came along, and arrested all that were in the field. Several men were making off with their hats and arms full when the Officer directed them to empty them into our sack, which was fully capable of holding a good many such additions." Once they had all dumped their loads of spuds, a burly corporal of the 72nd Indiana was ordered to carry the bag of potatoes to headquarters. The Hoosier artillerymen watched their feast march away. The provost marshal ordered the man carrying the sack of potatoes to stop and put the bag down while he went off to find a guard. "As soon as he disappeared, I told Orderly Sergeant Miller the fate our sack of potatoes had met," said Campbell. "He seeing the situation of affairs, and the probability of our scanty dinners, marched boldly up to the sack—just as if he had been ordered—shouldered and marched off with it." The pickets "seeing the joke, never said a word and when the Provost returned, he was so completely sold out that he made tracks with his guard as soon as possible. We had plenty of potatoes all thro the three days fighting that followed," concluded Campbell. He and his mates slept well that night with comfortably full stomachs.[36]

Fortunately for John Wilder and the Lightning Brigade, there were no Confederates in their immediate front. His men would not be tested with the rising of the sun on September 18, like Minty's would. If Bragg advanced on Alexander's Bridge, he would not do so until later in the day, and Wilder's network of videttes should provide him sufficient notice to prepare to receive their attack. That gave Wilder the luxury of having time during the day on September 18 to prepare to meet the enemy, which was an indulgence Minty would not have.

Minty spent the night sending galloper after galloper off to Crittenden's headquarters at Lee and Gordon's Mills, carrying the most current intelligence to the corps commander. Crittenden remained skeptical of the Englishman's reports and largely disregarded them. Minty, however,

36 Campbell, *Three Years in the Saddle*, 99-100.

Lee and Gordon's Mills as it would have looked at the time of the battle. *Library of Congress*

prepared to receive Bragg's host the next morning.[37] He noted that John Pegram's Confederate videttes were about nine miles up the Pea Vine Valley that evening.[38] The combination of the distance involved and the billowing clouds of dust that would be generated by the movement of the Confederates in the drought-ridden valley should give his men plenty of time to steel themselves to receive the approach of the grayclad horde. Only time would tell whether he and his 973 officers and men would be up to the heavy task that awaited them on the morning of September 18, 1863.[39]

37 Vale, *Minty and the Cavalry*, 224.

38 *OR* 30, pt. 1, 113.

39 Ibid., 923. Although this number varies from the reported strength of Minty's regiments from September 30, 1863 (those reports indicated more than 1,400 men present for duty), Minty's report of the battle of Chickamauga specifically stated he had 973 officers and men present for duty at Reed's Bridge on September 18. The only explanation for this difference of nearly 500 men—about one-third of Minty's total force—is that they were picketing at various points along the banks of Chickamauga Creek and they could not be spared to reinforce Minty's main body.

Chapter Four

The Ball Opens on the Reed's Bridge Road

Colonel Robert H. G. Minty arose very early on the cool and cloudy morning of September 18, 1863. Restless and concerned about his ability to hold off overwhelming numbers of Confederates who would soon come marching down the Reed's Bridge Road, Minty was a bundle of nervous energy. He ordered his men to saddle their horses at 4:00, and they waited for orders to move out.[1] His troopers were told to feed their horses, feed themselves, harness the artillery horses and mules, and pack and prepare the brigade's baggage to move out at a moment's notice.[2] At 5:00, he dashed off a quick note to Maj. Gen. Gordon Granger at Rossville, reporting "all quiet at this point during the night."[3]

Bushrod Johnson's Confederate infantry was also up early that morning. They had spent the evening of September 17 cooking two days' rations to add to the two days' worth already on hand, meaning they now had four full days' ready, a sure sign that a major battle loomed. With the booming of artillery echoing off the hills, the Confederate soldiers rested on their arms so they would be at hand instantly if needed.[4] They

1 Potter, diary, September 18, 1863.

2 Vale, *Minty and the Cavalry*, 224.

3 *OR* 30, pt. 3, 731.

4 Ibid., pt. 2, 471.

broke their camp near Catoosa Platform at 4:00 a.m. and marched to Ringgold.[5] They then moved out of Ringgold and headed toward Leet's Tanyard, trudging on through thick, choking dust, "little thinking what a terrible ordeal awaited us," admitted one of Johnson's Arkansans.[6]

About three miles into the march a courier from Bragg reined in with orders for Johnson to return to Ringgold and instead take the Reed's Bridge Road, where he was to "make a lodgment" on the west bank of the creek.[7] A detachment of cavalry under Nathan Bedford Forrest was to escort Johnson's infantry on its march.[8] After they had covered a few miles, another galloper arrived with further instructions: After crossing the Chickamauga at Reed's Bridge, Johnson was then to turn south and head along the creek to Lee and Gordon's Mills. Along the way he was to be reinforced by the troops of Walker and Buckner. The combined force would then attack Crittenden at the mills. The countermarching, however, added another 10 miles and several hours or so of marching to the day's itinerary, delaying the Confederate advance and further tiring out Johnson's men.[9] As the Confederate infantry wound its way along the Ringgold Road, civilian refugees streamed by, carrying whatever household goods they could manage, fleeing from the advance of the Army of the Cumberland, and competing with the Southern infantry for the road network.[10]

At 6:00 a.m., Minty sent 100 picked troopers of the 4th U.S. out toward Leet's Tanyard and another 100 troopers of the 4th Michigan and 7th Pennsylvania, under command of Capt. Heber S. Thompson of

5 Daniel Harris Reynolds, diary, September 17-18, 1863, Special Collections, University of Arkansas, Fayetteville, AR.

6 "History of Company H, 1st Arkansas Mounted Rifles," Mississippi Department of Archives and History, Jackson, Mississippi.

7 *OR* 30, pt. 2, 452.

8 Ibid., 524.

9 Ibid., 31, 467. This was the general order Bragg had issued the night before, just catching up to Johnson.

10 John Camden West, *A Texan in Search of a Fight: Being the Diary and Letters of a Private Soldier in Hood's Texas Brigade* (Waco, TX: Press of J. S. Hill & Co., 1901), 111-12.

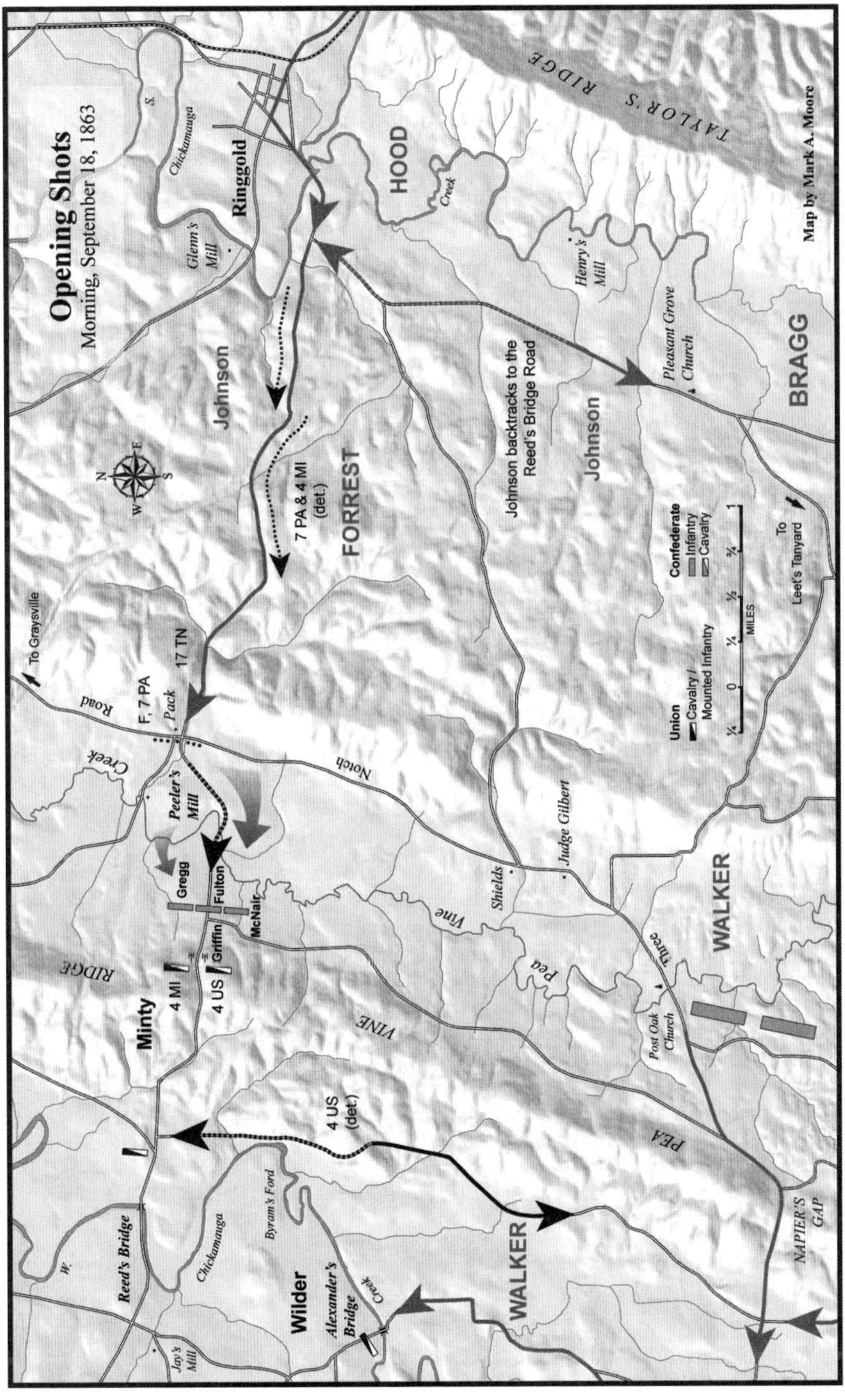

Opening shots, morning, September 18.

the 7th Pennsylvania, off toward Ringgold to scout the enemy.[11] Some of Forrest's cavalry were also scouting that morning. They encountered Thompson's detachment of the 7th Pennsylvania near Ringgold Gap. "The enemy had no advance guard, but were moving slowly," recalled one of them. "Our vedettes discovered them and fell back, unseen, to our main column. General Forrest placed 50 men in ambush, and instructed the officer in charge not to fire until he had heard three guns in front of him. At this signal they opened upon them rapidly." A detachment of an officer and 10 enlisted horse soldiers charged the Pennsylvanians and drove them back. The Keystone Staters reformed and countercharged, driving the grayclad troopers back to Forrest's ambush site. The dismounted Confederates opened on the surprised Pennsylvanians at point-blank range, driving them back in confusion, with the Confederate horsemen in pursuit. Johnson's infantry followed, heading for Reed's Bridge.[12] "The Morgan men boasted that their small force fired the first and last shots of that terrible battle," proudly claimed one of them.[13]

Four troopers of Company F, 7th Pennsylvania—Cpl. John Williams and Pvts. Amandus Womer, Samuel Waters, and John Ward—manned the critical vidette post farthest east on the Reed's Bridge Road, which was at the intersection of Reed's Bridge Road and Three Notch Roads. These four enlisted men were tasked with the essential job of providing an early

11 *OR* 30, pt. 1, 922. Twenty-two-year-old Capt. Heber S. Thompson was from Pottsville, Pennsylvania. He was an 1861 engineering graduate of Yale College who had enlisted in Company H of the 25th Pennsylvania Volunteer Infantry that spring after the fall of Fort Sumter, responding to Lincoln's initial call for volunteers to put down the rebellion. Thompson's company of the 25th Pennsylvania was one of the first volunteer infantry units to reach Washington, DC, earning the honorific "The First Defenders." When his three-month term of enlistment in the 25th Pennsylvania expired on July 29, 1861, he was commissioned a lieutenant in Company F of the 7th Pennsylvania Cavalry. He was promoted to captain of Company L on July 1, 1863. He was known as an officer of "tried courage, coolness and judgment." Thompson ended the war with the rank of major. *Schuylkill County, Pennsylvania: Genealogy—Family History—Biography, Containing Historical Sketches of Old Families and of Representative and Prominent Citizens, Past and Present*, 2 vols. (Chicago: J. H. Beers & Co., 1916), vol. 1, 33-34.

12 Thomas F. Berry, *Four Years with Morgan and Forrest* (Oklahoma City: Harlow-Ratcliff Co., 1914), 234-35.

13 James F. Corn, *Jim Witherspoon: A Soldier of the South, 1862-1865* (n.p., n.d.), James Franklin Witherspoon File, Civil War Collection, Tennessee State Library and Archives, Nashville, TN.

Capt. Heber S. Thompson of the 7th Pennsylvania Cavalry, whose men fired the first shots of the Battle of Chickamauga. *Sipes, The Seventh Pennsylvania Veteran Volunteer Cavalry: Its Record, Reminiscences and Roster*

warning system of the approach of the Southern infantry as they headed west toward the bridge.[14]

While Minty rode out to inspect his vidette posts, the rest of the Saber Brigade waited for orders. Although they had saddled up at 4:00 a.m., about the same time Minty sent his scouts out, the troopers left behind received orders to unsaddle and feed their horses.[15] Minty rode out to take personal command of his first line of defense on Pea Vine Ridge. "By 6:30 o'clock on the morning of the 18th, I was in position on the east slope of Pea Vine Ridge, ready to contest the advance of the approaching enemy," he recalled. He did not have long to wait.[16]

About 7:00 a.m., his scouts came galloping back to report the enemy was close behind and coming at them on the Ringgold and La Fayette Roads, deployed in a strong skirmish line and followed by heavy columns. Minty responded by strengthening his position along the La Fayette Road and advanced to the eastern slope of Pea Vine Ridge with all of the 4th Michigan, a battalion of the 4th U.S., and Lt. Trumbull D. Griffin's two-gun section of the Chicago Board of Trade Battery. Minty

14 George F. Steahlin, "Address and Historical Sketch," in *Pennsylvania at Chickamauga*, 309.

15 Potter, diary, September 18, 1863.

16 Robert H. G. Minty, "Minty's Saber Brigade—The Part They Took in the Chattanooga Campaign, Chickamauga—Holding the Creek Against Overwhelming Numbers, Left in the Lurch—The Saber Brigade the Last Troops to Enter Chattanooga," *National Tribune*, March 3, 1892.

also sent gallopers off to Maj. Gen. Gordon Granger at Rossville, to Wilder at Alexander's Bridge, to Wood at Lee and Gordon's Mills, and to Crittenden at Crawfish Springs.[17] He then prepared to receive the advance of the enemy.[18]

The 10 officers and 249 enlisted men of Lt. Col. Watt W. Floyd's 17th Tennessee Infantry of Col. John S. Fulton's brigade led Johnson's advance, with the rest of Fulton's brigade following behind.[19] Floyd's lead elements opened fire on Corporal Williams's picket post at the intersection of Reed's Bridge and Three Notch Roads. Private Samuel Williams of the 7th Pennsylvania Cavalry was situated at a nearby house. From a range of about 100 yards, he took aim with his Smith's carbine and squeezed off a shot at Floyd and another officer riding with him. He missed.[20]

"On reaching the bank of Pea Vine Creek, I discovered two Federal vedettes near a house about 150 yards from me," recounted Floyd. "One of them fired and I returned to the brigade to report the facts. Soon after this 15 or 20 more Federal cavalry came up and charged my pickets, but they were repulsed with a loss of 3 killed and 1 mortally wounded."[21] Floyd then reported his encounter with the Keystone Staters to Bushrod Johnson. The three dead Yankees noted by Floyd were Pvts. John Ward and Owen Brennan of Company F and Pvt. Jacob Stroup of Company H, all of the 7th Pennsylvania. Several other Pennsylvanians were wounded.

17 Crawfish Springs is in the modern town of Chickamauga, Georgia, directly across the street from the Gordon-Lee Mansion, where Rosecrans had his headquarters prior to the battle.

18 *OR* 30, pt. 1, 922.

19 The strength of the 17th Tennessee is found at ibid., pt. 2, 479. John S. Fulton was born in Fayetteville, Tennessee, on March 31, 1828. He attended Georgetown University in Washington, DC, and was admitted to the bar. He practiced law in Lincoln County, Tennessee, until the outbreak of the Civil War. He enlisted in Company F of the 44th Tennessee Infantry as a private on March 27, 1862, and was promoted to captain on April 14. He was wounded in action at the battle of Stones River. When he returned to duty, he was promoted to major on April 19, 1863, and then to colonel on May 5, 1863. With Bushrod Johnson temporarily in command of a division, Fulton, as the senior officer in Johnson's brigade, assumed command of the brigade. He was mortally wounded in action in the fighting around Petersburg, Virginia, on June 30, 1864, and died on July 4 at age 36. He was fondly remembered as being "loved by comrades and respected by officers." See Allardice, *Confederate Colonels*, 155.

20 Steahlin, "Address and Historical Sketch," 309.

21 *OR* 30, pt. 2, 479.

Privates Ward, Brennan, and Stroup were the first Union soldiers killed during the sanguinary battle of Chickamauga.[22]

Thompson and his small, mixed force of Wolverines and Keystone Staters fought a stubborn delaying action and slowly fell back. Keeping their horses nearby so they could fall back, the dismounted cavalrymen fought a classic delaying action. They formed a skirmish line and took advantage of their rapid-firing carbines and Colt's rifles to hold off the Confederates for as long as they could. When the Confederates threatened to flank them out of their position or threatened to overpower them with their vast numerical advantage, the blueclad troopers fell back a short distance, dismounted, formed their skirmish line anew, and resumed the fight. In this fashion, they greatly hindered the advance of Bushrod Johnson's infantry and bought critical time for Rosecrans. They employed the sorts of delay tactics taught by the army's outposting manual to

22 William B. Sipes, *The Seventh Pennsylvania Veteran Volunteer Cavalry: Its Record, Reminiscences and Roster* (Pottsville, PA: Pottsville Miner's Journal, 1905), 79. Lt. Col. Charles L. Greeno of the 7th Pennsylvania remembered Stroup fondly years after the war. "He was a bright active boy of about eighteen years of age; a brave soldier, always ready for duty," he declared at the dedication of the monument to the 7th Pennsylvania at Reed's Bridge in 1896. See Charles L. Greeno, "Address of Lt. Col. Charles L. Greeno," in *Pennsylvania at Chickamauga*, 312. The Compiled Military Service Records for Stroup indicate Jacob Stroup enlisted as a Private in Company H of the 7th Pennsylvania Cavalry on October 10, 1861, at Pittsburgh at the age of 21. No description was provided. Stroup was in Louisville, Kentucky, on detached service per the March April 1863 muster. He was killed in action on September 18, 1863, at Reed's Bridge at the battle of Chickamauga. He left no personal effects, and at the time of his death, he had last been paid to June 30, 1863. Records indicate that John Ward enlisted as a private in Company F of the 7th Pennsylvania Cavalry on October 29, 1861, at Pottsville at the age of 18. He had been born in Schuylkill County and was five-feet-seven-inches tall with gray eyes, sandy hair, and a light complexion. He was a laborer by occupation. Ward was hospitalized at Columbia, Tennessee, June 21, 1862. He returned to duty on July 3, 1862. Ward was killed in action on September 18, 1863, at Chickamauga. His body was never recovered from battlefield. Records indicate that Owen Brennan enlisted in Company F of the 7th Pennsylvania Cavalry in Donaldson on October 19, 1861, at the age of 42. Born in Ireland, Brennan was listed as five feet ten inches, light complexion, brown eyes, and sandy hair. No occupation was listed. He was noted to be hospitalized at Nashville, Tennessee, in the November-December 1862 muster roll and on detached service as a nurse in Nashville since February 4, 1863. He returned to duty on May 13, 1863. Brennan was killed in action on September 18, 1863, at Chickamauga. His body fell into enemy hands, and neither his body nor his effects were recovered.

Brig. Gen. John Gregg, who commanded one of the brigades assigned to Johnson's Provisional Division. He was badly wounded on September 20, but recovered and was assigned to lead Hood's Texas Brigade. After being wounded again in the Wilderness on May 6, he was killed outside Richmond on October 7, 1864. *Library of Congress*

perfection and achieved precisely the result that Minty hoped for when he designed his delaying action.[23]

The effectiveness of these delaying tactics is best illustrated by the words of a member of the 1st Arkansas Mounted Infantry of Brig. Gen. Evander McNair's brigade of Johnson's division. "From the movements we all knew that a fight was soon to occur," recalled the Arkansan. "We would move along for a short distance and halt, and about the time you had fairly sat down, and had got yourself into an easy posture, the order would be given—'fall in, forward' and then move up a short distance and halt again, and so it would go, consuming an hour or two, in making a mile or two, at the same time you had been on your feet all the while, for you would scarcely sit down until the line would be in motion again." Nobody liked that sort of marching because it wore out the men.[24]

Lieutenant James T. S. Thompson served in the 3rd Tennessee Infantry of Brig. Gen. John Gregg's brigade. Thompson echoed a similar note in describing the nature of the advance against Minty's defenders and the

23 When cavalry dismounts to fight on foot, something must be done with the horses, which are not permitted to roam free. One of every four men is detailed to hold the reins of his horse and three of his comrades' horses at the ready, so that the animals were out of the line of fire but near enough that the dismounted troopers could mount up and use them to escape quickly. This means the effective fighting strength of dismounted cavalry units is automatically reduced by 25 percent due to the horse holders. Horse-holding duty was very unpopular, because it meant the unfortunates who drew that duty did not participate in the action and had to watch from the rear. Although unpopular, it was nevertheless very important duty.

24 "History of Company H, 1st Arkansas Mounted Rifles."

textbook execution of the delaying action by the Federal troopers. "We proceeded a little, then fired a volley or two into the enemies ranks, and he began to retreat, but very stubbornly," he wrote. "He formed on every hill, as if he intended to give us battle; but as we steadily advanced he gave away to seek another position."[25] Minty's men were exposed to enemy fire only long enough to delay the advance of the Confederate infantry before falling back to the next position.

"Who of us survivors can ever forget the picture presented on that quiet September morning in the Pea Vine Valley," recalled Maj. Richard B. Robbins of the 4th Michigan Cavalry. "Directly in our front was the heavy line of skirmishers advancing; then the long, solid lines of infantry, with artillery flanked by cavalry. Further to our left heavy bodies of troops could be seen, all in motion, and still further, dense columns of dust; all indicating too plainly the coming battle. With the thousands of bayonets glistening in the first rays of the morning sun, and hundreds of battle flags kissing the morning breeze, it was a picture at once beautiful, grand and gloomy—grand in contemplation of military glory, gloomy in the reflection that the scene would soon change and many must die."[26]

About 10:45 a.m. approximately 200 of Forrest's cavalry joined Johnson's column. These forces consisted of Forrest's bodyguard and the 160 or so survivors of Brig. Gen. John Hunt Morgan's division who had made it back to the Army of Tennessee after a disastrous raid into Ohio and Indiana that summer.[27] Lieutenant Colonel Robert M. Martin of the 10th Kentucky Cavalry was the ranking officer of this detachment, and he was known as "a man of extraordinary dash and

25 Robert W. Ikard, ed., "Lieutenant Thompson Reports on Chickamauga: A Comparison of Immediate and Historical Perspectives of the Battle," *Tennessee Historical Quarterly* (1985), 419.

26 R. B. Robbins, "At Reed's Bridge: Splendid Work Done by the Cavalry on the Left at Chickamauga," *National Tribune*, November 14, 1895.

27 Morgan took approximately 2,500 Confederate cavalrymen on a raid deep into Indiana and Ohio during the summer of 1863. The raid lasted 46 days and covered more than 1,000 miles. Morgan violated Bragg's orders in going off on this expedition, and it wrecked a fine division. Morgan and over 2,000 of his men were captured, and only a fragment of his command safely made it back to duty with the Army of Tennessee. Obviously, a detailed discussion of Morgan's Indiana and Ohio raid strays far beyond the scope of this monograph. There is, however, no satisfactory full-length monograph devoted to Morgan's raid. For a decent study that features excellent maps, see David L. Mowery, *Morgan's Great Raid: The Remarkable Expedition from Kentucky to Ohio* (Charleston, SC: History Press, 2013).

resolution."[28] One of Morgan's men said: "Our small force was ordered to report to General Forrest, and did so about ten a.m. on the field. We were immediately deployed as skirmishers mounted." As the cavalrymen passed by Forrest alongside the road, the general "called to them in language which inspired them with still higher enthusiasm. He urged them to do their whole duty in battle. He spoke of their chief, who had been insulted in a felon's treatment, and was then lying in a penitentiary cell. He gave them 'Morgan' for a battle-cry, and bade them maintain their old reputation." These 200 or so grayclad horsemen were the only cavalry available to screen Johnson's advance, and they faced a real challenge that day in the face of Minty's active and diligent troopers. "The infantry objected to have 'the d—d cavalry' placed in front of them in a fight," the Confederate trooper continued. "But they did not easily catch up with 'the d—d cavalry.'"[29]

The Confederate horsemen drove in Minty's pickets and headed for the main line of battle. "We pushed on and found a regiment of cavalry in line to receive us," said one. "This fled upon the receipt of the first volley. The undergrowth was too thick for maneuvering on horseback, and we were dismounted and advanced at the double-quick. Our boys were anxious to drive the enemy and keep them going without letting the

28 Robert M. Martin was born in Greenville, Kentucky, on January 10, 1840. He helped operate his father's plantation there before the war. He acted as a scout for Forrest's cavalry in 1861-62, and on August 13, 1862, he was elected lieutenant colonel of the 10th Kentucky Cavalry. He served with Brig. Gen. Adam Johnson in partisan operations in Kentucky and was wounded in action at McMinnville, Tennessee, on April 19, 1863. Martin was promoted to colonel and was wounded in 1864 at Mount Sterling. After he recovered, he went to Canada to participate in clandestine operations there, including the scheme to burn New York City in 1864. He was paroled at Augusta, Georgia, on May 26, 1865, and was then held in New York City on arson charges arising from the 1864 scheme. He was eventually released and moved to Evansville, Indiana, where he operated a tobacco warehouse from 1866 to 1874. From 1874 to 1887 he was a tobacco inspector in Brooklyn, New York. He acted as a tobacco broker in Louisville after that, making and losing several fortunes along the way. He died on January 9, 1901, in New York City, where he had gone for treatment of a lung disease. See Allardice, *Confederate Colonels*, 254-55.

29 Basil W. Duke, *History of Morgan's Cavalry* (Cincinnati: Miami Printing & Publishing Co., 1867), 508. One of the traditional roles of cavalry is to screen the advance of infantry by having a force available to ascertain what enemy units await the arrival of the infantry. While Forrest typically had no talent for the traditional roles of cavalry, he performed an important role by doing so on September 18, 1863.

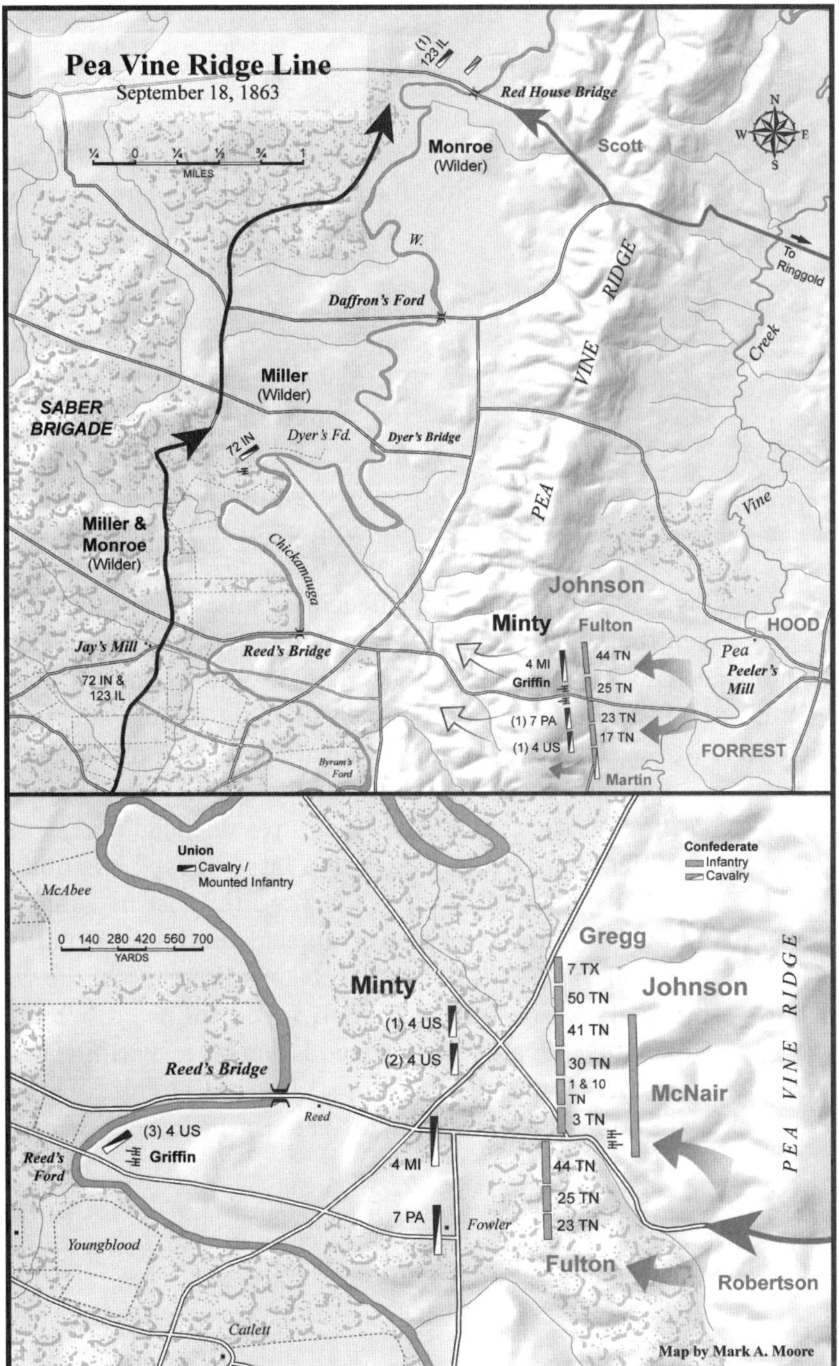

Pea Vine Ridge line, morning, September 18.

Brig. Gen. Evander McNair, the leader of one of the brigades assigned to Johnson's Provisional Division. *Museum of the Confederacy*

infantry overtake us."[30] Now came the first of several failures by Forrest that day. Instead of continuing to push Minty's men while mounted, Forrest dismounted his men and had them reinforce the infantry skirmish line.

They "made the vanguard, and they moved under fire for about six miles, while we marched in line of battle over hills and hollows to keep in supporting distance," recalled Capt. William H. Harder of the 23rd Tennessee Infantry.[31] The advancing Confederates quickly drove in Minty's pickets.[32] When the head of one of those columns came within range, Griffin opened fire on it with both of his pieces, "and so far as we could judge, did considerable execution. This checked the enemy and caused them to deploy," wrote Minty. "They evidently supposed that there was a strong force opposing them, and they occupied considerable time in getting into position."[33] The Confederates also strengthened their skirmish lines and then pulled their artillery back to a less-exposed position.[34]

With Forrest's detachment leading the way, the rest of Johnson's command cautiously followed behind in line of battle, with Fulton's brigade in the middle and Gregg's and McNair's brigades to the right and left, respectively. Robertson's Texas Brigade followed behind in support of the main line of battle. Heavy woods and other terrain features, however, dramatically slowed their advance, giving Minty plenty of time to fall back and establish his main line of battle near Reed's Bridge.

30 Ibid.

31 William Henry Harder, "Reminiscences of Captain William Henry Harder, Company D, 23d Tennessee Infantry Regiment," U.S. Army Command and General Staff College, Fort Leavenworth, KS.

32 *OR* 30, pt. 1, 922.

33 Minty, "Minty's Saber Brigade," *National Tribune*, March 3, 1892.

34 *OR* 30, pt. 1, 922; Larson, *Sergeant Larson*, 179.

Col. Abram Miller, commander of the 72nd Indiana Mounted Infantry of the Lightning Brigade. *USAHEC, Mass. MOLLUS Collection*

This meant Minty's plan was already working to perfection. By having Griffin open with his two guns, Minty forced Bushrod Johnson's infantry to halt and then deploy into line of battle from column of march, an action that could take as long as a couple of hours for an infantry division. By virtue of firing those two artillery shots, Minty deceived Johnson into believing a much larger force blocked his way, and that required the deployment of his entire division. In so doing, Minty delayed the Confederate advance for a couple of vital hours, throwing Bragg's timetable off schedule from the very onset of the battle. Thereafter, when they advanced again, they did so in a crescent-shaped continuous line of battle, extending from Dyer's Ford to the north, across Pea Vine Ridge, and into the Pea Vine Valley.[35]

Once it became obvious that Minty's troopers were going to be driven back from their position on Pea Vine Ridge and that they would have a hard fight at the bridge, Minty hastened over to a nearby house to warn the occupant that a desperate battle was about to unfold and that her quiet house would be in the thick of it. Minty urged the woman to take her children across the creek, where they would be out of the line of fire. She emphatically refused, said she was not afraid, and declared not only would she not leave her house, she would resist any attempt to remove her by force. Minty's staff officers urged her to evacuate her children to a picket post on the La Fayette Road, but she categorically refused to leave or even to remain inside the house. She spent most of the morning watching the fighting from her front yard.[36]

35 Robbins, "At Reed's Bridge," *National Tribune*, November 14, 1895.

36 Vale, *Minty and the Cavalry*, 233. Minty's staff officer Capt. Joseph G. Vale identified this woman as Jemima Reed; however, Vale recounted the death of this woman later in the day. As pointed out previously, Jemima Reed lived for many years after the

After being rebuffed by the woman, Minty spotted a heavy dust cloud billowing from the direction of Dyer's Ford to his north. The colonel dashed off a quick note to Wilder, asking the Hoosier to send a force to hold the ford and to cover his left flank. Wilder responded quickly, dispatching Col. Abram Miller of the 72nd Indiana with half of his regiment and the 123rd Illinois and two of Lilly's mountain howitzers to Minty's assistance. Minty directed Miller to take position picketing Dyer's Ford, which would block the column he had spotted advancing to the north.[37] These troops covered Minty's northern flank and held the important ford, but their departure left Wilder with only a regiment and a half to hold Alexander's Bridge. Minty ordered Griffin's guns to fall back to Reed's Bridge and Capt. Joseph G. Vale of the 7th Pennsylvania Cavalry, the brigade's acting inspector general, to lead the brigade's baggage train back to safety as well.[38] After leaving a strong skirmish line on Pea Vine Ridge, Minty pulled the remainder of his available forces back to the bridge.[39] "About 300 yards above the bridge there was a poor ford," wrote Minty, "near which was located Reed's house and orchard; here I posted my two guns, supported by Capt. [Thomas H.] McCormick's battalion of the 4th U.S. Cav."[40]

---

battle and died in 1881; she was buried at the Boynton Methodist Church near Pea Vine Creek. The identity of the woman whose death Vale reported remains unknown.

37 *OR* 30, pt.1, 922.

38 Vale, *Minty and the Cavalry*, 226.

39 *OR* 30, pt. 1, 922-23.

40 Minty, "Minty's Saber Brigade," *National Tribune*, March 3, 1892. The two companies of McCormick's battalion were Companies H and F. Thomas Hood McCormick was 27 years old in 1863. He graduated from Lafayette College with a law degree in 1855 and was working as an attorney in Lock Haven, Pennsylvania, when war came in 1861. Despite having no military training, he was commissioned as a second lieutenant in the 1st U.S. Cavalry on March 27, 1861. He was promoted to first lieutenant just two months later. When Capt. James McIntyre assumed command of the redesignated 4th U.S. Cavalry, McCormick assumed command of McIntyre's Company E. He was promoted to captain on August 7, 1862, and took command of Company A. On June 18, 1865, McCormick's military career came to an unpleasant and premature end when acting regimental commander Capt. John M. Thompson wrote, "I have the honor to state that at about 5 o'clock last evening Capt. Thos. H. McCormick 4th U.S. Cav was driven into this camp in an ambulance in a beastly or insensible state of intoxication—he was lying on his back on two seats with his head hanging down and totally unconscious of where he was or his condition. I believe several of the men saw him. Myself and Lieut. W. W. Webb saw him and conversed with the driver. The driver said he had been taken out of the cars in that condition by Col Eggleston and

About 11:00 a.m. Bushrod Johnson's column halted for a quick breather near Peeler's Mill. While the men rested for a few minutes, several farmers sought out Johnson to warn him that Union soldiers were in force about a mile in front of them. With that intelligence in mind, Johnson ordered McNair, Fulton, and Gregg and eight newly arrived guns to deploy into line of battle, with Robertson's Texans in reserve. In the meantime, Forrest and his staff arrived. They rode ahead to scout the Union position and to search for a weak spot. Johnson's troops resumed their advance, pushing across Pea Vine Creek, "which offered some obstruction to regular movements, and caused some delay in crossing the troops."[41]

During the halt, a girl approached some soldiers of the 3rd Tennessee Infantry of Brig. Gen. John Gregg's brigade.[42] She was about 10 years

himself aided by others at the depot. His condition was such that I could not permit him to be taken out in presence of the command and ordered the driver to take him to Wilson Hospital." The regimental surgeon, assistant surgeon Merritt S. Jones, concurred with Thompson's assessment, describing McCormick's condition as "insensible from intoxication. He was so entirely helpless that he had to be carried into the ward on a stretcher." Major General James H. Wilson recommended McCormick's immediate discharge for chronic drunkenness. "This is no new thing in his conduct," Wilson wrote. "His public disgrace by drunkenness is a matter of notoriety in service tho' hitherto he has managed to escape punishment. A Court Martial cannot well be convened to try him, and the credit of the public service, as well as its discipline and good order demands his summary dismissal." Major General George H. Thomas concurred and forwarded the recommendation. It was approved by Lt. Gen. U.S. Grant on July 12 and by the secretary of war on July 21. McCormick was dismissed on July 25, 1865, and he returned home to Lock Haven. He died on March 30, 1866. While brave in battle, McCormick's demons brought his military career to a premature end. See Don Caughey, "Fiddler's Green: Thomas Hood McCormick," Regular Cavalry in the Civil War, February 3, 2015, https://regularcavalryincivilwar.wordpress.com/2015/02/03/fiddlers-green-thomas-hood-mccormick/.

41 *OR* 30, pt. 2, 451.

42 Brigadier General John Gregg was born in Lawrence County, Alabama, on September 28, 1828. He studied at La Grange College and then attended law school in Tuscumbia, Alabama. Upon graduating, he moved to Fairfield, Texas, and opened a law office. He quickly became involved in local politics. He was a prosecession delegate at the state convention to determine whether Texas should secede from the Union. He was then elected to the Confederate Congress but gave up his seat to go home and organize the 7th Texas Infantry. Gregg surrendered with his regiment at Fort Donelson in February 1862, and he was eventually exchanged. His regiment was assigned to the defenses of Vicksburg, Mississippi. Gregg was promoted to brigadier general on September 27, 1862, and assumed command of a brigade consisting of the 7th Texas and 1st, 30th, 41st, and 50th Tennessee. His brigade fought with Gen. Joseph E. Johnston's army in its failed efforts to relieve Vicksburg in the spring of 1863. After the fall of Vicksburg,

old, and she was crying and obviously upset. The soldiers asked her what was wrong. "Oh, we are ruined," she cried. "They have just passed our house and taken everything we had. They have taken the dinner out of the pots, killed all our hogs and chickens and taken all our turnips and potatoes, and tore up everything on the place. We have not got anything at all to eat, and the rest of the family have all run away." The sympathetic Southerners offered her some of their rations, but she refused, declaring, "No, you keep what you have got to eat to yourselves, and go on and kill the last one of them."

Although they were tired, the girl's plight inspired the Tennesseans to spring to their feet and promise to pay the Yankees back. "We pointed out our good old colonel to her, and the last we saw of her she was standing by his horse, with streaming eyes she was telling him her woes." His eyes flashing with anger, the colonel called out, "Forward, March!" About a mile farther on they came upon the girl's home, which had been ransacked. A dead Union soldier lay in the yard, killed by Forrest's cavalrymen. He lay on his back in the hot sun, and the passing Confederates jeered at his corpse and sprinkled it with epithets as they marched by. Such were the horrors of war. The jaded Southerners marched on, all the more determined to deliver some vengeance.[43]

It took time for Bushrod Johnson's men to get into position to press the attack while preserving their formation as they made their way across Pea Vine Creek. While they did so, Johnson's chief of artillery, Maj. Felix Robertson, the son of Brig. Gen. Jerome B. Robertson, deployed four artillery pieces and a section of guns from Lt. William S. Everett's Battery E, 9th Georgia Artillery Battalion. The Southern gunners opened on Minty's dismounted cavalrymen, driving them back. Johnson then advanced to the top of Pea Vine Ridge, with Jerome Robertson's brigade of the Army of Northern Virginia supporting Brig. Gen. Evander McNair's brigade on the right, and they dislodged the stubborn Union horse soldiers

---

Gregg's brigade, along with the rest of Johnston's army, was sent to join Bragg, arriving in time for the battle of Chickamauga. "A rugged and unrelenting fighter, he was personally without fear, even looking the part of the rugged frontiersman with his 'spade' beard, high forehead, and fierce gaze." He was badly wounded at Chickamauga on September 19. Gregg went to Virginia with Longstreet after Chickamauga, and he was killed in action on October 7, 1864, during the siege of Petersburg. See Davis and Hoffman, *The Confederate General*, vol. 3, 36-39.

43 J. C. M., "A Story of the War," *The Sunny South*, August 15, 1896.

Brig. Gen. Jerome B. Robertson of Texas, who commanded Hood's old Texas Brigade from the Army of Northern Virginia. *USAHEC*

from a second position. "The cavalry on the right kept up the skirmishing during the ascent," noted Johnson.[44]

Minty estimated the advancing Confederates as having an effective strength of about 7,000; he counted 13 sets of regimental colors. "My left and rear being taken care of, I advanced to the support of the skirmishers, and the enemy's skirmish line was driven back on their line of battle in Pea Vine Valley." The Confederates regrouped and resumed their advance.[45] The terrain broke their advance into separate columns. "The rebel line advanced and I was steadily driven back across the ridge," wrote Minty.[46] Johnson's long line of battle overlapped Minty's right flank, forcing the thin line of troopers to fall back.

Seeing Johnson's long line of battle cresting the ridge, Minty realized he was in jeopardy. "The position of the brigade was now most perilous; it was in line on the east side of the Chickamauga, the only means of crossing which was the narrow bridge, only wide enough to allow two men to ride abreast, but the soldier-like steadiness of the men prevented any mishap." Enemy skirmishers began advancing down the ridge toward Reed's Bridge. The

44 *OR* 30, pt. 2, 452.

45 Minty, "Minty's Saber Brigade," *National Tribune*, March 3, 1892.

46 *OR* 30, pt. 1, 923.

west face of the ridge is "much more precipitous than the east," noted Minty. When he withdrew across Pea Vine Ridge, Minty briefly assumed a position in a cornfield.

Minty again rode over to urge Jemima Reed to leave. When she again refused, he ordered her, in peremptory terms, to "stay inside the house." She promised to obey, but she proved unable to do so.[47] After leaving her, Minty spotted another strong column of Confederate infantry moving out of the gap, and he ordered Griffin to open with his guns. His dismounted troopers resisted as long as they could, and they gave ground grudgingly, forcing Johnson's men to earn every foot they gained in the process.[48] The combination of Minty's artillery and the firepower of the Colt's rifles and the rapid firing breechloaders meant his command had bottled up the entrance to the gap through the ridge, which forced Johnson to order Brig. Gen. John Gregg's brigade to climb over the ridge in an effort to outflank the Federals.[49]

Minty's dismounted troopers continued to resist the Confederate advance, buying more time as they did, making effective use of the difficult terrain, which featured "very rough and broken ground," as Col. Robert B. Snowden of the 25th Tennessee Infantry of Fulton's brigade described the intervening ground between Pea Vine Creek and Reed's Bridge. "The difficulty now was to march in line of battle over the very rough and uneven ground, passing briar-thickets, many of the men being barefooted."[50]

"During the retreat to the bridge, and the period the latter was held, the brigade had some hard fighting to do," recorded the regimental historian of the 7th Pennsylvania Cavalry. "But it was impossible for the small force under Minty to stand against the heavy command pushing forward, in compliance with Bragg's orders, to cross the creek."[51]

Sergeant James Larson and his comrades from the 4th U.S. Cavalry were up early that morning and had settled in to cook the feast they had spent the night contemplating. While they cared for their horses, their cook

47 Vale, *Minty and the Cavalry*, 233-34.

48 Minty, "Minty's Saber Brigade," *National Tribune,* March 3, 1892.

49 *OR* 30, pt. 2, 488.

50 Ibid.

51 Sipes, *The Seventh Pennsylvania Veteran Volunteer Cavalry*, 79.

started a fire and began preparing the stew. He cut up the meat and set it boiling over a hot fire. He then added vegetables and "the kettle began to throw out a delightful odor," recalled Larson fondly, "which would have aroused the appetites of men far less eager to eat than we were. We were always hungry, and that particular morning we were hungrier than usual, but were willing to wait a little longer for our breakfast in view of the feast that was being prepared. As an accompaniment to the soup, the cook called in an assistant to make some pancakes and a more than usually large amount of extra strong coffee." They offered the leftover meat to some of the other troopers, who quickly began frying it. Those fellows had sufficient time to eat "and even had a little time to take a smoke when all of a sudden shots were fired at our picket post on the other side of the Chickamauga, soon followed by other shots which rapidly increased to volleys. Men at once ran to their horses and saddled up without waiting for orders, and the horses were all saddled when the trumpeter sounded 'boots and saddles'. As soon as the trumpeter had the last note of the call out of his trumpet he sounded 'to horse.'"

Larson noted, "That ended our cooking at once, and with it all chance of our mess having any breakfast at all. The meat was only half done. A drink of the soup might have been very good, but it was too hot to swallow in such a hurry. Only four pancakes were done, which was about half a pancake to each man, but they were divided, camp kettles kicked off the fire," and the regulars prepared for battle with half a pancake each for breakfast instead of the grand feast they had dreamed of all night.[52]

Larson and his fellow regulars swung into their saddles, formed a column of four, and moved out at a gallop. Reed's Bridge was too narrow for them to cross in a column of fours, so they had to cross in a column of twos, with the poorly constructed old bridge swaying "to and fro, creaking and groaning as if ready to fall at any moment." After crossing, the regulars moved east toward Pea Vine Ridge, where Minty's men "were disputing the enemy's advance on the road and as far to the sides as it was possible for so small a body of men to do." They were ordered to form skirmish lines by company, and they opened fire on the advancing Confederate infantry. After exchanging a few volleys with the Confederate skirmishers, the regulars could see Johnson's long lines of

52 Larson, *Sergeant Larson*, 175.

infantry forming for the advance, so they fell back across the tottering old bridge, "and that had to be done very slowly and carefully else it was likely to break down before half of the regiment had crossed." Once across the creek, the regulars were ordered to form a solid line across the open ground facing the enemy. They retained their formation of column of fours so that each company lined up behind the men on the skirmish line. This permitted them to fire over the heads of the men to their front, and the regulars opened a heavy fire on the advancing Confederates.[53]

The regulars retreated across the bridge one company at a time. "The movement was beautifully executed, and although under fire continually it was done as slowly and steadily as if on drill or parade," marveled Larson. "It would have been a grand sight for anyone to witness at a safe distance. For us it was a source of pride and it was undoubtedly a lesson to the enemy, which served to make them more cautious and prevented them from attempting to press us too hard, as they could see that they had steady troops to deal with." They then stood ready, waiting for further orders. Larson's horse was mortally wounded during the volleying with the Confederate infantry.[54]

With Minty's artillery, Griffin, described by one of the Wolverines as "an officer, efficient, and ever ready for duty," opened on the advancing Confederates with canister from his position among the Reed farm buildings.[55] "We were answered promptly by the rebels with four pieces—I could see them when they loaded," said a Michigan man. When the smoke cleared, the Wolverines received orders to fall back to rejoin the rest of their regiment, which they did quickly. They rejoined their comrades and deployed in line of battle to the left of the road and extending into the woods. Before the first squadron of the 4th U.S. could retreat across the bridge, the head of a column of enemy infantry appeared, carrying their arms at "right shoulder shift" and moving at the double quick, emerging from the gap about 500 yards from Reed's Bridge. The boom of Griffin's guns surprised the Confederates, who briefly halted and temporarily fell back in confusion.[56]

53 Ibid., 177.

54 Ibid., 178.

55 Robbins, "At Reed's Bridge," *National Tribune*, November 14, 1895.

56 Haines, "Record of Fourth Michigan Cavalry."

Captain Henry Potter of the 4th Michigan Cavalry received orders to take Company H and report to Capt. Benjamin D. Pritchard of Company L of the 4th Michigan so the squadron of Wolverines could reinforce the 7th Pennsylvania Cavalry, which was being pressed hard by enemy infantry. "When we came up, there was considerable skirmishing," noted Potter in his diary. "I was ordered to move to the right to prevent a flank movement—moved down in the camp we occupied the first night—& farther on into a road where we had a view of the rebel line." Potter saw the Confederates "were in strong force," with artillery in the road. He spotted a strong flanking party heading off toward the right, and he was ordered to fall back since the 4th U.S. was already in position on the right. The Wolverines rode into a cornfield on the right and then onto a hill, where they took a position to support Griffin's guns.[57]

"The position of the Seventh Pennsylvania, Fourth Michigan, and the section of artillery still on the east side—in all less than seven hundred men formed in a thin scant semi-circular line on the low ground at the bridge around Mr. Reed's house—was, at this time, perilous in the extreme," recalled an officer of the 7th Pennsylvania. "The line of mounted men was not more than two hundred yards in segment and about four hundred yards in total semi-circular length." That short line could be flanked, and with only the rickety bridge and a bad ford upstream, the position really was perilous. If pressed hard, there was nowhere for these troopers to go. Clearly, they would not be able to hold this exposed position for long.[58]

Johnson's right wing approached to within 200 yards of Reed's Bridge before halting at the booming of Griffin's guns, and now supported by their own artillery, they cautiously resumed their gradual advance. For a moment it looked like Minty's entire brigade might be cut off and captured. "The enemy was swarming again by thousands through the gap, pressing in a long, compact line, supported by heavy columns up the creek," observed Captain Vale. Using typical Napoleonic tactics to delay Johnson's advance, Minty ordered the 4th Michigan and 7th Pennsylvania to form a mounted line of battle, to draw sabers, and prepare to charge.

57 Potter, diary, September 18, 1863.

58 Vale, "Address of Capt. Joseph G. Vale," in *Pennsylvania at Chickamauga*, 304.

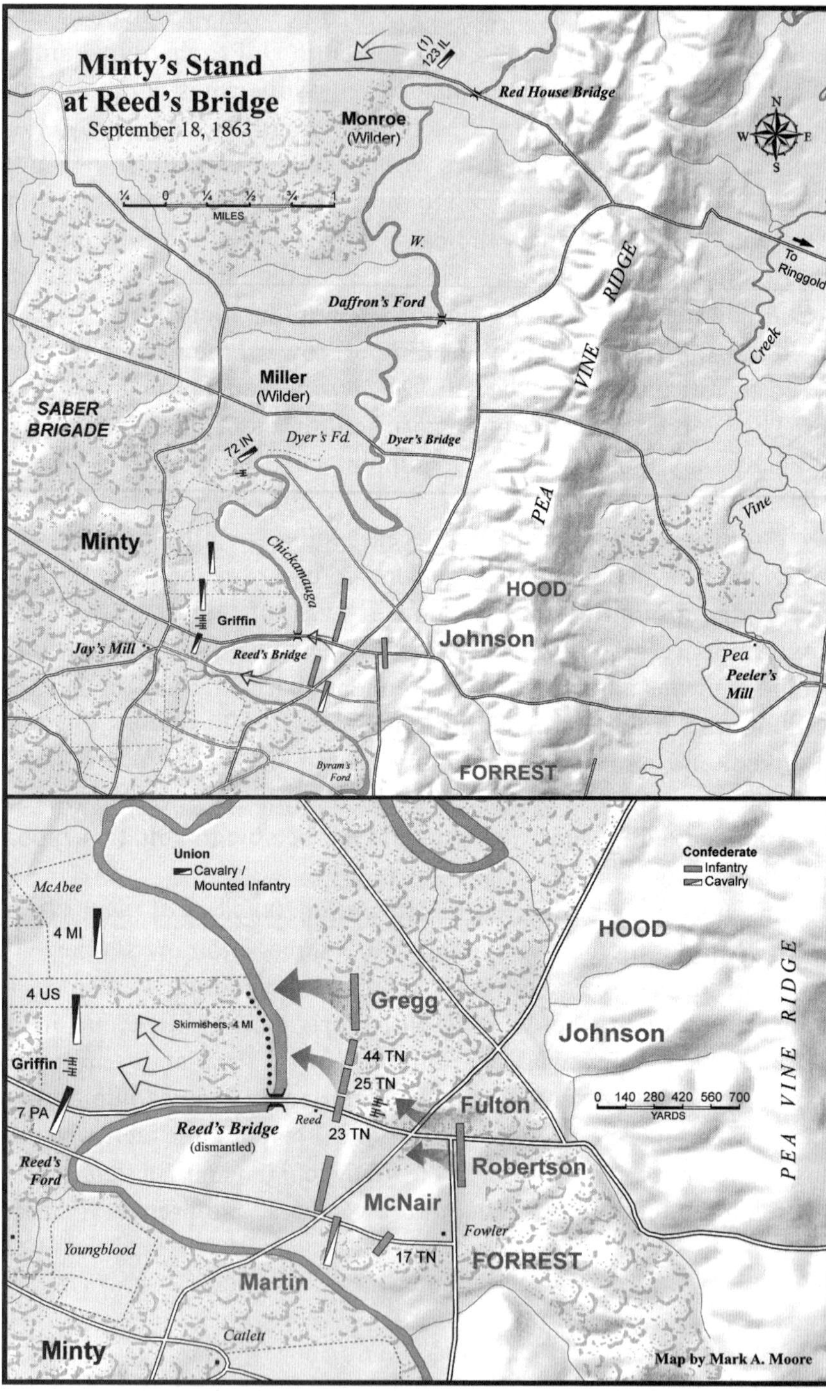

Minty's stand at Reed's Bridge.

They then feinted a charge, which forced Fulton to halt his advance and prepare to receive the charging horsemen.[59]

In the meantime, Minty's troopers drew heavy fire from the Confederate guns, which maintained a steady and accurate effect. "Their artillery fire sweeping the entire space from Mrs. Reed's house to the creek left no alternative but an immediate retreat," recalled Major Robbins of the 4th Michigan Cavalry. "This was accomplished successfully but at great risk, as the bridge over which we had to pass was frail and rickety."[60]

"Our skirmishers soon saw the rebel infantry—we dismounted half of the men & moved upon them—A smart skirmish ensued—but [we] were obliged to fall back by overpowering numbers formed in line again—again were driven back—passed thro our camp and past the 'Regulars'—toward the river—which we succeeded in crossing without loss," recounted Lieutenant Potter of the 4th Michigan. Once safely across the Chickamauga, they then formed a new line of battle on the left to cover the withdrawal of the 4th U.S. across Reed's Bridge, while the 7th Pennsylvania covered the right.[61]

The Wolverines followed most of the regulars across Reed's Bridge, leaving one squadron behind to cover the crossing of the 7th Pennsylvania. The advancing Confederate infantry cut off the retreat of a squadron of the 4th Michigan commanded by Lt. J. H. Simpson. "They made a gallant resistance and eventually swam the creek and escaped without the loss of a man," reported an officer of the 4th Michigan.[62]

Realizing he could not remain on the east bank of the Chickamauga much longer lest his command be cut off, Minty directed the 4th Michigan to form into a column of twos and then cross the rickety bridge to the

59 Vale, *Minty and the Cavalry*, 226. Vale claimed the 7th Pennsylvania and 4th Michigan made a mounted saber charge during this phase of the fighting, but Vale was not present, and although others have parroted Vale's account, this claim cannot be corroborated. Because it is not a reliable claim, I have elected not to include it in this narrative of the action on September 18, 1863. See James H. Shuster, "Holding Reed's Bridge," *National Tribune*, August 11, 1910. Shuster's account was published well after Vale's and was probably influenced by Vale's. Napoleon's maxim of war number 50 states: "Charges of cavalry are equally useful at the beginning, the middle, and the end of a battle. They should be made always, if possible, on the flanks of the infantry, especially when the latter is engaged in front."

60 Robbins, "At Reed's Bridge," *National Tribune*, November 14, 1895.

61 Potter, diary, September 18, 1863.

62 Haines, "Record of Fourth Michigan Cavalry."

west bank of the creek. The Wolverines trotted across to safety, after which Minty ordered the 7th Pennsylvania to form into a column of twos and follow the Wolverines. Griffin's two guns and caissons and limbers crossed the creek near the bridge at a spot that was supposed to be impassable but instead proved serviceable. Griffin unlimbered his guns on some high ground among the Reed farm buildings, where the dense woods screened their presence.

Meanwhile, Minty ordered Capt. Thomas H. McCormick of the 4th U.S. Cavalry to make a charge in order to buy time for the remaining elements of the Saber Brigade to make their way across Reed's Bridge. The regulars wheeled, formed, drew sabers, and feinted the charge. That feint, in turn, forced the Confederates to halt and allowed the blueclad troopers to make their way across the bridge to safety.[63]

Minty next ordered a squadron of the 4th U.S. Cavalry under the command of 2nd Lt. Wirt Davis to remove the planking from the bridge, which rendered it useless to any Confederate infantry for crossing the creek. Davis, described as "gallant," halted with a few of his men on the frail bridge while the Confederates raked it with artillery, watching his men tear up the rails and boards and toss those planks and fence rails into the creek below.[64] Davis later received a brevet to first lieutenant for his valor on Reed's Bridge that day.[65]

63 Vale, *Minty and the Cavalry*, 227. Vale claimed the regulars actually made a full saber charge, but there are no Confederate accounts to corroborate that an actual charge was made. Thus, while it seems obvious that something happened, it was likely a feint and not an actual charge. Consequently, it is treated as a feint here.

64 Ibid., 226-27. At least one Confederate claimed Minty's troopers set Reed's Bridge ablaze on September 18, but there is no evidence to suggest that the bridge was set on fire. See William C. Jordan, *Some Events and Incidents During the Civil War* (Montgomery, AL: Paragon Press, 1909), 50-51. After the war a veteran of the 4th Michigan Cavalry took up his pen to specifically deny the bridge was set ablaze. See J. W. Bradner, "Reed's Bridge: It Was Never Burned at All," *National Tribune*, November 15, 1914.

65 Heitman, *Historical Register*, vol. 1, 361. Davis, a Virginian, remained loyal to the Union. He had a long career in the regular army, enlisting as a private in the 4th U.S. in 1860. He was quickly promoted to corporal and sergeant and then, on April 22, 1863, to second lieutenant. Davis was promoted to first lieutenant on April 2, 1865, and served as regimental adjutant for three years. He was promoted to captain in 1868, major in 1890, lieutenant colonel in 1898, and colonel in 1900. Davis retired in 1900. Along the way he collected a number of brevets other than the one for the fight at Reed's Bridge. Davis was a gifted natural soldier who had a long and successful career in the regular army despite having no formal military training. See idem.

Once safely across, Minty formed his main line of battle on the high ground to the west of Chickamauga Creek. "[The] brigade now held a good position along the outskirts of the timber, with the battery in position on the open ground in front, and it would have been a costly affair for the enemy to attempt to cross the Chickamauga at Reed's Bridge," recalled Sergeant Larson. "In this position we had the advantage of heavy timber on our side of the Chickamauga and open country on the enemy's side. The banks of the ford were also very steep."[66]

By now Johnson realized he faced three or four regiments of mounted men and not Union infantry. A member of the 5th Texas Infantry of Brig. Gen. Jerome Robertson's Texas Brigade left a colorful description of the morning's fighting: "We ran into some Federal cavalry and knocked some of them off their horses; some of our men secured new cavalry hats." Nobody yet realized the serious business that lay ahead along the banks of the River of Death.[67]

At about noon, Forrest, with his escort and Martin's detachment of Morgan's division, arrived in front of the bridge. At this point, Forrest made his second significant error of the day. He spotted Union soldiers to the south of Reed's Bridge, probably picketing one of the fords. Believing those men represented Minty's camp, Forrest decided to attack. He asked Johnson for permission to take the 17th Tennessee Infantry and soon headed off to attack this unknown Union force, diverting about 600 of his men. Lt. Col. Watt W. Floyd, the commander of the 17th Tennessee, reported they marched about half a mile south but "before we got in range, the enemy fled."[68] This wild goose chase meant the 17th Tennessee did not make it back to participate in the fighting for Reed's Bridge. After seeing the Union soldiers flee, Forrest wheeled his cavalry and trotted back to the vicinity of Reed's bridge, where they immediately began skirmishing with Minty's troopers while they probed for weak points in the Englishman's position along the west bank of the creek.[69]

66 Larson, *Sergeant Larson*, 178.

67 J. M. Polk, *The Confederate Soldier and Ten Years in South America* (Austin, TX: Von Boeckmann-Jones Co., 1910), 23.

68 *OR* 30, pt. 2, 479.

69 John Allan Wyeth, *Life of Lieutenant-General Nathan Bedford Forrest* (New York: Harper & Bros., 1908), 246.

As the Confederates prepared to make their big push to drive off Minty's troopers, local citizens hastened to the rear, desperate to remove themselves from the line of fire. The soldiers watched with amusement as a girl repeatedly slipped and fell while trying to make her escape. The sight provided a moment of levity for the grayclad soldiers, who realized that more grim work lay ahead of them before they could rest that night.[70]

In the meantime, Bragg, unaware that Johnson had encountered stiff resistance from Minty's dismounted troopers and remembering how his plan to bag Thomas in McLemore's Cove had been stymied by the inertia of his subordinates, grew increasingly frustrated with what he viewed as delays on Johnson's part. At about 11:00 a.m. he sent a special order to Johnson, demanding that the Ohioan "proceed without delay." About 1:00 p.m., as Minty's men were firmly in position on the west bank of the creek, Bragg sent another galloper to Johnson, urging him to "push on vigorously and engage the enemy regardless of the force on your front."[71]

About 11:45 that morning, while the fighting for Reed's Bridge raged, vigilant Union signalmen atop Lookout Mountain reported to the Army of the Cumberland headquarters the progress of a massive dust cloud steadily moving toward the lower Chickamauga crossings at both Reed's and Alexander's Bridges, indicating that a large portion of Bragg's army was on the move in that area.[72]

Despite being outnumbered almost seven to one by Johnson's division and Forrest's cavalry, Minty was determined to make a stand on the west bank of Chickamauga Creek, hoping to further slow the advance of Johnson's Confederates. How long he could hold out against such overwhelming odds was an open question. But it would be answered soon enough. Johnson's Confederates were preparing to press their assault against Minty's razor-thin line of battle.

70 John C. West, "Fourth Texas Infantry at Chattanooga," *Houston Weekly Telegraph*, November 12, 1863.

71 *OR* 30, pt. 2, 467.

72 Robertson, "The Chickamauga Campaign," 44.

Chapter Five

Lightning at Alexander's Bridge

Confederate Maj. Gen. William H. T. "Shot-Pouch" Walker—so nicknamed for his propensity to collect enemy lead with his body—was frustrated on the morning of September 18, 1863.[1] "Gen. Walker had been

1 William Henry Talbot Walker was born in Augusta, Georgia, on November 16, 1816. He attended Richmond Academy in Augusta and then enrolled at West Point. He graduated 46th out of 50 in the class of 1837 and was commissioned in the 6th U.S. Infantry. He fought against the Seminoles in Florida and was wounded three times during the December 25, 1837, battle of Okeechobee, which forced him to resign from the army. He rejoined the army on November 18, 1849, and was promoted to captain five years later. He was seriously wounded at Molina del Rey during the Mexican War, and the wound was believed to be mortal at the time. He was brevetted to lieutenant colonel for his valor there. Walker recovered and filled several posts, including commandant of cadets at West Point and instructor in tactics. He resigned as a major on December 20, 1860, to take a commission in the Georgia state troops in April 1861. On May 25, he was commissioned a brigadier general in the Confederate army and was ordered to Pensacola, Florida, where he served under Bragg's command. Bragg requested that Walker be transferred to Richmond in August because of "feeble and failing" health. Walker commanded a brigade under Gen. Joseph E. Johnston during the fall of 1861, and then resigned his commission for health reasons. He was out of the service for about a year and then was commissioned a brigadier general on March 2, 1863, and assumed command of a brigade of Georgia troops. On May 5, his brigade was sent to reinforce Johnston's army in Mississippi, which was trying to break the siege of Vicksburg. At the request of Lt. Gen. John C. Pemberton, Walker was promoted to major general on June 27, 1863, and he assumed command of a division of six brigades. On August 23, Walker, with three brigades, was transferred to Bragg's army. Bragg assigned Walker to command the newly formed Reserve Corps of the Army of Tennessee, consisting of his old division and that of Brig. Gen. St. John Liddell. Liddell was a West Point classmate of Walker and said, "General Walker was well-known to be a crackbrained

Maj. Gen. William H. T. "Shot-Pouch" Walker led Bragg's Reserve Corps. Walker's command was new to the Army of Tennessee, and he did not think much of Bragg. *USAHEC*

desperately wounded on several occasions, but recovered, as he said, 'to spite the doctors,' although the permanent evidences of his sufferings remained in a painfully spare frame and a pale cadaverous complexion, which always suggested a ghost on horseback," recalled one observer.[2] His command was new to the Army of Tennessee—his troops had been transferred to Bragg's army from Johnston's command in Mississippi and had arrived only a few days before the battle of Chickamauga. He was unaccustomed to Bragg and to the dysfunctional command structure of the Army of Tennessee, and he chafed against it. In the days leading up the battle, Bragg constantly gave Walker and his command orders to march and countermarch, prompting Walker to complain to his wife that his corps had become a "shuttlecock concern," constantly being shifted every time Bragg contemplated launching an attack.[3] He also did not get along well with his West Point classmate, Brig. Gen. St. John Liddell, who commanded one of his divisions, adding additional friction to an already difficult command situation.

Bragg had ordered Walker and Maj. Gen. Simon B. Buckner to get their corps moving by 6:30 on the morning of September 18, 1863. Walker's command consisted of his old division, now commanded by

fire-eater, always captious or caviling about something whimsical or changeable and hardly reliable." Walker was killed in action during the battle of Atlanta on July 22, 1864. See Davis and Hoffman, The Confederate General, vol. 6, 98-99.

2 Henry E. Handerson, *Yankee in Gray: The Civil War Memoirs of Henry E. Handerson* (Cleveland, OH: Press of Case Western Reserve University, 1962), 33.

3 Quoted in Russell K. Brown, *To the Manor Born: The Life of General William H. T. Walker* (Athens: University of Georgia Press, 1994), 164.

Maj. Gen. Simon Bolivar Buckner, who led one of Bragg's infantry corps. *Library of Congress*

his senior brigade commander, Brig. Gen. Matthew D. Ector, and Liddell's division, numbering approximately 8,000 men.[4] Liddell's division consisted of the veteran brigades of Brig. Gen. Edward Walthall and Col. Daniel C. Govan (commanding Liddell's own brigade), made up of battle-hardened troops who had fought in all of the battles of the Army of Tennessee.

Walker was to cross the Chickamauga at either Alexander's Bridge or at Byram's Ford, about one and a half miles downstream, while Buckner was to cross at Thedford's Ford.[5] Neither Walker's nor Buckner's commands marched as scheduled, however, and it took them all morning to cover the eight miles between the last night's campsite and Alexander's Bridge.[6] The lack of progress greatly frustrated Walker, who had a short fuse for such things. The plan was not going well for his command that morning, and then more unwelcome news arrived to make the day even worse. "Before reaching the bridge I was informed that I would have to fight for it, as it was held by the enemy," he noted in his postaction report of the battle.[7] While Shot-Pouch Walker was never one to shy away from a fight, this prospect cannot have pleased him.

Because of the delayed march of Walker's corps that morning, the men of Col. John T. Wilder's Lightning Brigade waited while Minty's

4 Had he been present, Brig. Gen. States Rights Gist would have commanded this division on September 18. Gist did not arrive on the battlefield until September 20, leaving command of this division in Ector's hands until then.

5 *OR* 30, pt. 4, 663.

6 Ibid., pt. 2, 283.

7 Ibid., 239.

troopers fought it out along the Reed's Bridge Road. At about 10:00 that morning, most of Company A of the 72nd Indiana was on the south side of Chickamauga Creek, either foraging for food or manning vidette posts. Suddenly, Confederate cavalry making its way north to join Forrest at Reed's Bridge happened along, startling the Hoosiers. The grayclad horsemen spotted the Union men, drew sabers, and charged, scattering them. The Company A boys "came back like flying birds, with rebel pursuers close at their heels, yelling and shouting at every jump," recalled one of them. "The rebels got the advantage of them, cut them off from the bridge, and they had to plunge into the creek and swam across. A few shots from the boys at the bridge drove the rebels back."[8] The firepower of Wilder's Spencer rifles easily drove off the Southern horsemen, who resumed their trek north toward Reed's Bridge. There were no casualties in this brief encounter, and things immediately quieted down in Wilder's front once more.[9] The main body of Walker's rebel soldiers did not appear until almost noon, several hours after hostilities began in Minty's sector of the battlefield.

Without any enemy forces in their front, soldiers of the Lightning Brigade fanned out across the nearby countryside to forage for food. A few of them crossed Chickamauga Creek but came back before noon, reporting the presence of enemy troops approaching from the northeast. "Little attention was paid to these reports, and at noon, most of the command sat down to a good dinner brought in from the country that forenoon," fondly recalled Sgt. Benjamin Magee of the 72nd Indiana. "In our own mess we had eggs, chickens and potatoes and had just got coffee poured and our stomachs fixed for a large, square meal, when to our disgust the bugle began to blow 'boots and saddles' furiously, and immediately blew 'fall in.' We had only time to hastily swallow the coffee, gather our saddle and run." It took the Hoosiers ten minutes to saddle up and move out at a gallop.[10]

Responding to Minty's request that morning, and realizing that he would not be able to hold Alexander's Bridge if Minty were flanked out

8 Magee, *History of the Seventy-Second Regiment*, 168.

9 John T. Wilder, "Preliminary Movements of the Army of the Cumberland before the Battle of Chickamauga," *Sketches of War History, 1861-1865*, vol. 9, Ohio Commandery, Military Order of the Loyal Legion of the United States (Cincinnati: Monfort, 1911), 267.

10 Magee, *History of the Seventy-Second Regiment*, 167.

Lt. Col. Edward C. Kitchell, commander of the 98th Illinois Mounted Infantry of the Lightning Brigade. *USAHEC, Mass. MOLLUS Collection*

of his position at Reed's Bridge, Wilder ordered all but Company F of the 72nd Indiana, seven companies of the 123rd Illinois, and a section of Lilly's battery to go to reinforce the Englishman, who was worried about dust clouds billowing to the north of Reed's Bridge. This left only the 17th Indiana, Companies A and F of the 72nd Indiana, the 98th Illinois, and two sections—four guns—of Lilly's battery to defend Alexander's Bridge.[11] Those four guns dropped trail in a dominating position on a knoll near the log house of the Alexander family, about 400 yards southwest of and overlooking the bridge.[12] Lieutenant Colonel Edward Kitchell of the 98th Illinois then received orders to take Companies C and K of his regiment to guard Smith's Ford, from which spot Kitchell had a clear view of the enemy's advance on Alexander's Bridge.[13]

The rest of the 72nd Indiana and the detachment of the 123rd Illinois reported to Minty at Reed's Bridge. "We arrived their and found they were falling back," noted a member of the 72nd Indiana.[14] Following the Englishman's directive, these troops marched two miles farther downstream. The men of the 17th Indiana assumed a position where they could guard Dyer's Ford on the Chickamauga, while the Illini and one of Lilly's guns marched even farther to the left, extending all the way to Red House Bridge. Half an hour later, Minty ordered Col. Abram

11 *OR* 30, pt. 1, 447.

12 Rowell, *Yankee Artillerists*, 112.

13 Kitchell, diary, September 18, 1863.

14 Diary of unidentified soldier of the 72nd Indiana, entry for September 18, 1863, Indiana Historical Society, Indianapolis, IN.

Miller of the 17th Indiana to draw his command back from Dyer's Ford and to form a line of battle on his left because he was being flanked, dismount his men and send them forward as skirmishers.[15]

A single company of the 123rd Illinois was sent as far north as Red House Bridge. Upon arriving there, the Illini fell into an ambush set by Col. John Scott's cavalrymen, who were already across the west side of the Chickamauga (their movement had probably triggered the dust cloud spotted by Minty that morning), "and after a sharp skirmish" they were driven back with the loss of two or three men wounded while Scott's troopers lost one man in the fighting.[16] Lieutenant James Biggs and five privates of the 123rd Illinois were captured during the fighting with Scott's troopers—four of whom later died within a seven-week period in 1864 while confined at Andersonville prison in Georgia.[17] "We came very near being trapped and had to get out of that in a hurry," recorded Cpl. John Rippetoe, who served with the section of Lilly's Battery that was sent to reinforce Minty.[18]

A few minutes later, Lt. Col. Edward Kitchell, commanding the 123rd Illinois, received orders to withdraw and report to Minty, and Kitchell executed the difficult maneuver under fire. "We were obliged to fall back about two miles," recalled a member of the 123rd Illinois.[19] The 123rd Illinois then marched south to a point a mile and a half from Lee and Gordon's Mills.[20] Neither this detachment of the 17th Indiana nor the 123rd Illinois played any part in the coming fight for Alexander's Bridge. Wilder would soon have to make due with less than two full regiments and four guns to hinder the advance of Walker's entire corps.

15 *OR* 30, pt. 1, 464.

16 Allen, *Reminiscences of William G. Allen*, 6.

17 Baumgartner, *Blue Lightning*, 199. Biggs spent 15 months in four different Southern prisons and was finally paroled at Charleston, South Carolina, in December 1864. Only Pvt. Henry Nicholas returned to duty with the 123rd Illinois in October 1864 after being held at Belle Isle and Danville, Virginia.

18 John H. Rippetoe to his wife, October 5, 1863, John H. Rippetoe letters, Special Collections, Vigo County Public Library, Terre Haute, IN.

19 Christopher McManus, Thomas H. Inglis, and Otho James Hicks, eds., *Morning to Midnight in the Saddle: Civil War Letters of a Soldier in Wilder's Lightning Brigade* (Bloomington, IN: Xlibris, 2012), Kindle edition.

20 *OR* 30, pt. 1, 459-60.

Brig. Gen. St. John Liddell commanded one of the two divisions constituting Walker's Reserve Corps. *Library of Congress*

Walker's Confederate troops finally appeared in front of Alexander's Bridge about noon, with the 4,000 men of Liddell's division leading the way.[21] Pvt. J. N. Abbott of Company B of the 98th Illinois and another soldier manned Kitchell's farthest advanced vidette post at Dalton's Ford. "About 2 o'clock I discovered a skirmish line advancing across the Chickamauga, followed by a line of battle," recounted Abbott. "I fired first and my comrade next. We stayed until we had emptied our Spencers twice, and then fell back to the Company."[22] The advance of such a large force of the enemy meant that serious work remained to be done for Wilder's men if they were to continue to hold Alexander's Bridge.

21 St. John Richardson Liddell was born at Elmsley Plantation near Woodville, Mississippi, on September 6, 1815. He was appointed to the West Point but did not graduate for unspecified reasons that seem to stem from poor grades. His father purchased a plantation for him in Louisiana, and he farmed there. Along the way he became embroiled in a blood feud with Charles Jones, and the feud eventually cost Liddell his life in a postwar duel. Liddell had been tried and acquitted of the murder of two of Jones's friends. He knew many of the Confederate high command before the outbreak of the Civil War and served at the battle of Bull Run on July 21, 1861, as a volunteer aide. He was commissioned the colonel of a Missouri regiment and served as a staff officer until May 1862, when he was given command of a two-regiment brigade at Corinth, Mississippi. He was promoted to brigadier general on June 17, 1862, and commanded a brigade of Arkansas infantry at the October 8, 1862, battle of Perryville, where his brigade earned praise for its solid performance. His brigade performed especially well at the battle of Stones River, where it broke two Union lines and again earned the praise of the Confederate high command. Liddell was promoted to division command in the days just before Chickamauga, and his division suffered nearly 50 percent casualties during the three days' fighting there. Liddell was a solid subordinate commander, but he was prone to carping and did not get along with many of his superiors. See Davis and Hoffman, *The Confederate General*, vol. 4, 74-75.

22 J. N. Abbott, "Opening of Chickamauga Fight," *National Tribune*, April 9, 1914.

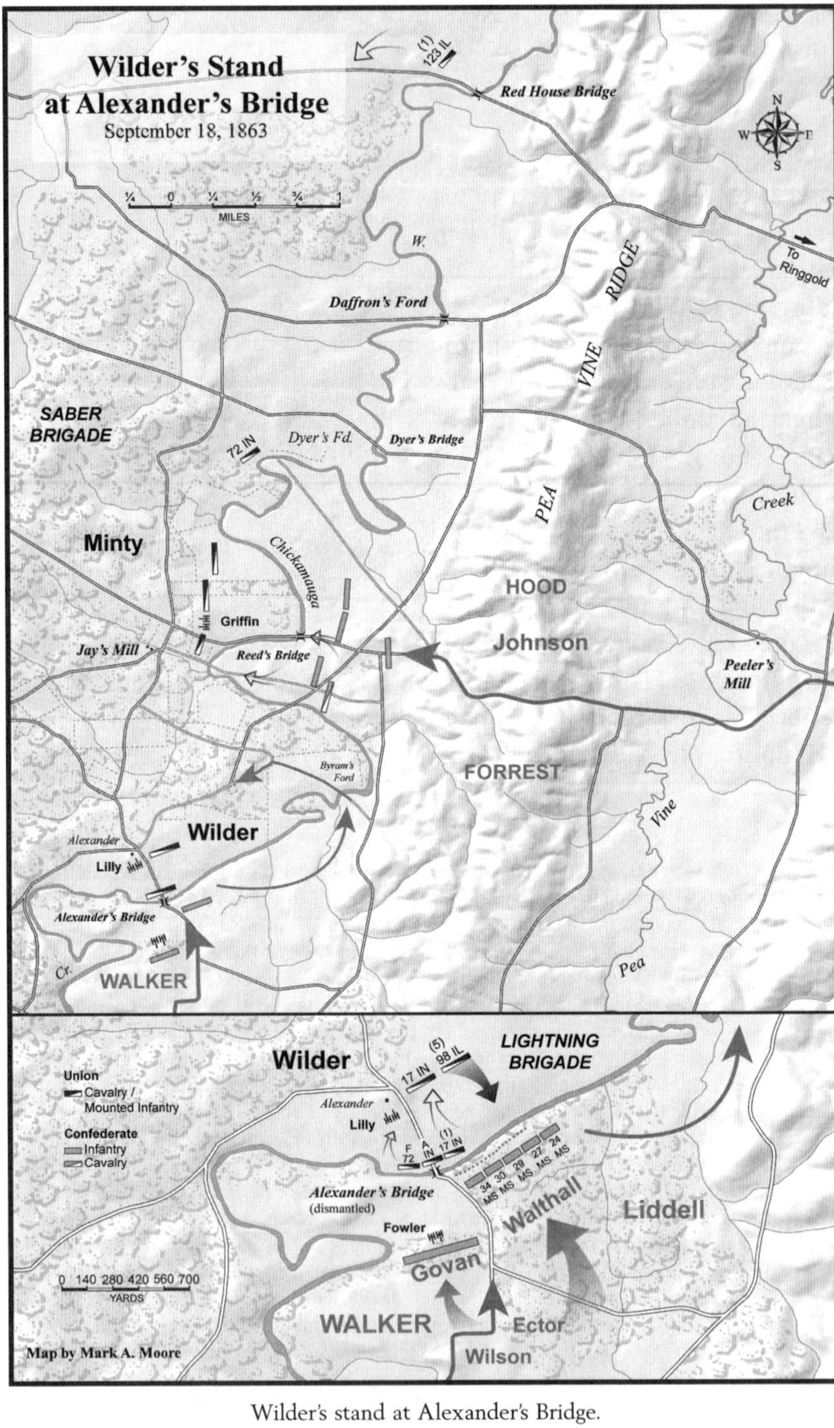

Wilder's stand at Alexander's Bridge.

Picket shots rang out from Wilder's videttes, the men of the Lightning Brigade did not have time to send their horses to the rear with holders, so they tied them to nearby trees, exposing them to Confederate fire. "The rebs came on us so sudden we hadent time to mount our horses," wrote one of them, "but we concealed ourselves thay best we could and fought them till they shot all our horses but at last we was ordered to fall back and done so under a heavy shower of bullets. Lost mule blankets haversack canteen and every thing except my gun."[23]

The sudden rattle of the videttes' Spencers caused the rest of the Lightning Brigade to prepare to receive the oncoming attack. "We quit our meal and formed into line," complained a soldier of the 17th Indiana, who resented having his lunch interrupted by the appearance of Walker's infantry.[24] The men of Company A of the 72nd Indiana tore up the planking from the bridge and used it to construct a lunette in the middle of the road on the west side of Alexander's Bridge. They then built earthen ramparts around the wooden planks to further fortify their lunette, determined to hold the bridge at all costs.[25] The entire company then took up position inside their hasty fortification, where they could concentrate the fire of their Spencers on any enemy forces that might approach the bridge. "The company was composed of the sort of men that would stand firmly," recalled the regimental historian.[26]

About 2:00 on the afternoon of September 18, Walker ordered Liddell to take Alexander's Bridge, with Brig. Gen. Daniel C. Govan's brigade supporting them. Liddell rode forward to get a good look at the lay of the land and examine the enemy's defenses as best he could. "The reconnaissance I made was a very hasty and imperfect one," reported Liddell, "and relying chiefly upon the information obtained from General Pegram, I instructed Brigadier-General Walthall, of my division, to make an attack upon the enemy, in possession of the bridge."[27] Walthall's veteran brigade of Mississippi troops was a good choice; it carried the

23 John M. Bernard to his wife, September 26, 1863, John M. Bernard letter, Indiana Historical Society, Indianapolis, Indiana.

24 William H. Kemper, diary, September 18, 1863, William H. Kemper Papers, Archives, Ohio Historical Society, Columbus, OH.

25 A lunette is a crescent-shaped earthwork usually employed to protect artillery.

26 Magee, *History of the Seventy-Second Regiment*, 158-59.

27 *OR* 30, pt. 2, 251.

Col. Daniel C. Govan led Liddell's other brigade. Govan's men were not heavily engaged at Alexander's Bridge. *Alabama Department of Archives and History*

proud moniker of "first in and last out."[28]

The gray-haired, bespectacled Liddell, described as "a typical old school Southern gentleman" who was a "good brigadier," ordered Walthall to form a line of battle with the left of his brigade resting on the Alexander's Bridge Road and then to move forward, guiding left and keeping the road to his left.[29] "The line was formed almost at right angle to the road, the right slightly retired, and skirmishers covering my entire front were thrown forward about 200 yards," reported Walthall. "These dispositions made, I moved forward through a dense thicket, and after advancing about a quarter of a mile the enemy's skirmishers were encountered in front of my left and center."[30] The two regiments

28 E. A. Smith, *Records of Walthall's Brigade of Mississippians* (Brewton, AL: n.p., 1904), 4.

29 Nathaniel Cheairs Hughes Jr., ed., *The Civil War Memoir of Philip Dangerfield Stephenson, D.D.* (Baton Rouge: Louisiana State University Press, 1995), 112.

30 Edward C. Walthall was born in Richmond, Virginia, on April 4, 1831. In 1841 the family relocated to Holly Springs, Mississippi. Walthall was educated at St. Thomas Hall. He apprenticed at his brother-in-law's law office before finishing his studies and serving as deputy clerk of the Marshall County Circuit Court. He was admitted to the bar in 1852 and opened a practice in Coffeeville. He was elected prosecuting attorney for the state's 10th Judicial District in 1856 and was reelected in 1859. Soon after Mississippi seceded from the Union in the spring of 1861, he resigned and organized an infantry company, which elected him lieutenant. On July 21 he was promoted to lieutenant colonel, and his regiment, the 15th Mississippi, joined the army of Brig. Gen. Felix Zollicoffer in Tennessee. His first combat was at Camp Wildcat on October 21, 1861, and he commanded the 15th Mississippi at the battle of Mill Springs on January 19, 1862, where his men held out against determined Union assaults for an hour. On April 11 he was elected colonel of the newly mustered 29th Mississippi and served at Corinth that spring. His regiment participated in the attacks at Munfordville, Kentucky, that September and helped to force the surrender of John T. Wilder's troops there. Walthall's command did not participate in the battle of Perryville. He was given

Brig. Gen. Edward C. Walthall led one of St. John Liddell's brigades. Walthall's men did the bulk of the fighting for Alexander's Bridge. *Alabama Department of Archives and History*

on the right—the 24th Mississippi and the 27th Mississippi—advanced at the double-quick for nearly a mile. "In this movement the regiment became much confused and scattered, and did not arrive on the line at the river in time to take any part in the engagement that took place there" other than taking a few potshots at Wilder's skirmishers. Only the two companies on the left of the 27th Mississippi met any resistance during this advance.[31]

Govan threw forward skirmishers to support Walthall's attack. As they advanced, they heard the unfamiliar rattle of the Spencers, which they had never before experienced. One of them said, "These treacherous Yankees now had a gun they could load on Sunday and shoot all week."[32] They also heard the gunfire from the fighting at Reed's Bridge, realized it was not just random picket fire and that a battle was underway. These skirmishers were thrown forward along the creek to Walthall's left, extending the Confederate skirmish line well to the south of Alexander's

command of a brigade of Mississippi and Alabama troops on November 13, 1862. Walthall was promoted to brigadier general on January 17, 1863, despite missing Stones River due to illness. His brigade was assigned to Polk's corps and saw much marching and fighting in the Tullahoma campaign during the spring of 1863. During the fourth week of July his brigade was sent to Atlanta and then returned in mid-September, joining Liddell's division. He eventually achieved division command and led the final attack of the Army of Tennessee at the battle of Bentonville on March 19, 1865. After the war, Walthall served as a U.S. senator for his home state of Mississippi. He died on April 21, 1898, and was buried at Holly Springs. See Davis and Hoffman, *The Confederate General*, 6:105-7.

31 *OR* 30, pt. 2, 271-72, 277, and 281.

32 Floyd R. Barnhill Sr., *The Fighting Fifth: Pat Cleburne's Cutting Edge: The Fifth Arkansas Infantry Regiment, C. S. A.* (Jonesboro, AR: Privately published, 1990), 98.

Bridge. They drew fire, but nothing like the severity of that faced by Walthall's men, and their casualties demonstrate that plainly; Govan's skirmishers, who were the only portion of his men engaged, suffered only onc man killed and five wounded in the fighting for Alexander's Bridge.[33]

Lilly's guns opened on the long gray lines as they moved toward the bridge. Their accurate fire tore gaping holes in those neatly dressed lines. Sgt. William O. Crouse later claimed credit for firing the first artillery shots of the battle of Chickamauga, but Griffin's section of the Chicago Board of Trade Battery had earned that honor earlier that morning.[34] Nevertheless, the accurate fire of Lilly's two sections prompted Liddell to plant the guns of Capt. William H. Fowler's battery to engage with Lilly's guns. Fowler's guns unlimbered. So, too, did Swett's Battery, commanded by Lt. Henry Shannon. The Confederate gunners only got off a couple of rounds per gun because "we made it too hot for them,"

33 Ibid., 257. Daniel Chevilette Govan was born in Northampton County, North Carolina, on July 4, 1829. His father, Andrew R. Govan, had served in the U.S. House of Representatives in the 1820s. The family settled in Somerville, in 1830 in West Tennessee. The family then moved to Mississippi in 1832. Daniel spent his youth on the family plantation and received an education from a family tutor. He enrolled in South Carolina College (now the University of South Carolina) in the class of 1848, but he left before graduating. In 1859 he joined his cousin, future Confederate Gen. Benjamin McCullough, and went west to California. When McCullough was elected sheriff, he appointed Govan as his deputy. Govan returned to Mississippi in 1852 and married the following year. He established a plantation in Arkansas and was working there when war came in 1861. He raised a company of volunteers and was elected captain of Company F of the 2nd Arkansas on June 5, 1861. On January 28, 1862, he was promoted to colonel and commanded the regiment throughout the campaigns of 1862 and 1863 as part of Maj. Gen. Patrick R. Cleburne's hard-fighting division. When St. John Liddell became a division commander, Govan assumed command of his old brigade. On February 5, 1864, he was promoted to brigadier general and assigned command of the Arkansas brigade he had led at Chickamauga. Govan was captured during the battle of Jonesboro in August 1864 but quickly exchanged for Maj. Gen. George Stoneman. He was with Cleburne at the battle of Franklin when the latter was mortally wounded. Govan was wounded at Nashville on December 16, 1864, but he returned to duty that winter. Joseph E. Johnston surrendered Govan's command at Bennett Place, North Carolina, in April 1865. Govan resumed life as a planter in Arkansas after the war. In 1894 he received a political appointment from President Grover Cleveland as government Indian agent at the Tulalip Agency near Everett, Washington. Govan died on March 12, 1911. See Davis and Hoffman, *The Confederate General*, 3:37-39.

34 *Lafayette Journal and Courier*, July 8, 1926.

Bugler Henry Campbell of Lilly's Battery. Campbell left a detailed account of his service in the Civil War. *Eli S. Lilly & Co. company archives*

Bugler Henry Campbell, one of Lilly's men, recalled.[35] The accurate and deadly fire of Lilly's guns killed two of Fowler's horses and scattered the men. Even though Liddell himself ordered one of Fowler's sections to move closer to the creek, the combination of accurate artillery fire and the deadly effect of the Spencer rifles made it impossible for Fowler's men to man their guns.[36]

The first shot by the Southern cannons hit in front of Lilly's guns and ricocheted against the corner of the Alexander log house. It then bounced back among the Federal cannoneers, its fuse still hissing. Pvt. Sidney Speed picked up the shell and threw it over the house before it exploded, saving Lilly's gunners from serious injury.[37] Henry Campbell recalled, "I don't think I will ever forget the awful, unearthly screeching—that shell made—as it approached us. It seemed as if it never would strike it was so long coming." Campbell and "four or five of the boys doubled down behind a little bit of a sapling not big enough to stop a small bullitt," he recalled. "We all knew from the sound of it, it would strike some place close by, and it was a great relieve when it crashed in

35 Henry Campbell, "The 18th Ind. Battery," *The National Tribune*, November 1, 1906. George A. Grammer, however, who served with Swett's Battery, claimed in his diary that Swett's Battery fired about 30 rounds that day, which is quite a few more than the four rounds claimed by Lilly's men. See George A. Grammer, diary, September 18, 1863, CCNMP.

36 *OR* 30, pt. 2, 255.

37 Ibid., pt. 1, 466.

Pvt. Sidney Speed of Lilly's Battery. Speed indicated that he would only accept a Medal of Honor for his service at Chickamauga if it meant an increase in his pension. *Eli S. Lilly & Co. company archives*

the logs above our heads."[38] Years after the war, Lilly's grandson and another member of the battery tried to get a Medal of Honor for Speed, who demurred.[39] The Alexander house burned to the ground that evening, probably as a consequence of being struck by Confederate artillery shells.[40]

The Confederate artillery fire wounded only one of Wilder's men: Lt. John T. Drury of the 17th Indiana, who served as Wilder's ordnance officer. Drury was struck on the ankle by a Confederate shell that so mangled his ankle that the foot had to be amputated that night.[41] Drury had been sent with orders to move the brigade's ordnance wagon train to a safer place. He was struck shortly after reaching the train. "He rode up to the side of one of the ammunition wagons and was helped off of his horse into the wagon,"

38 Campbell, "The 18th Ind. Battery."

39 Rowell, *Yankee Artillerists*, 113. According to Rowell, Speed wrote Lilly that he "didn't give two hoots for the medal" but that if receiving the honor meant he would receive an additional pension, Speed was "willing to have the medal forced on me" (idem). Apparently, Speed was quite a character.

40 Minnich, "Unique Experiences in the Chickamauga Campaign," 381.

41 *Indianapolis Daily Journal*, October 22, 1863.

Lt. John T. Drury, Wilder's ordnance officer, who lost a foot to a Confederate artillery shell during the fighting for Alexander's Bridge. *Indiana State Library*

recalled Wilder's orderly, Henry Tutewiler. "I bid him good bye and saw him no more. He was the first of [Wilder's] staff to be wounded."[42]

Some of Walthall's infantry advanced toward the creek, but they had to pass through what one Mississippi soldier described as "one of the most impenetrable thickets I ever saw."[43] The steady fire of Walthall's skirmishers drove the skirmishers of Company F of the 72nd Indiana, and the 123rd Indiana back from the banks of the creek. "They came up in splendid style, lines well dressed, step firm, even and steady, bayonets fixed and gleaming in the sun." Despite this intimidating sight, the men of Company A waited patiently. "The company held its fire until the advancing enemy were so close that they could see their eyes bat, then opened upon them with their Spencers, which belched such a constant and awful stream of well-aimed balls that the rebels were completely surprised, faltered, wavered, and then retreated."[44] The advancing Confederates were met by "volley after volley from the lines posted along the banks of the creek and from Lilly's Battery."[45]

The Alexander's Bridge Road turns to the right 200 to 300 yards from the bridge itself, forming a right angle. At this point, two of Walthall's regiments, the 30th and 34th Mississippi, advanced across the road into an open field to the left of the road. Walthall's old regiment, the 29th

42 Quoted in Baumgartner, *Blue Lightning*, 206.

43 J. D. Smith, "Walthall's Brigade at Chickamauga," *Confederate Veteran* 11 (1904): 483.

44 *OR* 30, pt. 2, 272.

45 Benefiel, *Souvenir of the Seventeenth Indiana Regiment*, 8.

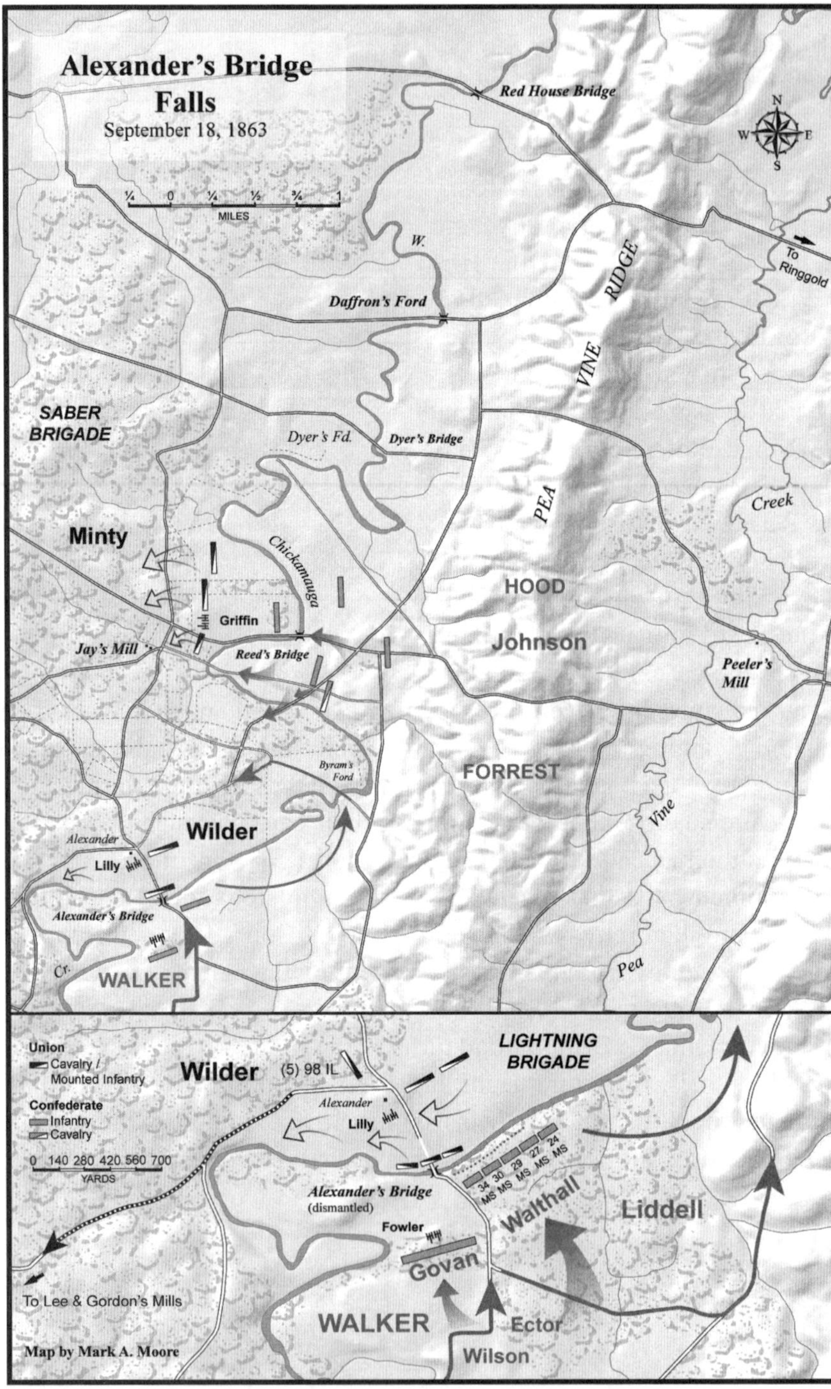

Alexander's Bridge falls, afternoon, September 18.

Mississippi, had the difficult task of fighting Wilder's skirmishers directly in front of the bridge itself. The 29th Mississippi "stubbornly resisted for about fifteen minutes, and in the meantime the regiments to the left of this, driving the skirmishers of the enemy before them, swung round under the enemy's artillery fire through an open field until the line they formed was nearly at [a] right angle to that formed by the other three regiments, conforming in the main to the general direction of the creek." Sgt. David R. Childers of Company A of the 34th Mississippi described the fire of Wilder's men as being a "murderous volley." He continued, "We charged through an open field—shot, shell, grape and Ball coming in and among us—many a brave man bit the dust."[46]

The 29th Mississippi then assaulted Alexander's Bridge under a heavy fire from Wilder's men posted on the west bank of the creek, "which along my line was narrow, but deep, with steep banks and impassable. The bridge had been torn up by the enemy, but this fact, owing to the density of the undergrowth, could not be ascertained until the bank of the creek was occupied." A soldier of the 17th Indiana remembered, "The fire from our Spencer rifles…was so terrific that, notwithstanding the enemy made frequent rushes to cross the bridge they were as often repulsed."[47] Wilder directed Maj. David D. Marquis and five companies of the 98th Illinois to go forward to reinforce the men at Alexander's Bridge. The combined firepower of these additional men only added to the intensity of the volleys being laid down by the Federals. So far the men of the Lightning Brigade had repulsed two determined attacks by Walthall's infantrymen. The 29th Mississippi suffered 56 men killed and wounded during the severe fighting with Wilder's men, and the 34th Mississippi lost one officer and another 24 enlisted men wounded.[48]

The Confederate flanking movements exposed the horses of Company A of the 72nd Indiana to Walthall's severe fire. The men of Company F of the 72nd Indiana and the 123rd Illinois saw the horses were about to be captured by the Confederates, so they opened a fierce fire on the horses, killing most of them in order to keep them from falling into

46 David R. Childers to M. V. Barksdale, September 27, 1863, Sallie B. Veal Collection, Georgia Department of Archives, Atlanta, GA.

47 Benefiel, *Souvenir Seventeenth Indiana Regiment*, 8.

48 *OR* 30, pt. 2, 272.

enemy hands. Still protected by their makeshift lunette, the men of Company A "punished the enemy so severely in front that he gave way a second time, but on the flanks he still continued to advance," recalled a member of the 72nd Indiana. Company A, however, was in danger of being encircled and captured. Colonel Miller sent his orderly, Genio Lawrence, to warn them of the looming danger. Lawrence was described as a "brave boy," and he cried out, "Company A, get out of here, the enemy are surrounding you" and then dashed off under a hail of gunfire. The men of Company A could not pull back en masse, because doing so would expose all of them to capture, so they slipped out by ones and twos until only a handful were left. Sgt. Joseph R. Higginbotham was shot five times while running the gauntlet to escape, including once in the head and once in the face.[49]

Only Sgts. William R. Stewart and James H. Barnes and Pvt. George Baily remained in the lunette. Baily "was a boy 17 years old, had fought bravely, and being the last to get the word to fall back, would not go but turned and shot a rebel who fell," recalled Stewart. "Another rebel ran up to aid the fallen man and Baily shot him also. I, having got a shell fast in my gun, kept urging Baily to fall back. I got the shell out and we both gave the enemy a farewell shot and ran. My horse was killed where he was tied, but Baily's was not, and cutting him loose, he mounted and rode away in a shower of bullets. Both got out safely." They made their way out in a northerly direction, and soon got lost in the dense woods. Company A had made an epic stand in their rough lunette, suffering two men wounded and 31 of its 37 horses killed during the fierce firefight.[50]

East of the bridge, the commanders of the 30th and 34th Mississippi halted their regiments in the open field and ordered the men to lie down behind the shelter of an "abrupt hill" because they had become so far separated from the rest of the brigade.[51] "I then directed the skirmishers of these regiments, which I had previously ordered to be pressed forward, to be recalled and the regiments to move by the right flank until they closed up an interval between the Thirtieth and Twenty-ninth near the

49 Magee, *History of the Seventy-Second Regiment*, 158-59. Higginbotham actually survived his five wounds and eventually returned to duty. He was killed in action in 1864.

50 *OR* 30, pt. 2, 259.

51 Ibid., 283.

angle in the line," reported Walthall. The Confederate brigade commander also deployed Fowler's battery on an eminence to the left of his line, where the guns opened a severe counterbattery fire with Lilly's guns, which withdrew to a position near the Alexander farm buildings about a quarter of a mile up the hill from Alexander's Bridge.[52]

"After it was found to be impossible for the command to cross the creek on the aforesaid bridge, I received orders to march by the flank, together with the whole brigade, to Byram's Ford, about 1½ miles below the bridge, where a crossing was effected without opposition," reported Col. William F. Brantly of the 29th Mississippi. "By the time we had fairly gotten over the creek it was night, and, in obedience to an order I received through a staff officer of [Liddell], I directed my command to move out of the road to the left, build small fires, and rest until further orders." They had had a tough slog.[53]

Eventually, some men of the 29th Mississippi made it to the south bank of the creek. From there they could see the planking had been removed from Alexander's Bridge, rendering it unusable even if they had succeeded in driving off Wilder's men. "The assaulting column, emerging from the woods, could not walk on thin air," one of Walthall's Mississippians facetiously observed.[54] Word of the impassable condition of the bridge quickly made its way back to General Walker, who directed Walthall to break off the engagement at Alexander's Bridge and instead march for Byram's Ford, which was one mile downstream and which was inexplicably unguarded. If Walthall's men could cross the Chickamauga there, they would be able to return south and outflank Wilder's men at Alexander's bridge. About sundown, "we waded across on the enemy's side" at Byram's Ford, one of Walthall's Mississippians reported.[55] Another Mississippi soldier noted that he and his comrades, before wading, "stripped off all but our shirts" and joked about what "a fine

52 Ibid., 272.

53 Ibid., 281.

54 Smith, *Records of Walthall's Brigade*, 4.

55 William B. Honnoll to Robert S. Honnoll, September 28, 1863, Honnoll Family Papers, Special Collections, Robert W. Woodruff Library, Emory University, Atlanta, GA.

looking set" the filthy, tired soldiers made.[56] Once across, they began to move down the north side of Chickamauga Creek, hoping to encircle and capture Wilder's command.[57]

The stout stand by Wilder's men meant the advance of Buckner's corps was also delayed. Buckner's troops swept away the detachment of Union pickets guarding Thedford's Ford and then splashed their way across the Chickamauga at both Thedford's and unguarded Dalton's Fords at about 2:00 p.m. "I awaited the movements of Walker on my right," said Buckner in his after-action report of the battle. Hence, by delaying Walker's advance, the men of the Lightning Brigade also delayed the advance of Buckner's waiting troops, who were not even engaged in the fighting.[58]

Bragg's frustration and impatience bubbled over once more. He sent a series of dispatches to both Buckner and Walker urging them on. That afternoon he told Walker that a "junction tonight with General Johnson is of vital importance." Later, he directed Walker to "effect a junction . . . which . . . no doubt . . . you have already done." Finally, at 7:30, even though neither Walker nor Buckner had gotten their entire commands across the creek, Bragg made his wishes clear: "The Commanding General directs that you effect that passage in force at daylight tomorrow morning."[59]

While Walthall's flanking movement to bypass Alexander's Bridge posed a threat to Wilder's brigade, a more serious and more immediate danger was developing two and a half miles to the north at Reed's Bridge.

56 John H. Freeman, diary, September 18, 1863, Civil War Collection, Tennessee State Library and Archives, Nashville, TN.

57 *OR* 30, pt. 2, 272.

58 Ibid., 357. Specifically, Buckner wrote, "On the morning of the 18th, I moved from a point on Pea Vine Creek, midway between Pea Vine Church and Rock Spring Church, under orders to cross the West Chickamauga River at Thedford's Ford, after Major General Walker's division had succeeded in crossing below me. Part of my route being common with that of Walker's column, my march was somewhat retarded by the encounter of the two columns. But notwithstanding this I occupied, about 2 p.m., with Stewart's division, after a brisk skirmish, the crossing at Thedford's Ford, and, with Preston's division, without opposition, the crossing at Hunt's (or Dalton's) Ford. In this position, holding both banks of the stream, I awaited the movements of Walker on my right."

59 Brent to Walker and Brent to Walker and Buckner, September 18, 1863, Bragg Papers.

Chapter Six

Reed's Bridge Falls

At 12:40 that afternoon, Rosecrans's chief of staff, Brig. Gen. James A. Garfield, reported that Minty's horse soldiers "were heavily engaged in the vicinity of Reed's Bridge, and that a major Confederate turning movement was probably in progress." At last, army headquarters understood the nature of the threat posed by Bragg's advance that day. The question now was whether Minty could hold on long enough to permit Rosecrans to shift his army to meet the broader oncoming threat.[1]

At approximately 2:00 p.m., Johnson was finally ready to launch his assault on Reed's Bridge. With Fulton's brigade attacking straight down the road, headed directly at the bridge, they ran into Col. Robert H. G. Minty and his determined band of cavalrymen, who stoutly contested the advance. Having successfully pulled his entire command across Chickamauga Creek onto the west bank, Minty became "hotly engaged," as he put it.[2] The historian of the Saber Brigade wrote, "Minty now formed line on the high ground west of the creek, and disputed the passage for over two hours, holding the whole rebel force in check the while."[3] The

1 Robertson, "The Chickamauga Campaign," 44.

2 *OR* 30, pt. 1, 923.

3 Vale, *Minty and the Cavalry*, 227.

historian of Forrest's command recalled that "another sharp affair, with severe loss, occurred, before the bridge was seized."[4]

"About four o'clock in the afternoon, we left the main road and diverged into an open field, where we found our comrade, Capt. Wm. Everett, with his battery unlimbered, and ready for action," noted a soldier of the 1st Arkansas Mounted Rifles of Brig. Gen. Evander McNair's brigade. "He would occasionally order a shell to be thrown over into a clump of woods. We were told that there was a body of Federals over in those woods, and that we would be forced to charge them. Preparations were soon made, all the surplus were soon deposited into a pile, and men left to take charge of them, cartridge boxes were brought around in front, guns loaded, and seen that they were in proper shape, and the order given to march."[5]

As the Confederates prepared to make their attack, Maj. Gen. Nathan Bedford Forrest rode over to Col. John S. Fulton of the 44th Tennessee, who was commanding Johnson's brigade, and ordered Fulton to detach a portion of the 17th Tennessee from his command. Forrest inexplicably sent the detachment of the 17th Tennessee off to the left "perhaps to ascertain his locality," surmised Maj. G. M. Crawford, the Tennesseans' commander.[6] Forrest and his cavalry then rode off to the left, hoping to get around Minty's left flank, where they could make a lot of trouble for the Englishman.[7] Forrest later claimed that after "crossing the creek at a ford above the bridge, the country was scoured for a mile west of the bridge."[8]

With his brigade reduced by the redirected 17th Tennessee, Fulton ordered the rest of his command to attack. Led by the 23rd Tennessee and with the Rebel yell quavering, the grayclad wave surged forward. The 23rd Tennessee's skirmishers surged across the bridge and deployed on the west bank of Chickamauga Creek, followed by the 44th, 25th, and the rest of the 23rd Tennessee, which filed off 300 to 400 yards

4 Thomas Jordan and J. P. Pryor, *The Campaigns of Lieut.-Gen. N. B. Forrest and of Forrest's Cavalry* (New Orleans: Blelock & Co., 1868), 313.

5 "History of Company H, 1st Arkansas Mounted Rifles."

6 *OR* 30, pt. 2, 472, 492.

7 Vale, "Address of Capt. Joseph G. Vale," 306.

8 *OR* 30, pt. 2, 524.

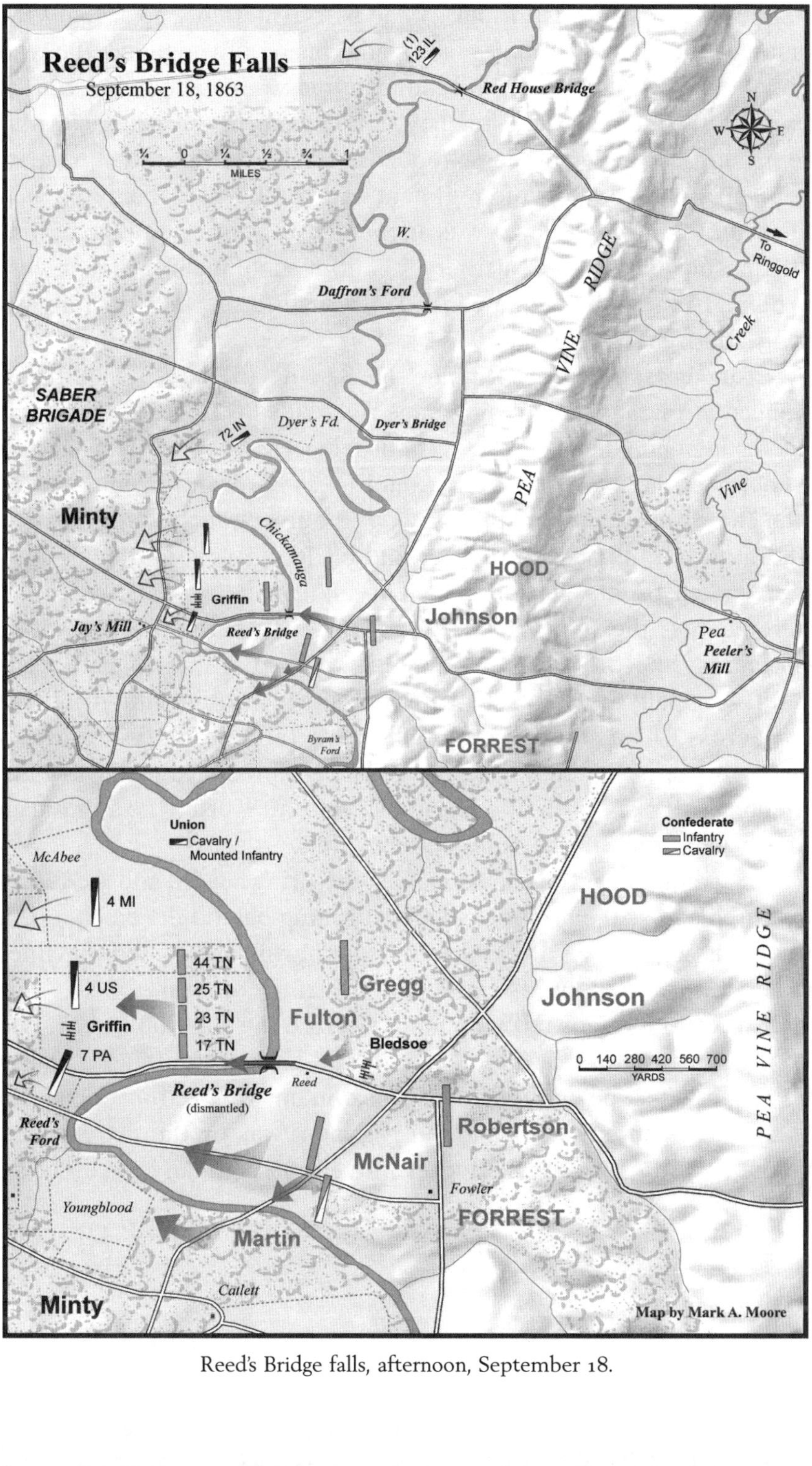

Reed's Bridge falls, afternoon, September 18.

to the right through a cornfield.[9] "The skirmishers of the Twenty-third Tennessee Regiment [of Fulton's brigade] becoming engaged, the whole regiment, supported by the brigade, charged with a shout and run, and drove off the Yankees before they could destroy the bridge," taking five casualties in the process, reported Bushrod Johnson. "After our skirmishers and some of the regiment had passed, the enemy opened a battery on the bridge, which was silenced by a section of [Capt. Hiram M.] Bledsoe's [Missouri] artillery," continued Johnson. A fragment of one of Griffin's shells wounded Lt. J. H. Hastings of the 17th Tennessee during this fighting.[10]

Before crossing, Col. Richard H. Keeble of the 23rd Tennessee advanced through the cornfield on the right side of the road, with his left flank resting upon the road. "My skirmishers were now hotly engaged with the enemy at the bank of the river, and I was suffering from the effects of the enemy's fire, when all at once, without a command, the regiment with one accord charged the river and bridge at double-quick and put the enemy to flight," he reported. "My skirmishers were immediately ordered across the river and thrown forward. I then moved by the left flank across the bridge and immediately formed line of battle upon my left company, the Twenty-fifth Tennessee forming upon my right when across." The color-bearer of the 23rd Tennessee, Pvt. A. Melton, was wounded in the leg during the advance on the bridge. "Carry them through the thickest of battle ahead of everything else," he admonished the man who took up the colors after he fell.[11]

"On arriving near the Chickamauga, the firing ceased and the federals had retired across the bridge, and after forming behind the creek, opened on us with great fury with grape and small arms and halted our lines," recalled Capt. William H. Harder of the 23rd Tennessee. "The color bearer of our regiment fell wounded, I seized the flag to carry it, when one of the men volunteered to carry it, so I gave it to him. We charged the lines, but unexpectedly met the creek on our whole front. The bridge was to the left of our wing and our regiment was on the extreme left." Without waiting for orders, Harder moved his company to the bridge,

9 Ibid., 472.

10 Ibid., 452.

11 Ibid., 484.

trying to repair the damage done by the Union troops, "by replacing the planks the federal rear had torn up, and under a heavy grape shot fire from the federal lines about three hundred yards distant. While I was on the bridge it was splintered with the grape shot."[12]

Just as Harder's men finished replacing the planks, Forrest clattered up onto the bridge on horseback, smiled, put a hand on the captain's shoulder, and said, "You are a brave gallant captain, what is your name and regiment?" Harder answered and Forrest rode forward. Harder called to warn Forrest to be careful, but the general merely laughed. Harder asked if his company should cross, and Forrest pointed to the spot where he wanted Harder to form his men. Accompanied by a single officer, he then rode to within 100 yards of the Union line, halted, and examined Minty's position, "while discharge of grape and canister dashed by him." Forrest finished his examination, turned, and slowly rode back.

In the meantime, Harder found Colonel Keeble and suggested Keeble get Forrest's permission to attack Griffin's guns. Forrest gave the order, and as Harder began moving his company out, Colonel Fulton ordered another company of the 23rd Tennessee to work through the thicket and charge the guns. This company attacked "rapidly and after some delay cutting through the briars and vines emerged to the open ground on the flank of the battery . . . opened fire on it, and after the first fire charged it, but the federal had done limbered up and moved the battery behind the infantry line," Harder recalled. It looked like Minty was going to counterattack, but when Fulton's entire brigade formed to receive the attack, the Englishman thought better of it and instead pulled his beleaguered troopers farther back.[13]

When the final Confederate attack kicked off and drove Minty's troopers back, a woman in the house near the bridge could no longer contain herself. She rushed into the road, shouting, "You Yanks are running! Our army is coming! Our friends will not hurt me!" As she stood there shouting at the retreating cavalrymen, Bledsoe's Battery took position to sweep the area between Reed's Bridge and the La Fayette Road with enfilading fire. The first blast of canister by the Show Me State men struck the woman "and laid her a mangled corpse in front of her door."

12 Harder, "Reminiscences of Captain William Henry Harder."

13 Ibid.

Maj. Gen. John Bell Hood, who commanded a division in Longstreet's First Corps in the Army of Northern Virginia. Hood was just returning to duty after a serious arm wound suffered at Gettysburg. He sustained an even worse wound at Chickamauga that cost him his leg and nearly his life. *Library of Congress*

When Minty learned of the feisty woman's fate, he "deeply regretted not having had her forcibly removed, which he intended doing, but the rapid advance of the enemy in their final attack gave him no opportunity." Neither Minty nor his staff ever learned the fate of her children.[14] Eventually Bledsoe's severe and accurate fire drove Griffin's two guns off their knoll.[15]

As the first Confederate infantrymen gingerly made their way across Reed's Bridge, Maj. Gen. John Bell Hood, his mangled arm still in a sling from his Gettysburg wound, arrived on the scene much to the delight of the men of his division, who had not seen their general since July 2. As Hood unexpectedly trotted past his old command, the Texas Brigade, on his way to the front, the men "raised their hats in silent tribute at the sight of their commander, still suffering from his wounds, galloping into action."[16] As Hood and his staff passed, he called out, "Remember, boys, we are here to whip them."[17]

Hood left an account of his discussions with Bushrod Johnson when he arrived at the front. "After a few words of greeting exchanged with General Johnson, I assumed command in accordance with the instructions I had received, ordered the line to be broken by filing into the road, sent

14 Vale, *Minty and the Cavalry*, 234.

15 *OR* 30, pt. 2, 472.

16 Calvin L. Collier, *First In—Last Out: The Capitol Guards, Ark. Brigade* (Little Rock, AR: Pioneer Press, 1961), 156.

17 Jordan, *Some Events and Incidents During the Civil War*, 51.

a few picked men to the front in support of Forrest's cavalry, and began to drive the enemy at a rapid pace," he declared, taking all the credit for driving Minty's pesky and determined cavalrymen from their strong position on the knoll overlooking Reed's Bridge.[18]

Capt. Henry Potter of the 4th Michigan Cavalry and his men came under that heavy and accurate Confederate artillery fire. "Crash! Came their artillery in the midst of us," he recalled. "A shell passed a few feet over my head, & wounded one of my men seriously. Chas. Hall and two horses—we broke to the right under cover of the woods." Captain Benjamin D. Pritchard of the 4th Michigan was wounded in the arm by a shell fragment and had to leave the field. "Again we formed & dismounted to fight on foot, sending the men toward & along the river—from the left where I was sent to watch for them, I saw three separate lines of their infantry move from the left & swing around towards the bridge," Potter recounted. "I sent word to Major Gray, to that effect & he moved the regiment back once more into a piece of woods, skirmishing all the time."[19]

Private John C. McLain served in Company C of the 4th Michigan. A Confederate shell killed McLain's horse from under him. The dismounted private carried his saddle back to the brigade's supply wagons so it would be safe. While he was gone, another well-aimed shell killed McLain's friend Charley Rickard and wounded another man. Knowing that McLain had lost his mount, the men still on the front line sent Rickard's horse to McLain and sent the other wounded man's mount to Pvt. George Munger, who had also lost his mount to the accurate and deadly fire of Bledsoe's guns.[20]

Another trooper of Company C of the 4th Michigan was killed just to the left of the approach to the bridge. "Some tall weeds grew there, and the body was not found when the dead were picked up by the rebels after the fight," noted J. W. Bradner, the first sergeant of Company B. Two months later, when they were again in the area, "Some of his

18 John Bell Hood, *Advance and Retreat: Personal Experiences in the United States and Confederate States Armies* (New Orleans: G. T. Beauregard, 1880), 61. Because of the severe wound he suffered on September 20, Hood never wrote a formal after-action report of his division's role in the battle of Chickamauga.

19 Potter, diary, September 18, 1863.

20 McLain, diary, September 18, 1863.

company, knowing where he was last seen in the fight, went there and found him lying just as he fell, his watch, picture, letters, and belongings not being disturbed."[21]

The troopers of the 7th Pennsylvania Cavalry had just as difficult a fight. Lieutenant Jacob Sigmund of Company E commanded the skirmish line. Although his exposed position took enfilading fire from both sides, the lieutenant refused to yield any ground to the Confederate advance. Seeing this, the regimental adjutant dashed forward and shouted, "Sigmund, why don't you fall back?"

"My instructions are to hold this hill," replied the lieutenant. "And I meant to hold it until I was ordered to fall back." And so he did. His skirmish line held until it was finally flanked out of its position.[22]

After crossing Reed's Bridge, Forrest, his escort, and the detachment of Morgan's division found Minty's men "formed in the edge of a woods, in front of which was an open field. This field was fought over again and again, each side charging alternately, and forced back," recalled Capt. James E. Cantrill of the 5th Kentucky Cavalry.[23] "Gen. Forrest was closely following our line and, being mounted on a gray horse, was plainly attracting the enemy's fire," recalled another of Morgan's men. "As he rode near where I had halted by a tree to reload, I said to him, 'General, you had better get back. I am afraid you'll be killed.' The bullets were flying thick and fast about him, but his only reply was: 'Push 'em; push 'em.'" Under such unrelenting pressure, Minty's line began to give way.[24] "At last a charge upon our part, led by Lieutenant Colonel Martin, was successful," concluded Cantrill. "The enemy fell back still further. We now saw clearly from many indications, and were told by prisoners, that the Federal line of battle, the main force, was not far off. We, therefore, moved more cautiously."[25]

21 Bradner, "Reed's Bridge," *National Tribune*, November 15, 1914.

22 Thomas F. Dornblaser, *Sabre Strokes of the Pennsylvania Dragoons in the War of 1861-1865* (Philadelphia: Lutheran Publication Society, 1884), 131-32.

23 Duke, *History of Morgan's Cavalry*, 377.

24 Anonymous, "The First Gun at Chickamauga and Its Opening Scenes," *The Sunny South*, June 29, 1895.

25 Duke, *History of Morgan's Cavalry*, 377.

Minty had sent his ordnance officer, Capt. Joseph G. Vale of the 7th Pennsylvania Cavalry, to Lee and Gordon's Mills to escort his wagon train out of harm's way. Minty also ordered Vale to scout for good ground where the Saber Brigade might make another stand, to place whatever forces might be available there to hold the position, and to report any movement occurring on his flank and rear.[26] After discovering that Walker's infantry had flanked Wilder out of position at Alexander's Bridge, Vale dashed off a note and sent it back to Minty: "Colonel Wilder has fallen back from Alexander's Bridge to Gordon's Mills and the enemy are crossing at all points in force."[27]

When Vale arrived at the mills, he reported to General Wood and said, "We had been attacked at 7 a.m. and had been fighting for 3 or 4 hours." Amused, Wood asked Vale what time he supposed it to be. Vale shrugged and said he thought it to be about 11:00. Wood responded with a grin, "Look at your watch." When Vale did so, he discovered it was actually 5:00 in the afternoon and not 11:00 in the morning. "Time flies when men are so engaged," correctly observed Lt. Col. Richard B. Robbins of the 4th Michigan.[28]

Minty realized this turn of events meant both of his flanks could be turned and the position at Reed's Bridge was no longer tenable. One of his horse soldiers reported, "We were flanked on both sides before we gave up the position."[29] Minty sent a galloper to Colonel Miller with orders to join him without delay.[30] "I held my ground until his arrival about 4:30 p.m.," remembered Minty.[31] After the detachment of the 72nd Indiana arrived, Minty ordered his command to fall back. His cavalrymen called for their horses, mounted up, and pulled back a few hundred yards to the site of Jay's Sawmill. Their hasty departure meant

26 Vale, *Minty and the Cavalry*, 227-28.

27 *OR* 30, pt. 1, 923.

28 Richard B. Robbins, Account of the Battle of Chickamauga, September 18, 1863, Bentley Historical Library, University of Michigan, Ann Arbor, MI.

29 James Vernor to His Brother, September 23, 1863, James Vernor Letters, Detroit Public Library, Detroit, MI. In the years after the war, James Vernor ran a drug store and soda fountain, invented Vernor's Ginger Ale, and established the company that continues to produce that ginger ale to this day.

30 *OR* 30, pt. 1, 923.

31 Minty, "Minty's Saber Brigade," *National Tribune*, March 3, 1892.

that a few horses, many blankets, oilcloths, boxes of hardtack, and other supplies were abandoned to the pursuing Confederates.[32]

Lieutenant Griffin's two guns of the Chicago Board of Trade Battery also had to limber up and leave, a process that took more time than it took the cavalrymen to mount up and move out. While Griffin's artillerists tried to limber their guns, a well-aimed shot by one of Bledsoe's cannons shattered a wheel of one of Griffin's guns, dropping the end of the axle and the barrel onto the ground. The sergeant in command of the piece limbered up anyway and dragged the cannon off under severe fire, and although it took a long time to do so, he reported with both guns to the new position that the guns took up that night. Griffin's men put a new wheel on the gun, and it resumed its place in the line.[33]

Colonel Keeble led his 23rd Tennessee on a flanking movement, covering 300 to 400 yards before making a left-wheel maneuver over the crest of a hill "where it was supposed the enemy had rallied." The colonel was surprised to learn that the Federal horse soldiers "had, however, left the field."[34] The same thing happened when McNair's brigade made its attack. "Into the woods we went expecting every step to receive their volley, but on reaching the top we found only one or two dead Federals," recalled a member of the 1st Arkansas Mounted Rifles. "It seems that Robertson's Texas brigade had preceded us, and after a small resistance had driven them away."[35] As the cavalrymen pulled back, the rest of Hood's men poured across the Chickamauga at Reed's Bridge and at the bad ford situated about 300 yards upstream.

The combined force of the Saber Brigade and Miller's detachment of the 72nd Indiana made their next stand at Jay's Sawmill, where the Reed's Bridge Road intersects with two roads that lead directly to Alexander's Bridge. Johnson had "ordered the formation to be preserved and the line of battle, extending across the right-hand or western road, to move forward." The newly arrived Hood, however, countermanded this order and instead directed one of Gregg's regiments to march in a line

32 *OR* 30, pt. 2, 488.

33 Sylvanus H. Stevens to Edgar D. Swain, n.d., CCNMP.

34 *OR* 30, pt. 2, 484.

35 Frank T. Ryan Reminiscences, Georgia Department of Archives and History, Atlanta, Georgia.

of battle, extended across the road to the left, and the other regiments to be moved in the rear along that road in column of companies.[36] "The whole brigade . . . were dismounted and took position in line as infantry," noted Sgt. James Larson of the 4th U.S. Cavalry.[37]

The men of the 72nd Indiana ended up fighting a two-front battle there. The Hoosiers formed a line of battle alongside Minty's horse soldiers, not realizing their position was next to a large nest of yellow jackets. "The rebel shells bursting over us and the Yellow Jackets stinging our horses and us made it anything but comfortable," complained one of them.[38] This two-front fight wore on the Indiana men, but they remained resolute in their determination to hold that position for as long as possible.

Thus, Minty's troopers stubbornly held at Jay's Mill for about an hour before Hood's dispositions flanked the Saber Brigade out of position once again. They drove the cavalrymen westward until they broke off the engagement, with Forrest's cavalry in close pursuit. Minty's troopers skirmished with Forrest's pursuing horsemen the whole way to the edge of the Viniard property line. Minty "had to continually turn and check them," the colonel later recalled.[39] Capt. Henry Potter of the 4th Michigan recorded in his diary that the enemy followed "us closely, & firing in our rear" caused the retreating Wolverines to be concerned about being cut off.[40]

After flanking Minty out of his position at Jay's Sawmill, and with John Bell Hood leading the way, the Confederate infantry marched down the road toward the Alexander farm. They passed the burning Alexander farmhouse, "penetrating between the enemy and the Chickamauga to a point nearly opposite their center, about 2½ miles from the steam saw-mill and about 1 mile west of Dalton's Ford," recalled Johnson.[41] Minty's weary horsemen buzzed around the flanks of Hood's marching column like a swarm of angry bees as it made its way toward Alexander's Bridge. The fight for Reed's Bridge was finally over, 10 hours after it began.

36 *OR* 30, pt. 2, 452.

37 Larson, *Sergeant Larson*, 179-80.

38 Linville, *Battles, Skirmishes, Events and Scenes*, 81.

39 Minty, "Minty's Saber Brigade," *National Tribune*, March 3, 1892.

40 Potter, diary, September 18, 1863.

41 *OR* 30, pt. 2, 452.

When Hood ordered his command to head for Alexander's Bridge, he lost a great opportunity. Had he instead continued another mile and a half or so farther west to the La Fayette Road, they would have created real problems for Rosecrans, who was simply not prepared for a general engagement late on the day of September 18. Hood also would have placed his command squarely athwart Rosecrans's primary route of supply, being the direct route to Chattanooga, and cut off the Army of the Cumberland's route of retreat. While it is likely Hood had no knowledge of this situation, it was nevertheless a shining example of a lost opportunity for Bragg to shatter Rosecrans's army before the Ohioan was ready to receive such an attack. Minty's determined stand contributed greatly to avoiding this catastrophe and severely hindered the execution of the well-designed battle plan Bragg had spent so much time developing.

After finally driving Minty's troopers from their position at Jay's Sawmill, Bushrod Johnson sent a galloper to Bragg to inform him that his entire Provisional Division was now on the west side of the Chickamauga. Bragg then passed this information on to Polk: "Brig. Gen. B. R. Johnson, commanding Hood's division, has crossed at Reed's Bridge, and is now on the west bank of the Chickamauga. Generals Walker and Buckner have been directed to cross at once and co-operate with him." Bragg expected Polk to begin his movement now that the bulk of the Army of Tennessee was across the creek.[42]

As Minty quite proudly put it, "With 973 men, the First Brigade had disputed the advance of 7,000 rebels from 7 o'clock in the morning until 5 in the evening, and at the end of that time had fallen back only 5 miles."[43] Years later, the Englishman wrote, "One hundred and two rebel graves at Reed's Bridge attest the effectiveness of our resistance at that point."[44] One of his veterans noted that the Saber Brigade was "outnumbered about four to one" throughout its gallant efforts to delay the advance of Bushrod Johnson and his command on September 18, 1863.[45] Without a doubt, the determined stand of Minty and his troopers

42 Ibid., pt. 4, 663.

43 Ibid., pt. 1, 923.

44 Minty, "Minty's Saber Brigade," *National Tribune*, March 3, 1892.

45 Bradner, "Reed's Bridge," *National Tribune*, November 15, 1914.

compelled Bragg to change his plans for the coming battle. In doing so, Minty had achieved something remarkable.

More fighting, however, remained to be done by both Wilder's Lightning Brigade and Minty's Saber Brigade before they would find some hard-earned rest.

Chapter Seven

Night Falls Across the Battlefield

At 3:00 p.m. one of his pickets informed Col. John T. Wilder there was a strong force of enemy infantry in his rear. Wilder understood this presence in his rear meant his command was in danger of being encircled and cut off. He scribbled a situation report and sent a galloper to warn Rosecrans. "Colonel Minty has fallen back after being reinforced by two regiments and two pieces of artillery of mine," wrote the Hoosier. "A rebel infantry force has crossed Chickamauga between Alexander's Bridge and Reed's Bridge, getting in my rear. I held the rebels at Alexander's Bridge until they outnumbered me on every side. I got off my artillery, and am falling back on General Wood."[1] In order to avoid being encircled and captured, Wilder had no choice but to break off and withdraw, leaving Alexander's Bridge to Shot-Pouch Walker's men.

After making a determined stand against the Confederates men for two hours, Wilder gave orders for the Lightning Brigade and Lilly's Battery to withdraw. "Having driven the enemy away from a ford below me, I immediately commenced withdrawing my forces in the direction of Gordon's Mills, and intercepted the force that was trying to surround me," wrote Wilder. "When, being reinforced by two regiments of infantry from General Woods' division and Colonel Miller [and the 72nd Indiana] returning to my assistance, we held the rebels from farther advance

1 *OR*, pt. 3, 725.

until morning."[2] Wilder directed Maj. David D. Marquis and his five companies of the 98th Illinois to serve as the brigade's rear guard as he withdrew. These Illini soldiers were already taking fire from Bushrod Johnson's and Forrest's men, who had turned south after crossing the Chickamauga downstream at Reed's Bridge.[3]

Once Wilder's men fell back from Alexander's Bridge, some of Walthall's infantry swam the creek and replaced the planking on the bridge, thus allowing the Confederate infantry to swarm across in force.[4] Forrest and his cavalry were now operating on the west side of Chickamauga Creek, and Confederate infantry was pouring across at various points. "The rebels were now pressing us in such superior force that we had no time to form line of battle, but our brigade and battery formed column by regiments and retreated by the right flank, the battery in the centre with two regiments on either side, swinging back to the rear in a line a little west of south toward the camp we occupied in the morning," recalled a member of the 72nd Indiana.[5] "I had to run like the Devil to keep up," reported John M. Barnard of the 72nd Indiana, whose horse was killed earlier during the severe fighting around the lunette.[6]

"Mounted infantry is supposed to do its fighting from the ground, but this time we were so hard pressed and the emergency was so great that we remained on our horses ready to fall back rapidly if the pressure became too great," wrote Pvt. Theodore Petzoldt of the 17th Indiana. "We did not know at any minute when the enemy might appear at the right or left out of the darkness. My horse was not accustomed to firing from his back and every time I would fire he would jump so that he would nearly throw me off. It was dark enough so that I could see the fire stream from the muzzle of my gun every time I shot."[7] Sgt. George Wilson served in the same company as Petzoldt, and was nearby, also firing while mounted. "When they got within a hundred yards or so we opened a fusillade," he recalled. "But I doubt if we hit a single man.

2 Ibid., pt. 1, 447.

3 Baumgartner, *Blue Lightning*, 207.

4 Magee, *History of the Seventy-Second Regiment*, 159.

5 Ibid., 160.

6 Barnard to His Wife, September 26, 1863.

7 Theodore Petzoldt, reminiscences, CCNMP.

We needed to be on the ground to properly get in our work. The rebels seemed to make a special point of pushing us in indecent haste. We could hear their officers urging on their men, and I grieve to say that they were a fearfully profane set."[8]

"The rebels planted artillery in every available position, and completely enfiladed our position, making it untenable," recounted Sgt. William O. Crouse of the 18th Indiana Battery.[9] With no other alternative, Lilly's four guns withdrew from the knoll at the Alexander house and fell back to a church at the intersection of the Jay's Mill Road and a farm road that led to the Viniard farmhouse, which was situated on the La Fayette Road. The gunners cut down and cleared trees to create fields of fire so they could cover Thedford's Ford, upstream from Alexander's Bridge, where Brig. Gen. William B. Bate's division was preparing to cross the Chickamauga. They took position in a cornfield on a slight hill. Lilly's guns "opened out hot and made the shell fly through the woods driving the rebels and greatly relieving the 17th [Indiana] who then had time to strengthen their position."[10] That severe and accurate fire by Lilly's gunners prevented Bate's division from utilizing Thedford's Ford in time to participate in the first day's fighting.[11]

Wilder ordered Lieutenant Colonel Kitchell and his detachment of the 98th Illinois to fall back up the creek if possible. "We fell back and Cos. C, K, I, one co. 72nd Ind. & 2 cos. of 17th Ind. as rear skirmishers, supported by two regts. of Wood's Division in support," noted Kitchell in his diary. "The enemy made a charge on Co. I, 72nd Ind. on foot & horseback. We fell back firing as we retired."[12] The men of the 17th Indiana, who had defended Alexander's Bridge so effectively, conducted a fighting withdrawal as they withdrew from the River of Death, taking artillery fire the whole way.[13] "The firing was intense, causing considerable

8 Wilson, "Wilder's Brigade of Mounted Infantry in the Tullahoma-Chickamauga Campaigns." *National Tribune*, October 12 and 26, 1893

9 Crouse, journal, September 18, 1863.

10 Quoted in Rowell, *Yankee Artillerymen*, 114.

11 *OR* 30, pt. 2, 383.

12 Kitchell, diary, September 18, 1863.

13 George W. Kemper to His Cousin, September 27, 1863, George W. Kemper Papers, Special Collections, Ball State University, Muncie, IN.

confusion among our troops," recalled Pvt. William H. Kemper of the 17th Indiana. "We all fell back and formed on the left of Wood's division" on the eastern boundary of the Viniard farmstead not far from the La Fayette Road.[14] Wilder's men dismounted and sent their horses into the safety of the deep woods and formed a line of battle.[15]

With Forrest's cavalry in pursuit, "We had to return on a trot to keep them from cutting us off," noted Pvt. Alva C. Greist of Company B of the 72nd Indiana—which had been sent to reinforce Minty—in his diary that night. "They followed us closely. Fell back until we gained a good position, when we hastily dismounted and formed a line of battle, sent our horses to the rear."[16] Sergeant Benjamin Magee of the 72nd Indiana recalled, "It was about sundown when we dismounted, and we immediately went to work with a will and in a few minutes threw up a line of works of old logs and rails."[17] Deprived of their lavish breakfast that morning, the hungry and weary soldiers of the Lightning Brigade had no dinner that night either.[18]

At 5:00 p.m. Maj. Gen. Simon B. Buckner was at Thedford's Ford and passed along a report to Polk about Walker's whereabouts: "I still quietly hold this ford. General Walker, on my right, after a brisk skirmish, took the position at the bridge [Alexander's] below here, but found it destroyed by the enemy. He is now moving to Byram's Ford, below that bridge about 1½ miles. He cannot get in position before dark He will await further orders from General Bragg." Here was proof of the disruptive effect on Bragg's carefully laid battle plans of Wilder's determined fight to hold Alexander's Bridge.[19]

14 Kemper, diary, September 18, 1863. The Viniard farm is about half a mile south of the Brotherton house along the La Fayette Road, but on the east side of the road (the Brotherton house is on the west side of the La Fayette Road a bit south of the battlefield visitor center). Little is known about the Viniard family. Although some of the hardest and most desperate fighting of the battle occurred on the grounds of the Viniard farm, the family had only settled there a short time before the battle. See Sartain, *History of Walker County*, 108.

15 Linville, *Battles, Skirmishes, Events and Scenes*, 83.

16 Greist, diary, September 18, 1863.

17 Magee, *History of the Seventy-Second Indiana Regiment*, 160.

18 Benefiel, *Souvenir the Seventeenth Indiana Regiment*, 8.

19 *OR* 30, pt. 4, 664.

At Alexander's Bridge 105 dead and wounded Confederates littered the road and fields, providing silent testimony to the severity of the fire laid down by the Spencer rifles of the Lightning Brigade during their defense of the bridge that day. "I can only account for this disproportion from the efficiency of this new weapon, our attacks having been made through thick woods and cedar underbrush, rendering the artillery of the enemy that was used on the occasion comparatively harmless," declared Liddell, who was terribly frustrated by his division's ordeal that day.[20] His weary men halted about half a mile from where they forded the Chickamauga, formed a double line of battle, and then slept on their arms that night, knowing that "tomorrow would bring a heavy and deadly conflict."[21]

By contrast, only one of Wilder's men was killed during all the severe fighting. Private Jonathan Tuggle of Company F of the 98th Illinois was killed during the withdrawal from Alexander's Bridge.[22] "How well do I remember your defense of the line of the Chickamauga River on that dusty Friday before the great battle was joined, when both armies were sweeping toward the goal of strife—Chattanooga," declared John T. Wilder years after the war. "Your thin line opposed to two grand army corps, struggling to hold them back until 'Thomas could come.'"[23] The Lightning Brigade had held. Wilder's determined defense of Alexander's Bridge delayed Walker's advance for the entire day of September 18, which had far-reaching consequences for both sides.

As pointed out in the previous chapter, however, Wilder's withdrawal exposed Minty's position to being flanked, thus forcing Minty to withdraw to Jay's Sawmill and then from the area around the bridge entirely. His withdrawal in turn permitted Hood's infantry to march down the Jay's Sawmill Road toward the Alexander farm. "We all expected a volley every moment and went through all the fears and motions incident to entering a charge," recalled one of Hood's Texans. "We were much relieved at only finding some cavalry who discharged a few shots too high to hit

20 Ibid., pt. 2, 251.

21 Barnhill, *The Fighting Fifth*, 98.

22 Baumgartner, *Blue Lightning*, 207.

23 Benefiel, *Souvenir the Seventeenth Indiana Regiment*, 4.

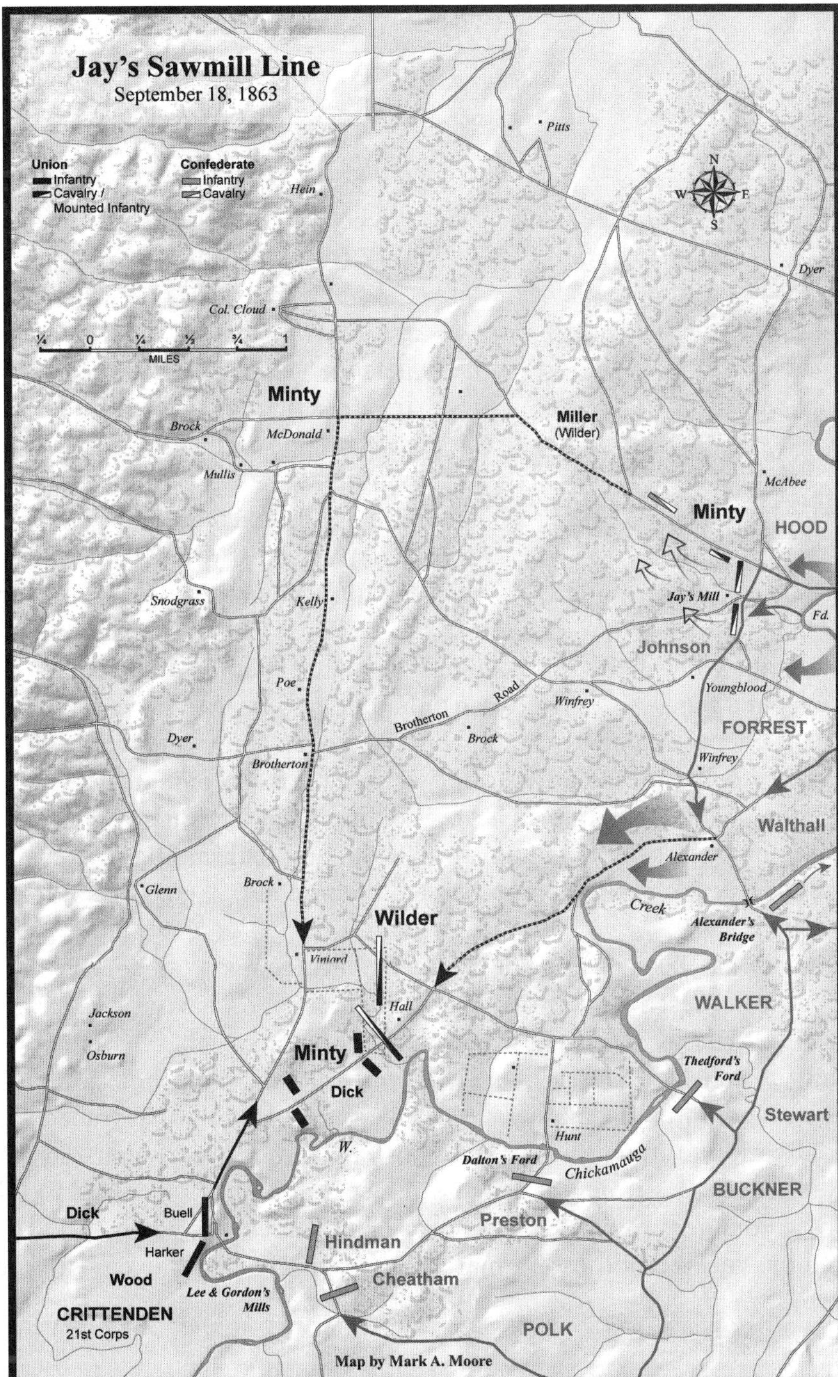

Jay's Sawmill line, late afternoon, September 18.

Col. Daniel McCook, Jr., commander of the Second Brigade, Second Division of Granger's Reserve Corps. McCook was the younger brother of 20th Corps commander Maj. Gen. Alexander McCook. *Library of Congress*

anybody and disappeared without a shot from our side."[24]

Father Patrick Trecy, chaplain of the 4th U.S. Cavalry and Rosecrans's personal confessor, had been riding the lines that afternoon. Wilder sent him to find Brig. Gen. Thomas J. Wood, whose headquarters were still at Lee and Gordon's Mills. The priest arrived at Wood's headquarters at 4:40 p.m. and reported that Minty and Wilder had formed a junction with their two brigades and, "though they are falling back they have not yet reached the [La Fayette Road], though very near to it. Father Trecy says the enemy apparently outnumber our troops 4 to 1, and that he drove us very vigorously for a time, but when he left the pursuit was not so vigorous." Wood then related Trecy's opinion that "the enemy appears to have infantry, artillery, and cavalry."[25] This critical intelligence chilled Rosecrans, who finally comprehended the dire and exposed position of his army.

Minty had been asking for infantry reinforcements for several days, but each request met with the same response: "We have no infantry to spare." His increasingly urgent reports on September 18, however, finally persuaded Rosecrans and the rest of the Union high command that a severe threat faced them at Reed's Bridge and that they needed to pay attention to it. On the afternoon of September 18, 29-year-old Col. Daniel McCook, a member of the famed Fighting McCooks of Ohio and the younger brother of 20th Corps commander Maj. Gen. Alexander McCook, received orders to march his 2nd Brigade, 2nd Division, of

24 West, *A Texan in Search of a Fight*, 112.

25 *OR* 30, pt. 3, 728.

Granger's Reserve Corps from its camps around Rossville to support Minty and to burn Reed's Bridge if possible in the hope of depriving Bragg's army of its use.[26]

About 2:00 p.m. Maj. James T. Holmes, commanding McCook's 52nd Ohio, received orders to ensure that every man of his command had a least 60 rounds of ammunition in his cartridge box and to be ready to march at a moment's notice. The Buckeyes quickly complied, and the order to move soon arrived.[27] Accompanied by Capt. Charles M. Barnett's Battery I, 2nd Illinois Light Artillery, and augmented by the addition of the 69th Ohio Volunteer Infantry, McCook's brigade left Rossville at 3:00 p.m. They marched about five miles down the La Fayette Road, and upon arriving at the intersection of the La Fayette Road and the Reed's Bridge Road, they turned left and made for Reed's Bridge itself, unaware that Minty had already withdrawn, leaving this area in the firm

26 Ibid., pt. 1, 871. Daniel McCook Jr. was born on July 22, 1834, at Carrollton, Ohio. He graduated from Alabama University in Florence, Alabama, in 1858 and then studied law in Steubenville, Ohio. In 1860 he moved to Leavenworth, Kansas, where he opened a law office with William T. Sherman and Sherman's brother-in-law, Thomas Ewing. With the outbreak of the war, the office was closed and all three partners joined the Union army. During the summer of 1861 McCook served as captain of the 1st Kansas Infantry and fought in the August 1861 battle of Wilson's Creek in Missouri. He then served as George H. Thomas's chief of stuff during the Shiloh campaign and was commissioned colonel of the 52nd Ohio Volunteer Infantry on July 15, 1862. He was immediately assigned to command a brigade under his old law partner, Sherman. At Perryville, his brigade was part of Maj. Gen. Philip H. Sheridan's division, and at Stones River it was part of Brig. Gen. Speed S. Fry's 3rd Division of Thomas's corps but did not participate in the battle because McCook's troops were guarding wagon trains. His brigade regularly consisted of the 52nd Ohio and the 85th, 86th, and 125th Illinois Infantry. For the battle of Chickamauga, the 69th Ohio Volunteer Infantry was assigned to serve with his brigade. After the battle of Chickamauga, they pursued Bragg's defeated army toward Ringgold and then marched to relieve the siege of Maj. Gen. Ambrose E. Burnside's troops at Knoxville. His command was then assigned to Jefferson C. Davis's 14th Corps division for the Atlanta campaign. McCook was promoted to brigadier general on July 16, 1864, one day before he died of wounds sustained in the June 27 assault on the Confederate works at Kennesaw Mountain. McCook was buried in Spring Grove Cemetery in Cincinnati. His father and namesake, Maj. Daniel McCook Sr., was killed in action by some of Morgan's troopers at the July 19, 1863, battle of Buffington Island in Meigs County, Ohio, during Morgan's Indiana and Ohio raid. See Warner, *Generals in Blue*, 295. For more about the McCook family's numerous contributions to the Union victory in the Civil War, see Charles Whalen and Barbara Whalen, *The Fighting McCooks: America's Famous Fighting Family* (Bethesda, MD: Westmoreland Press, 2006).

27 *OR* 30, pt. 1, 579-80.

control of Hood's Confederates.[28] "We naturally expected soon to get in touch with our friends who were supposed to be guarding the bridge," observed Capt. Lewis E. Hicks of the 69th Ohio, "but instead of that we got in touch with the enemy!"[29]

As darkness fell, the head of McCook's column came within a mile of the bridge, passing through "a cedar thicket along either side of the road so close and dense that a horse could not have been turned around in it."[30] McCook's men unexpectedly ran into the rear of Evander McNair's brigade, which was passing through the area to turn onto the Jay's Sawmill Road. McCook captured 22 prisoners—mostly musicians and surgeons—and then quietly got his troops into position on a knoll to the west of the mill, unaware that their position precariously lay between two divisions of Confederates who did not know they were there. The musicians had been marching behind a wagon train that made a tempting target. "The rebble wagon train, eight in number, we could have captured but it would have brought on an engagement," declared a member of the 86th Illinois, "which would frustrate our plans to destroy the bridge."[31] A member of the 125th Illinois noted, "The meeting of this wagon train was as much a surprise to us as it probably was to them, for we had no skirmishers out and were marching along in everyday style."[32]

As quietly and as quickly as possible, McCook deployed his troops into a line of battle and deployed Barnett's battery on both sides of the Reed's Bridge Road. He ordered that no fires be built, threw out strong pickets, and decided to wait until morning, when he could see what lay in front of him.[33] "We laid between two divisions of the Rebels,"

28 Ibid., 871.

29 L. E. Hicks, "The Capture of Reed's Bridge: A Check to Bragg's Flank Movement at Chickamauga," 69th Ohio Volunteer Infantry unit file, CCNMP.

30 Robert M. Rogers, *The 125th Regiment Illinois Volunteer Infantry: Attention Battalion!* (Champaign, IL: Gazette Steam Print, 1882), 77.

31 Allen L. Fahnstock to Henry V. Boynton, February 24, 1894, 86th Illinois unit file, CCNMP.

32 Rogers, *The 125th Regiment Illinois Volunteer Infantry*, 77.

33 *OR* 30, pt. 1, 871.

shuddered a soldier of the 52nd Ohio. "We run against their pickets but we didn't known there was such a heavy force there."[34]

Joseph Swan served in Company G of the 52nd Ohio. After dark, Swan spotted Dan McCook talking to Maj. James T. Holmes, the commander of his regiment. McCook told Holmes that one of the brigade's ordnance wagons had gotten hung up on a stump in very close proximity to the Confederate lines. Holmes ordered Swan to get it off. "I was not in a very good humor," recalled Swan, "however I followed directions, and was engaged in getting it off when Col. Dan McCook came up and began to swear and order me to hurry up. It made me mad, and I told him if he wanted my job, to get it off himself." McCook responded, "Well, get it off as quick as you can; the rebs are all around us." Swan somehow managed to disengage the wagon from the stump and then settled down for a long, unpleasant night.[35]

Private William P. Rea served in Company K of the 69th Ohio. When he arrived near Jay's Sawmill, he spotted a dead cavalryman of the 7th Pennsylvania and a dead horse lying in a nearby fence corner among some bushes. "I took a good look and am sure it was a 7th Pa. Cavalryman," he declared. "We had been with them quite a little, and I wanted to see if I knew him. It was by this stop I found the Johnnies were across the creek, as here was a big lot of them in the field just below me, and that was what made me run so fast, as I was alone, the regiment being fully a quarter of a mile from me."[36]

"Chill winds were moaning among the pines," an officer of the 69th Ohio colorfully remembered.[37] The men spent the chilly night under strict orders not to speak above a whisper and to maintain strict silence in their movements. They were to rely upon the movements of the men to their right if they had to move at all.[38] Although they had had nothing to eat,

34 Thomas M. Burns to His Father, October 4, 1863, Thomas M. Burns Letters, Special Collections, Virginia Polytechnic Institute, Blacksburg, VA.

35 Joseph Swan, "At Chickamauga: A Few Observations and Criticisms Regarding That Battle," *National Tribune*, November 30, 1893.

36 William P. Rea, "Roasted Bacon at the Bridge: 69th Ohio Man Helped Set the Bridge on Fire," *National Tribune*, October 15, 1914.

37 Hicks, "The Capture of Reed's Bridge."

38 L. E. Chenoweth to J. H. Brigham, December 6, 1901, Brigham Family Papers, Center for Archival Collections, Bowling Green State University, Bowling Green, OH.

their long march on the dry, dusty roads wore them out, and most tried to get some sleep. "In this condition we rested on our arms, without fire, for the night," said Col. Caleb J. Dilworth of the 85th Illinois. "During the night I could distinctively hear the rattle of wagons or artillery."[39] A soldier of the 52nd Ohio recounted, "[We] had only lain down when we were ordered to rally on the Battery. Did so and were moved ½ mile into a field filled with soldiers. Were ordered to support two pieces of artillery." He concluded: "Slept uncomfortably on account of the cold. The coldest night of the fall."[40] All anticipated a major battle the next morning, and Capt. L. E. Hicks of the 69th Ohio observed, "Besides the frosty air our perilous situation tended to produce shivery sensations in the bones."[41]

About 11:00 that night McCook received reinforcements. Col. Robert G. Mitchell's brigade of the 1st Division of the Reserve Corps joined his brigade along the Reed's Bridge Road after marching about seven miles from Rossville at about 7:00 that evening. They pitched their camp on the opposite side of the road from McCook's camp. "There were two rebel camps near by, one on either side, the fires of which could be plainly seen," noted a gunner of Battery M, 1st Illinois Light Artillery. "We made very little noise during the night."[42]

Meanwhile, a mile and a half from Lee and Gordon's Mills, Minty found Wilder's Lightning Brigade in a line of battle and facing northeast. Minty rode over to Wilder and asked, "Where do you want me?" The Hoosier replied, "I think your best position will be to my right." Minty immediately dismounted his troopers and had them deploy to Wilder's right in a field to the west of Hall's Ford, extending the Union battle line. Two regiments of infantry filled the gap between Wilder and Minty. These troops held the far left flank of the Army of the Cumberland's position near the La Fayette Road.[43] They quickly set about building some crude breastworks that were completed not a moment too soon.

39 *OR* 30, pt. 1, 873.

40 Theodore W. Blackburn, *Letters from the Front: A Union "Preacher" Regiment (74th Ohio) in the Civil War* (Dayton, OH: Morningside Bookshop, 1981), 150.

41 Hicks, "The Capture of Reed's Bridge."

42 "Capsule History of Battery M, 1st Illinois Light Artillery, 8/12/62-7/26/65," CCNMP.

43 Minty, "Minty's Saber Brigade," *National Tribune*, March 3, 1892.

After placing his men in line alongside Wilder's, Minty galloped over to Lee and Gordon's Mills to find General Tom Wood, who was speaking with one of his brigade leaders, Colonel Charles G. Harker. When Minty approached, Harker sprang to his feet and said, "General, here is Col. Minty now." Wood looked up and said, "I am glad to see you. I have just reported to Gen. Crittenden that your brigade had been cut off and captured."

"My brigade is all right, General," replied Minty, "and is now with Wilder's, covering your position."

Wood scrawled a postscript to his dispatch: "Col. Minty has just come in with his brigade." The general handed the dispatch to an orderly, who galloped off with it. The division commander then turned back to the Englishman. "Well, Minty, what have you been doing all day?"

> "Fighting the enemy," came the retort.
>
> "What have you been fighting?"
>
> "Everything—infantry, artillery and cavalry."
>
> "Where are they?"
>
> "Close to your present position, which is now covered by Wilder's brigade and mine."
>
> "Do you mean on our side of the creek?"
>
> "On our side of the creek, General."
>
> "Well, come along, and we'll drive them back across to their own side."

Wood and Minty then mounted their horses and, accompanied by a couple of orderlies, rode to the front. As they approached the Lightning Brigade, Wood haled Wilder and asked, "Where are they, Wilder?"

"Ride forward about a dozen paces, General, and you will see them," replied the Hoosier.

Just then a roar of musketry blazed in front of Minty's position, followed by the quavering sound of the Rebel yell. Wood turned to see Hood's infantrymen charging. With a stunned look on his face, Wood declared, "By God, they *are* here," realizing for the first time just how endangered the Army of the Cumberland was. Wood wheeled his horse and galloped back to his command to get it ready to give battle.[44]

As dusk settled over the dense woods, Hood ordered an attack upon the Union right, against the positions of the 44th Indiana and 59th

44 Ibid.

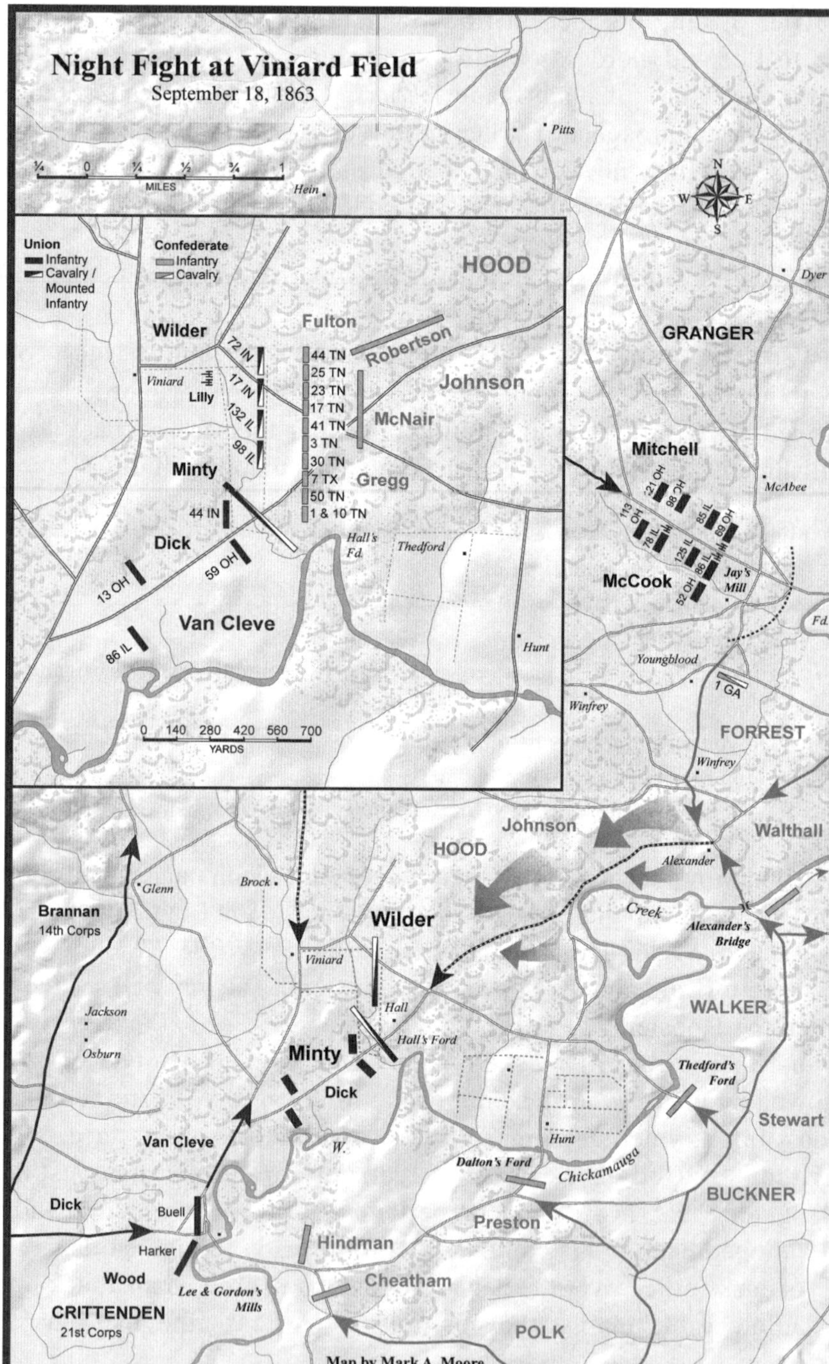

The night fight at Viniard Field, September 18-19.

Col. George F. Dick, commander of the Second Brigade of Van Cleve's division. *USAHEC*

Ohio regiments of Col. George F. Dick's brigade of Van Cleve's division of Crittenden's corps.[45] John Gregg's brigade of Bushrod Johnson's Provisional Division led the way. Dick reported to Wilder, who ordered him to take position on his right and to hold the approaches from the two fords that intersected the main road nearby. "The advance of the enemy then showed themselves to [Wilder's mounted] skirmishers, who had been thrown out in front of my regiments," reported Dick. "They were immediately driven back." Three of Gregg's skirmishers were wounded, one mortally, in this unexpected exchange. Johnson deployed the balance of Gregg's brigade and then brought up McNair's and Fulton's brigades, which took time to deploy, facing southwest and in support of Gregg. Robertson's brigade formed near the wagon train in the rear, facing northwest, while the 44th Tennessee of Fulton's brigade remained as a rear guard.[46] Johnson had deployed his three brigades wisely; they were in a defensive formation and facing three directions in case an attack came. His provisional division, however, was nearly as exposed as the Union troops facing them.

At about 9:00 p.m., just before the initial probes by Gregg's brigade, Wilder's orderly, Henry Tutewiler, finally returned to the Lightning Brigade's position after having to make his way through the woods to avoid the pursuing Confederate infantry. He realized that Maj. David D. Marquis and his detachment of the 98th Illinois had already pulled back and that he was now alone, caught "between the Rebel advance and their main army. I was within one hundred yards and in plain

45 *OR* 30, pt. 1, 822. Dick's orders were to report to Wilder and "to support him and hold the road at all hazards."

46 Ibid., pt. 2, 452.

sight of thousands of them." Luckily, Tutewiler wore "a semi-military suit" and was mistaken for a Confederate in the gathering dusk as a result. "By falling in behind the advance I got into the woods and worked my way off to the left until out of sight." Once darkness fell, he finally found Wilder's line in the woods. Lieutenant Francis Van Pelt of Company G of the 17th Indiana had earlier reported Tutewiler as "lying dead at the foot of a tree, [so] I received a royal welcome." Wilder embraced his orderly, "thank[ing] God that I was back safe and sound," said Tutewiler. "It made an impression on my mind that I can never forget."[47]

It took about half an hour for the Confederates to deploy. Gregg's brigade, now fully deployed, joined the attack, and a "sharp skirmish" ensued.[48] Wilder's skirmishers fell back, and the infantrymen opened their ranks to permit them to pass through. The foot soldiers then closed ranks. "Our Colonel gave the order to open fire on them," recalled Pvt. W. C. Salt of Company H of the 59th Ohio.[49] Although the 59th Ohio's heavy volley broke the line in front, the length of the Confederate line overlapped the end of Dick's line, thus forcing the 59th Ohio to fall back.[50] The Confederate infantry "made a very stubborn fight and was only driven back after one of our regiments, the 98th Illinois, and two companies of the72nd [Indiana] went to the relief of Col. Dick," noted a soldier of the 72nd. "The rebels lost considerable here. Our loss was light."[51]

Minty's and Wilder's men opened fire, and their rapid firepower quickly blunted Hood's attack, driving the head of his column back on its supports. The stout resistance surprised Bushrod Johnson, convincing him that "the whole Yankee army was in our front," and he therefore called off the attack.[52] "The rebel yell ceased, the

47 Quoted in Baumgartner, *Blue Lightning*, 212.

48 John H. Rerick, letter, September 29, 1863, published in *Lagrange Standard*, October 13, 1863.

49 W. C. Salt, "Among the First," *National Tribune*, November 29, 1917.

50 *OR* 30, pt. 1, 822.

51 J. E. R., "The Battle of Chickamauga," *Daily Courier* (Lafayette, IN), October 4, 1863. In fact, the 59th Indiana lost one man severely wounded and two men captured, both of whom managed to escape their captors during the night. See *OR* 30, pt. 1, 832.

52 *OR* 30, pt. 2, 453.

charging line halted, turned, and went back considerably faster than it had advanced," wrote Minty. "It was now very dark, and the opposing soldiers were so close that they could hear every movement being made."[53] Although the 59th Ohio bore the brunt of this attack, Wilder's men also saw some heavy firing that night. "Having the entire brigade together and having been enforced by two regiments of Dick's brigade, the enemy was repulsed and the line on the east end of the Viniard field remained."[54]

"We opened upon him and in two minutes the cloud of smoke from our rifles made it quite dark," recalled Sgt. Benjamin Magee of the 72nd Indiana. "Soon after encountering our brigade he also attacked the infantry on our right. A single volley from the whole line closed the work for the day, and enemy ceased firing," although sporadic firing continued well into the night.[55] By holding this line, Minty and Wilder kept the La Fayette Road open and available to the Army of the Cumberland, permitting Rosecrans to move Thomas's 14th Corps into position to receive an attack the next morning. Their stand meant that Rosecrans's route of escape to Chattanooga remained open and accessible if needed. Dick's infantrymen were understandably proud of their contribution that night. "Our claim is that if not the first infantry engaged in the Chickamauga battle, we were among the first, and as we checked this advance, we saved the Lafayette Road for the passage of troops to the left during the night."[56]

About 9:15 that night, after the repulse of Hood's night attack, Wilder scribbled a note to Thomas. A civilian from the Rossville area reported on the Confederate dispositions, and Wilder sent the civilian to Thomas so the corps commander could hear the man's information for himself. "The rebels are across Chickamauga and are found in force on any of the roads leading off to the right, at a quarter of a mile," he wrote. "They are planting artillery in my front, and our lines of skirmishers are mixed together. My main line and theirs is not more than 200 yards apart, and not more than 600 yards from the road from Gordon's Mills to

53 Minty, "Minty's Saber Brigade," *National Tribune*, March 3, 1892.

54 Benefiel, *Souvenir the Seventeenth Indiana Regiment*, 8.

55 Magee, *History of the Seventy-Second Regiment*, 160.

56 Salt, "Among the First," *National Tribune*, November 29, 1917.

Maj. Gen. George H. Thomas, "The Rock of Chickamauga," commanded the Army of the Cumberland's 14th Corps. Wilder's "Lightning Brigade" was assigned to the 14th Corps. *Library of Congress*

Chattanooga, 1¼ miles from Gordon's Mills." He concluded, "I have no position for artillery, and if my right is not strengthened, am in danger of being driven back. They attacked us at dark with cheers, but were

Capt. Charles C. Davis of the 7th Pennsylvania Cavalry was awarded a Medal of Honor for leading Minty's brigade in the devastating saber charge at Shelbyville on June 27, 1863.
Kenneth C. Turner

held in check. Their force is nearly all infantry, and from appearances it is a large one."[57]

With that, Minty's and Wilder's tired men hunkered down for a long, cold night on the front lines, with a very large enemy force just a couple of hundred yards in their front. "As our tents and blankets were always fastened to our saddles, we never saw horses, tents or blankets again until the 20th," remembered Sergeant Magee.[58] "We lay in position all night," recounted Minty, "and were without fires, although the night was bitterly cold."[59] Captain Charles C. Davis commanded a company of the 7th Pennsylvania Cavalry. "We went into camp after dark . . . and . . . you all know what a cold night it was for that season of the year in the State of Georgia," he said with a shudder. "No fires were allowed, no match to be struck, and our guns pointed to the enemy during the night." He also pointed out, "You know how tired and worn out we were after marching all of the night of the 17th to join our brigade a half a mile south of Chickamauga Creek."[60] A trooper of the 4th Michigan shivered, "Such a cold night is seldom felt at home in September."[61] It got so cold

57 *OR* 30, pt. 2, 725.

58 Magee, *History of the Seventy-Second Regiment*, 160.

59 *OR* 30, pt. 1, 923.

60 Charles C. Davis, "Address of Major Charles C. Davis," in *Pennsylvania at Chickamauga*, 314.

61 Potter, diary, September 18, 1863.

that the water in the canteens of Minty's troopers froze.[62] "I shook from head to foot as though I had a fit of ague," said a foot soldier of the 44th Indiana, "and O how I wished that it was the case, for then I knew it would be followed by the heat of fever."[63]

Sergeant James Larson of the 4th U.S. Cavalry left a detailed account: "There we remained all night in line of battle as infantry, a night never to be forgotten by the men who shivered and shook until daylight. A spat with the Rebs on the other side of the fence occasionally would have been a preferable change during the night. In our light marching order we had no overcoats and our ponchos and extra saddle blankets were with the horses far back in the woods." He continued, "We were not allowed to get up and walk, but had to lie close to the damp and cold ground and keep very quiet, as the enemy was so close that the least sound in the still night air could be heard and might precipitate a night attack. The officers were anxious to avoid that. The usual order to keep awake was also given, but there was really no necessity for the order because the men were all too busy shaking with cold to find time or inclination for sleep."[64]

A member of the 72nd Indiana of Wilder's brigade recalled, "About two oclock in the morning away in the far distance we could begin to hear the heavy rumbling of Rosecrans Artillery which brought the joyful tidings that reinforcements were coming. In our front we could hear the rebels chopping trees making roads and building breast works. We were anxious that the infantry would get up in time for we knew that the battle would commence in earnest in the morning."[65] Sergeant Magee left a more colorful description. "The night was clear, and thousands of sounds for many miles around were audible, while those coming from the south were omens of good to us, those coming from the north and east were presages of disaster and defeat," he wrote. "Between these conflicting sounds, and the feeling engendered by each in turn, we

62 Othniel Gooding to Nancy, September 26, 1863, Othniel Gooding Letters, Special Collections, Michigan State University, East Lansing, MI.

63 Julia A. Doyle, John David Smith, and Richard M. McMurry, eds., *This Wilderness of War: The Civil War Letters of George W. Squier, Hoosier Volunteer* (Knoxville: University of Tennessee Press, 1998), 69.

64 Larson, *Sergeant Larson*, 180.

65 Linville, *Battles, Skirmishes, Events and Scenes*, 83.

wore the hours of the night away. We had ample time to reflect upon the bloody battle which had fairly begun the day before."[66] There was little rest for the weary.

Wilder established his temporary headquarters in the nearby Viniard log farmhouse along the La Fayette Road. "We had to tie the Headquarters horses in the rear of the house to save them from the enemies bullets," recalled Wilder's orderly, Henry Tutewiler. "Whatever force was in our front, they were held in check and prevented from taking possession of the road which seemed to be their objective point."[67] Wilder also passed a long, uncomfortable night. "How anxiously we waited that long, starless night," he remembered years later. "I heard the rumbling of heavy wheels, as of Artillery, moving towards Chattanooga. Sending scouts to learn the cause, they reported at daylight that Gen. Thomas was moving his corps north on the Crawfish Springs road & about a mile and a half to my rear." Their stand had kept the La Fayette Road open long enough for Rosecrans to shift his forces to meet the threat posed by Bragg's army.[68]

During the afternoon of September 18 elements of Longstreet's corps continued to filter in from Catoosa Platform. Brigadier General Evander M. Law's brigade of Alabamians of Hood's division arrived on September 17 and then camped in Ringgold for the night. Colonel William C. Oates commanded the 15th Alabama Infantry of Law's brigade. Oates's men had marched out of Ringgold while the fighting for Reed's Bridge continued on the afternoon of September 18. "We marched westward several miles, and passed over ground where Hood, who had preceded us, with a part of his division and Forrest's cavalry, had fought and driven the Union cavalry," wrote Oates. "A dead man was occasionally found. We marched and we marched, along the dustiest roads I ever saw. We got on the wrong road and we marched I don't know where to and camped; got up the next morning and marched back again." They had exhausted the rations they carried with them, so Longstreet's men were hungry, parched from the choking dust, and tired from their

66 Magee, *History of the Seventy-Second Regiment*, 160-61.

67 Quoted in Baumgartner, *Blue Lightning*, 214.

68 Commissioners for the Chickamauga and Chattanooga National Park, *Indiana at Chickamauga*, 110.

travels. But they would be ready to go into battle the next day, just as they always were.[69]

As Bushrod Johnson recalled, "One-third of our forces was required to remain awake during the night, and the rest slept upon their arms. Obstructions to cavalry were hastily placed in our front, skirmishers were thrown out to the field east of Viniard's house, 150 yards in front of our left flank, and scouts were sent out nearly to the road to Lee and Gordon's Mills."[70] The Confederates faced the same problems as their Union counterparts: They did not have tents or blankets, and they also slept on their arms that night. "The night was extremely cold for the season, but we were ordered to keep very quiet, with no fires to disclose our position," John T. Goodrich of Gregg's brigade recalled.[71] "The Autumnal Equinox was evidently heralding its advent," quipped another Confederate.[72] An officer of the 3rd Tennessee noted that because no fires were permitted, "the boys had to drag out a miserable night, the most of them being wet up to the knees from wading the creeks that came in their way during the days march. The night was cold and many of the boys only kept themselves comfortably warm by building up breastworks of logs, to keep off the enemies cavalry if they attempted to charge during night."[73]

The grayclad soldiers could plainly hear the rumbling of the Union artillery and troops just as clearly as their Union counterparts, and those ominous sounds chilled the Confederates just as they did the Union men across the way. "All night we could hear the Federal Army moving into position with infantry artillery & to be ready for battle the next day," reported Lt. Col. James J. Turner of the 30th Tennessee Infantry of Gregg's brigade.[74] One of Robertson's Texans sounded a similar note: "Judging by the moving of troops and the rumbling of artillery during

69 William C. Oates, *The War Between the Union and the Confederacy and Its Lost Opportunities with a History of the 15th Alabama Regiment and the Forty-Eight Battles in Which It Was Engaged* (New York: Neale Publishing Co., 1905), 253-54.

70 *OR* 30, pt. 2, 453.

71 John T. Goodrich, "Gregg's Brigade in the Battle of Chickamauga," *Confederate Veteran* 22, no. 6 (June 1914): 264.

72 Terrill to His Brother, September 22, 1863.

73 Ikard, "Lieutenant Thompson Reports on Chickamauga," 419-20.

74 Postwar report of Col. J. J. Turner, 30th Tennessee Infantry, CCNMP.

the night, I felt pretty sure that 'the wool-tearing' would come off in the morning."[75] The night was just as long for the Confederates as it was for the Union soldiers.

Lieutenant Colonel Granville A. Frambes commanded the 59th Ohio Volunteer Infantry of Dick's brigade.[76] After repulsing Hood's attack, his men had fallen back to a ravine about 100 yards behind their original position. "During the night circumstances convinced me that the enemy was in our immediate front in force," he wrote. "I reported these facts to Colonels Wilder, Dick and Minty, and stated that our line was too weak to hold the position that we occupied, and that we had better fall back across the open field to the [La Fayette] road before daylight and avoid the necessity of being driven back in the morning." Wilder and Dick instructed Frambes to fall back and take position on the west side of the La Fayette Road on the edge of the woods and to deploy his skirmishers along the road. The Hoosiers spent the rest of the night there.[77]

Sergeant Silas K. Freeman of Company H, 44th Indiana, grew concerned when the gunfire intensified. "We could plainly hear the rebs cheering when our men run—they came down and outflanked the 59th who fell back after giving them a volley or two, and we were left there in the woods alone," he recalled. "We fixed our bayonets and peered out

75 West, *A Texan in Search of a Fight*, 112.

76 Granville Augustus Frambes was a very interesting man. He was the tenth child of Joseph and Eleanor Frambes and born in Washington Township, Clermont County, Ohio, on May 10, 1834. After his mother died, his farmer father remarried. He and his brother Oliver were both educated at Ohio Wesleyan College in Delaware. He then became a schoolteacher and was so engaged when the war came. On September 27, 1861, the 27-year-old Frambes was commissioned captain of Company B, 59th Ohio Volunteer Infantry. Less than a month later he was promoted to major, and on March 9, 1863, he was promoted to lieutenant colonel. When the regimental commander's health declined, Frambes assumed command of the regiment and remained in command of the 59th Ohio until he mustered out on October 31, 1864. He then founded a school in Sunbury, Ohio, and eventually became assistant superintendent of public schools in Columbus, Ohio, which he held for much of his adult life. Frambes invested in a large parcel of land in Franklin County. About 1890 Frambes sold his property to a nearby agricultural college, which later became known as Ohio State University. After he was caught up in a Freemason scandal, he died penniless in 1901. His brother Oliver paid for his burial. Oliver founded the University of Southern California in Los Angeles. Frambes Avenue runs close to the Ohio State University athletic facilities in Columbus. See Michael Arace, "OSU, USC Roots Lie with Ohio Brothers," *Columbus Dispatch*, September 12, 2008.

77 *OR* 30, pt. 1, 832.

into the darkness, expecting to see [them] dashing down on us. If they had known that we were there they could have taken us all prisoners." The Hoosiers did not have to wait long. The order for them to fall back soon arrived.[78]

As the unseasonably frigid night dragged on and fueled by Frambes's report, Minty grew more and more concerned about his exposed position since no further reinforcements had been sent to his support. "I well knew that if we remained in our then position until after daylight, nothing but a miracle could save us," he wrote. "The overwhelming numbers of the enemy could have crushed us in a moment."[79]

By 2:00 a.m. Minty could no longer stand it. He swung into his saddle and rode back toward Lee and Gordon's Mills to try to find some assistance. After going just a short distance, he encountered Maj. Gen. John M. Palmer, commander of Crittenden's 2nd Division. "Before I had time to say a word he asked me about the position of the opposing armies," recalled Minty. "I rapidly gave him a sketch of the day's work, and, describing the then position of my brigade, I told him that I was on my way to either Crittenden or Wood to ask for relief or support for my almost worn out command." Palmer turned to one of his staff officers and said, "Tell Gen. Hazen to move forward at once and relieve Col. Minty's brigade."

"Thank you, General," replied Minty. "My poor fellows have not had a bite to eat nor a moment's rest for 21 hours, and this will be a most acceptable relief to them, but Wilder is on my left and is in exactly the same condition; he has been opposing one of Longstreet's Corps since yesterday afternoon." Palmer immediately ordered another brigade to relieve Wilder. "I have always felt grateful to this gallant and distinguished soldier for his prompt action on that occasion," Minty said years later.[80]

Near daybreak, Wilder received orders from Rosecrans to take up a position "on the right fighting flank of our army and keep the department commander advised of events in that vicinity." About 4:00 a.m. Wilder pulled the Lightning Brigade from its exposed position back to the woods at the edge of the Viniard farm property on the west side of the

78 S. K. Freeman, letter to the editor, *Lagrange Standard*, October 10, 1863.

79 Minty, "Minty's Saber Brigade," *National Tribune*, March 3, 1892.

80 Ibid.

road from Lee and Gordon's Mills to Rossville, near where the road from Alexander's Bridge and the fords near Napier's Gap through Pea Vine Ridge converge, as Wilder expected this to be the area from which the enemy attack would come. His men threw up crude breastworks of fence rails and the like and prepared to meet a determined attack by Bragg's infantry.[81]

A few moments later, Wilder rode off to find General Thomas. "The enemy in my front, having drawn back at dawn, I immediately galloped over to Gen. Thomas . . . & explained the situation to him," recalled Wilder. "He directed me to draw my command back to Vineyards on the LaFayette road, & keep that road open to troops from Lee & Gordon's Mills."[82] Of course, had Crittenden taken more seriously the reports coming in from both Minty and Wilder, none of the last-minute shuffling of troops would have been necessary. "These reports were pooh-poohed," declared Maj. James Connolly of the 123rd Illinois. "It was intimated at the Corps headquarters that there was nothing but cavalry in our front and that we shouldn't be frightened. Finally, the urgency of Wilder compelled the Corps Commander, a little after daylight that morning, to come where he was on the field." Connolly concluded, "Wilder himself, and many of the subordinate officers warned the Corps Commander and told him what they heard and saw during the night, to all of which he listened with an incredulous air, and finally turning to a staff officer, said 'Go and tell General Palmer to send [Col. William] Grose's Brigade up here.' The staff officer started off hastily, while the Corps Commander remained with Wilder." Once the infantry reinforcements arrived, Crittenden was standing near Wilder's brigade and "his ears were saluted with the cries of our men: 'What do you think now? Do you think we were scared by cavalry now? We told you so,' and much more of the same sort, interlarded with the picturesque and comical comments which the enlisted men were so full of. The Corps Commander, mounting, posted off in hot haste to the rest of his command."[83]

81 *OR* 30, pt. 1, 447, 465.

82 John T. Wilder, "Revised Report for the Battle of Chickamauga," November 26, 1888, CCNMP.

83 Kilborn, *Dedication of the Wilder Brigade Monument on Chickamauga Battlefield*, 12.

"Daylight disclosed the fact that the main part of our army had moved round to our left to counteract a similar movement on the part of the enemy," observed a member of the 98th Illinois of Wilder's brigade.[84] The determined and successful stand by the combined forces of Wilder's and Minty's brigades and the infantry of Dick's brigade had kept the La Fayette Road open for use by the Army of the Cumberland and permitted Rosecrans to, at last, shift forces to meet the threat posed by Bragg's army. It took all night for Thomas's 14th Corps to move past Crittenden's 21st Corps and for two of Thomas's divisions to take position near the Kelly house, north of Wilder's position on the Viniard farms. Because of the movement of Thomas's corps, Wilder's Lightning Brigade now found itself on the right of the battle line, whereas it had been on the far left on the night of September 18.

At about the same time that Wilder pulled his brigade back from its exposed position on the eastern edge of the Viniard farm property, Palmer's infantrymen arrived to relieve Minty's weary horse soldiers. "I then moved to the rear and procured forage for the horses and rations for the men, who had been entirely without since early the previous morning," wrote Minty.[85] His command arrived at Lee and Gordon's Mills about 7:00 on the morning of September 19, fed their horses, and "got the first mouthful of food we had had for 26 hours." As Minty finished his coffee, a courier told him to report to Rosecrans, and the weary little colonel mounted up and rode off.[86]

About 4:00 a.m. McCook ordered Lt. Col. Joseph H. Brigham to take his 69th Ohio and surprise and burn Reed's Bridge. "By swift and stealthy approach we succeeded in taking the Confederate pickets completely by surprise," recalled Capt. Lewis E. Hicks of the 69th Ohio, who commanded the detachment that seized the bridge. "Some of them lying by a fire on our side of the river were captured; those on actual duty at the bridgehead ran away closely followed by our vanguard charging across with

84 McManus, Inglis, and Hicks, *Morning to Midnight in the Saddle*.

85 *OR* 30, pt. 1, 923.

86 Minty, "Minty's Saber Brigade," *National Tribune*, March 3, 1892. I have simplified the narrative of the Union troops on the night of September 18, as many of those movements are not relevant to this narrative. Those aspects that do not address the events surrounding the fighting at either Reed's Bridge or Alexander's Bridge are not addressed here. For a detailed discussion of these events, see Powell, *The Chickamauga Campaign*, 269-87.

fixed bayonets." The Buckeyes tore up the planks and piled them across the beams with some dry cedar rails from the cornfield fence. They then set it ablaze and withdrew under heavy fire.[87] By boldly setting Reed's Bridge ablaze, Brigham's Buckeyes deprived Bragg of its use, forcing him to use the bad ford 300 yards north of the bridge instead, suffering the loss of 2 killed, 14 wounded, and 13 prisoners.[88]

"Near morning we were aroused by the sound of musketry, but it not being followed up by any further attack, we rested quietly until daybreak," noted Colonel Dilworth of the 85th Illinois. The assault on Reed's Bridge did not even rouse the rest of McCook's command.[89] About 7:00 McCook received orders to withdraw back to Rossville. "This order came not a minute too soon," he declared, "for I have since learned that one division of Longstreet's corps was in my front, another in my rear, only three-quarters of a mile distant, and the third on my left flank, just across the creek."[90]

Before they could head out toward Rossville, however, a heavy skirmish began between McCook's infantry and the Confederates, meaning that the opening shots of the main engagement at Chickamauga began along the Reed's Bridge Road and involved Dan McCook's infantrymen. The main battle was now on. "Dan wanted to fight them," observed a soldier of the 52nd Ohio, "but he had strict orders not to. We got out of there on the double quick, and it was a good thing we did or we would have been gobbled before we got out of hearing."[91]

On the night of September 18, West Chickamauga Creek split Bragg's Army of Tennessee, with Hood's division, Col. Robert C. Trigg's brigade of Buckner's corps, and Forrest's cavalry separated from the rest of the army as a result of Minty's stout stand at Reed's Bridge that day.

Both his supply wagons and the remaining infantry of Longstreet's corps were still moving toward Reed's Bridge from Ringgold, so Hood was worried about keeping that vital road open. He gave Forrest specific

87 Hicks, "The Capture of Reed's Bridge," CCNMP.

88 *OR* 30, pt. 1, 871-72. The bridge was quickly repaired and put back into service. Interestingly, Confederate accounts do not mention the burning of the bridge.

89 Ibid., 873.

90 Ibid., 871.

91 Burns to His Father, October 4, 1863.

orders to "move out on my right and protect my right flank and ordnance train."[92] Forrest failed miserably, meaning that Hood's critical supply route remained threatened by the presence of those Union troops all night. Scott's brigade pulled back across the Chickamauga at Red House Bridge and then moved off to join Pegram near Alexander's Bridge, leaving the road to Ringgold dangerously unguarded. Instead of obeying Hood's order, Forrest ordered Pegram's brigade to recross the Chickamauga near Alexander's Bridge and to go into camp nearby. Forrest joined Pegram there, as did Scott's brigade. Forrest had chosen a position several miles away from Jay's Sawmill, away from the threat, and on the wrong side of the creek, meaning that he did little to fulfill Hood's orders.

W. F. Shropshire served in the 1st Georgia Cavalry of Pegram's division. His regiment cautiously moved up the road toward the sawmill, "seeking as advance position as possible . . . [when] reaching some 300 yards from the saw mill . . . [we were] fired into by the enemy from ambush." The grayclad horsemen wisely pulled back out of range, leaving the road intersection and Reed's Bridge in Union hands even after the sacrifice incurred in taking it earlier that day.[93]

Brigadier General John Pegram then decided to see for himself. He personally led a patrol up the Reed's Bridge Road. "During the night of the 18th, our Gallant General Pegram, wishing to reconnoiter, crossed [Alexander's] bridge accompanied by his staff and bodyguard, and to his surprise found himself in a lane between two large camps," recalled a Confederate horse artillerist. "He addressed a party of soldiers inquiring the name of the command and was informed that an Ohio regiment occupied one side of the lane, while an Illinois regiment camped on the other side. Without showing alarm or surprise, he turned his horse's head, and recrossed safely Alexander's Bridge." Pegram had accidentally blundered into McCook's camp and that of Mitchell's Reserve Corps brigade.[94] Pegram reported this encounter to Bragg's headquarters, and that ended the Confederate cavalry's efforts to fulfill Hood's orders,

92 H. B. Clay, "On the Right at Chickamauga," *Confederate Veteran* 21 (1913): 439-40.

93 Curtis Green, "Sixth Georgia Cavalry at Chickamauga," *Confederate Veteran* 8 (1900): 324; W. F. Shropshire, "Reminiscences," *Confederate Veteran* Papers, Special Collections, Perkins Library, Duke University, Durham, NC.

94 *OR* 30, pt. 1, 867.

and Reed's Bridge thus fell back into Union hands. Forrest had failed miserably.[95]

At 2:00 a.m. Col. John Scott's brigade of Pegram's cavalry division, which was resting at Leet's Tanyard, received orders to seize and hold Red House Bridge. "Travel was slow going," recalled Trooper William G. Allen of the 5th Tennessee Cavalry. "It was near sunrise Saturday morning when we reached the bridge." Upon arriving, they received orders to charge and seize the bridge, which they did. Scott's troopers encountered Union infantry pickets, who opened on them, dropping 10 to 12 of the Southern horsemen and some of their mounts, halting them in their tracks. A flanking movement succeeded in driving the blueclad pickets back into their main line, and soon the fighting began in earnest.[96]

Brigadier General John M. Brannan commanded the 3rd Division of the 14th Corps. About 5:00 p.m. on September 18, Brannan received orders to break his camp at Gower's Ford on the Chickamauga. He marched to a position above Crawfish Springs and then took the La Fayette Road about two and a half miles to a position near the Elisha Kelly farmhouse.[97] "I was much retarded in this march, which continued the entire night," groused Brannan, "by the delay of the Twenty-First Corps in getting into position, having frequently to halt for a considerable time to enable portions of the command to come up from the rear of my column."[98] The march was extremely frustrating for Brannan's troops. "We were continually starting and halting and it is impossible to estimate the distance correctly," noted Capt. John D. Inskeep of 17th Ohio in his diary. "The whole country is alive with soldiers pushing forward as rapidly as the roads would permit."[99] The all-night ordeal suffered by

95 Postwar account of Gustave A. Huwald, October 7, 1866. Dave Powell addresses Forrest's miserable failures at Chickamauga in great detail in *Failure in the Saddle* (2010).

96 William Gibbs Allen memoir, Tennessee State Library and Archives, Nashville, Tennessee.

97 Elisha Kelly and his family lived in this house, though it was owned by Kelly's brother Elijah and is situated in Kelly's field, where much of the second day's hardest fighting occurred. Thomas established his headquarters there on the night of September 19. See Sartain, *History of Walker County, Georgia*, 104-5.

98 *OR* 30, pt. 1, 400.

99 John D. Inskeep, diary, September 18, 1863, John D. Inskeep Papers, Ohio Historical Society, Columbus, OH.

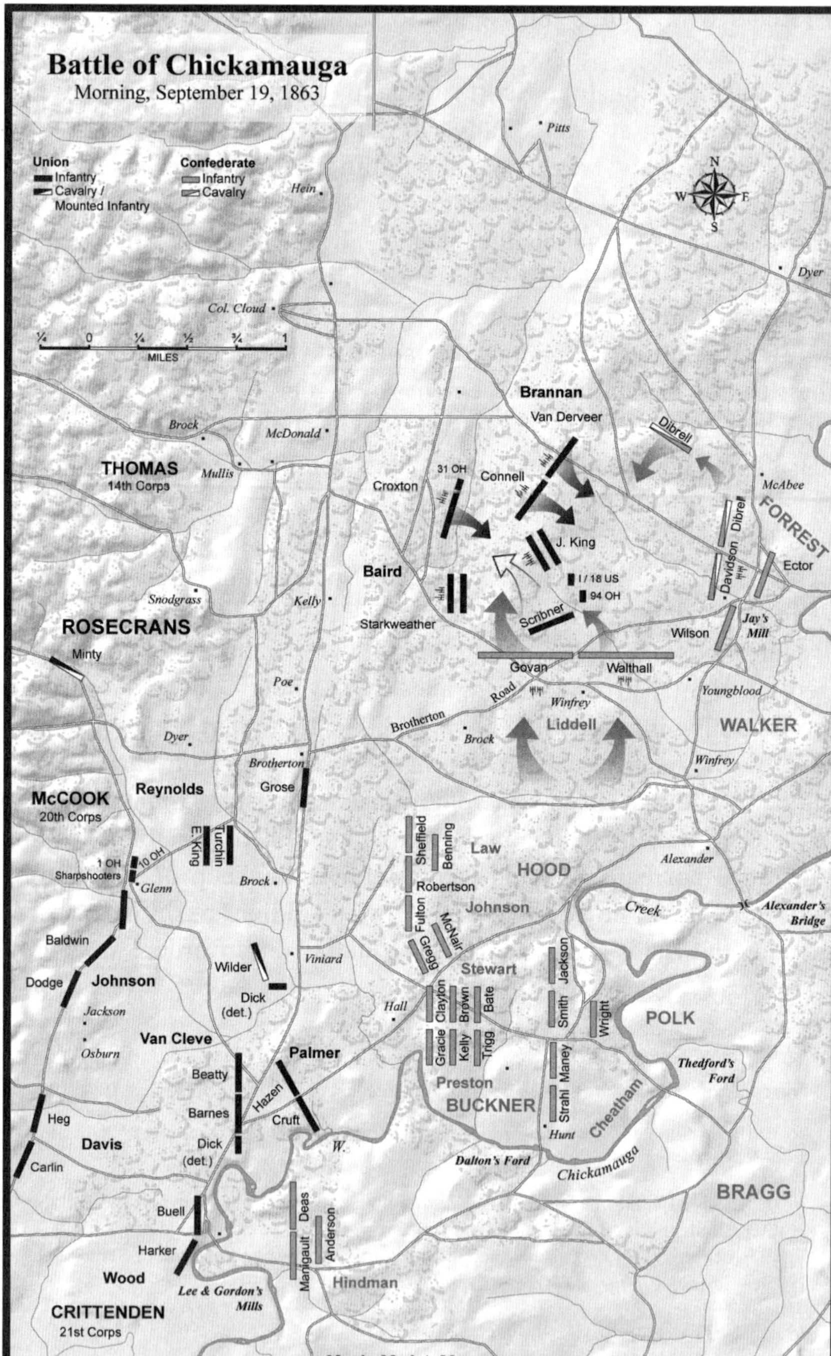

Battle of Chickamauga, morning, September 19.

Brannan's foot soldiers, however, was only the beginning of the challenge that faced them the next morning.

Shortly before daylight on the morning of September 19, Thomas ordered Brannan and his tired division to advance to "capture, if possible, a rebel force represented by Col. Dan. McCook to be a brigade cut off on the west side of Chickamauga Creek; failing in this, to drive it across the creek." Not realizing that a major portion of the Army of Tennessee was in his front, Brannan ordered Col. John T. Croxton and his 2nd Brigade to attack Forrest's troopers about dawn.[100] "This morning the enemy attempted to regain the ford and fought Forrest's cavalry very stubbornly," noted artillerist George Grammer of Swett's Missouri Battery in his diary.[101] "The battle raged, cavalry dismounted, driving Federals from every stand they made," claimed William G. Allen of the 5th Tennessee Cavalry of Pegram's division.[102] Croxton's determined attack prompted Hood to commit two divisions of infantry to the fight to reinforce Forrest's hard-pressed troopers, and the battle of Chickamauga began in deadly earnest.

Describing the fateful morning of September 19, 1863, a Confederate colonel eloquently but prophetically wrote, "The day was bright and beautiful, and the world never seemed so attractive before, now that there was a good chance for leaving it soon."[103] The gates of hell had finally swung open. They would not slam shut again until sundown the next day, September 20, 1863, when the butcher's bill had finally been paid. Both sides would incur nearly 35,000 casualties. But the full story of that bloody, desperate conflagration is told in other books.

100 *OR* 30, pt. 1, 400.

101 Grammer, diary, September 19, 1863.

102 Allen, *Reminiscences of William G. Allen*, 6-7.

103 James L. Cooper Memoirs, Civil War Collection, Tennessee State Library and Archives, Nashville, TN.

Conclusion

General Braxton Bragg, the commander of the Army of Tennessee, was the best person to describe the consequences of the stands of Minty's Saber Brigade at Reed's Bridge and Wilder's Lightning Brigade at Alexander's Bridge. Regarding Minty's stout stand, he wrote, "The resistance offered by the enemy's cavalry and the difficulties arising from the bad and narrow country roads caused unexpected delays in the execution of these movements [ordered for September 18]. Though the commander of the right column [Bushrod Johnson] was several times urged to press forward, his crossing was not effected until late afternoon."[1] Bragg raised a red herring by blaming the roads for the derailing of his battle plan for September 18, as will be discussed below. He seemed unwilling to give Minty's lone small brigade credit for throwing off his entire plan of battle.

About Wilder's stand at Alexander's Bridge, Bragg wrote, "Alexander's Bridge was hotly contested and finally broken up by the enemy just as General Walker secured possession. He moved down stream, however, a short distance, and crossed, as directed, at Byram's Ford, and thus secured a junction with Hood after night."[2] Again Bragg grudgingly acknowledged the stalwart resistance by Wilder's Lightning Brigade while downplaying its role in the unraveling of his carefully laid plan of attack for that day.

1 *OR* 30, pt. 2, 31-32.

2 Ibid., 32.

Bragg believed he had managed to get more than 20,000 men of Hood's, Walker's, and Buckner's corps onto Rosecrans's left flank without Rosecrans realizing it. Bragg also was prepared to move at dawn once Polk's additional 13,000 men finished their movement toward the flank. When word from Forrest arrived, however, that a significant force of Union infantry threatened Hood's right and rear near Reed's Bridge, Bragg froze. Their presence there could ruin his entire plan, so the army commander asked for better information. He ordered Forrest to advance up the Reed's Bridge Road early in the morning and to determine the precise nature of the threat. Bragg believed he could not attack until this important question was resolved, meaning the entire schedule for the battle for September 19 had to be completely reworked. Instead, Forrest's movement to Jay's Sawmill opened the battle in earnest when he ran into Brannan's infantry there.[3] Further, the burning of Reed's Bridge by Union soldiers meant that Confederate troops had to be detailed for bridge-building duty and to make the bad ford 300 yards from Reed's Bridge ready for military operations, further delaying Bragg's advance.[4]

Together, the approximately 3,200 officers and men of Wilder's and Minty's brigades, the six guns of Capt. Eli Lilly's battery, and the two guns of the Chicago Board of Trade Battery held off approximately 17,000 Confederate troops. More important, the stands of Minty and Wilder and two regiments of Dick's infantry brigade on the Viniard property after dark that night prevented Confederate infantry from reaching the La Fayette Road and interdicting Rosecrans's line of supply, communication, and route of retreat to Chattanooga. With Rosecrans finally alerted to and understanding the dire threat to his army, the stubborn stands of these Union soldiers gave the Army of the Cumberland's commander time to shift troops—especially Maj. Gen. George H. Thomas's 14th Corps—to meet the threat and to be in position to fight on the morning of September 19. "The holding of the line on the east of the Vinard field was the saving of Rosecrans's army," declared a member of the 17th Indiana Infantry of Wilder's brigade.[5] He was right.

3 Ibid., 524.

4 Jordan, *Some Events and Incidents of the Civil War*, 50-51.

5 Commissioners for the Chickamauga and Chattanooga National Park, *Indiana at Chickamauga*, 143.

Sergeant Nixon B. Stewart, who served in Col. Daniel McCook Jr.'s own 52nd Ohio Volunteer Infantry and who was present for the late-night skirmishing at Reed's Bridge, wrote, "Our mounted troops saved Crittenden's corps on the first day, by their resistance of the enemies approach to our lines." Even the infantry, which was known to disparage the cavalry by hooting such things as "whoever saw a dead cavalryman" at passing horse soldiers, recognized the valiant role played by Minty and Wilder on September 18.[6]

Minty left a cogent analysis of the important roles played by both Wilder and himself. "If Wilder's Brigade at Alexander's Bridge and Minty's at Reed's Bridge had not made the stubborn fight they did, which fact is attested by the 105 rebel dead left at Alexander's Bridge and 102 rebel dead left at Reed's Bridge and the unknown number left in the Pea Vine Valley, at Dyer's Ford, on the line of retreat from Reed's Bridge to Gordon's Mill, and in front of our position near that place, and by the loss of the entire day to Gen. Bragg, what would have been the result to that glorious army, the Army of the Cumberland?" he asked.

"If Bragg had been allowed to carry out his well-planned order of battle, as laid down in his order of the 18th, Crittenden's corps would have been struck on its left flank by the corps of Hood, Walker and Buckner, while his front would have been attacked by Polk, and must have been annihilated before Thomas could have got within supporting distance, and Chattanooga, which had been won in such a masterly manner by our command, that illustrious leader, Gen. W. S. Rosecrans, would have been lost," he correctly claimed. "The fruits of two successful campaigns, those of Tullahoma and Chattanooga, would have been snatched from us."[7]

In a postwar speech at the dedication of the Chickamauga and Chattanooga National Military Park, Minty also correctly declared, "Whether history does us justice or not, we have the proud and gratifying knowledge, that, by the performance of our whole duty, in the hour of danger and necessity, we saved the Army of the Cumberland from terrible disaster, if not from annihilation."[8]

6 Nixon B. Stewart, *Dan McCook's Regiment, 52nd O. V. I. A History of the Regiment, Its Campaigns and Battles, From 1862-1865* (Alliance, OH: Review Print, 1900), 61.

7 Minty, "Minty's Saber Brigade," *National Tribune*, March 3, 1892.

8 Minty, *Remarks of Brevet Major General R. H. G. Minty*, 10.

A number of other commentators agreed with Minty's opinion. A Confederate of the Army of Tennessee noted, "Preston's Division effected an unobstructed crossing at Hunt's [Dalton's] Ford; not so with Johnson and Walker at Reed's and Alexander's Bridges, and without them there was no sweeping up the Chickamauga and vigorously pressing the enemy's flank and rear."[9] Captain Joseph G. Vale of the 7th Pennsylvania Cavalry, who served on Minty's staff, carefully chronicled the history of the Saber Brigade after the war. Writing about the events of September 18, Vale stated, "The importance of this day's operations of Minty's and Wilder's Brigades can only be appreciated by remembering that it was Bragg's intention to have thrown Hood, Walker, Buckner, Forrest, and Pegram on Crittenden's left flank, in determined assault as early as 8 or 10 o'clock in the morning of the 18th, when Polk's Corps was to overwhelm him in an assault from the front; and having disposed of him, pen Thomas up in McLemore's Cove, thus defeating the army in detail." Vale concluded, "The persistent fighting and daring charges of Minty's men, of which the 102 rebel graves at Reed's Bridge are to-day mute but undeniable witnesses, compelled him to fight a long, determined battle before crossing; and to slow, cautious movements, with frequent halts and deployments in his after progress, so hampered and delayed his march that there was no 'sweeping up the creek,' and prevented the blow that was planned to fall on Crittenden."[10]

At the 1895 dedication of the monument to the 7th Pennsylvania Cavalry on the Chickamauga battlefield, Vale dispelled Bragg's blaming the delay on anything but the stiff resistance by Minty's troopers:

1. What of "bad roads"? It was the 18th day of September, during a remarkably dry spell; no rain of any account had fallen since the preceding July and the roads were dry and hard, and on the line of Johnson's advance were not even rough or rocky. With the exception of the short, sharp activity of Pea Vine Ridge the march was over a comparatively level country. Pea Vine Creek, where he halted and maneuvered in the face of less than 100 men under Captain Thompson, is an insignificant stream which at that time a man could step across.

9 Minty, "Minty's Saber Brigade," *National Tribune*, March 3, 1892.

10 Vale, *Minty and the Cavalry*, 231.

2. As to the "narrow country roads." With the exception of a short distance over the Pea Vine Valley at Peeler's Mill, about a mile and a half in all, the whole distance was through an open wooded country, and, in point of face, wherever we saw the advance it was in line and parallel columns, sweeping over the country without regard to roads or their condition. Again, even if confined to roads, no wagon road is so narrow but that it gives space enough for a movement of infantry "by fours." The whole force moving on Reed's Bridge was 4,700 infantry and 3 batteries of artillery. This infantry force can move comfortably in a column two miles long, and with the artillery would be about two and one half miles. In this formation it can and should move at the rate of three miles an hour, and this rate at least Johnson's report shows he actually maintained for the first six or eight miles; that is, from Ringgold and Catoosa Station to near Peeler's Mill. He says he started at 5:00 a.m., and reached Pea Vine Creek at about seven. From Peeler's Mill to Reed's Bridge is less than three miles, but it took him five hours to cover that distance. It took him, with over 7,000 infantry and 4 batteries of artillery, besides Forrest's cavalry, more than four hours to drive Minty, with less than 1,000 sabers and 2 pieces of artillery, from the bridge; and then took him, re-enforced by 2 more full brigades, in all over 10,000 infantry, supported on the right by Forrest's cavalry, and on the left by Buckner's division of Polk's corps, five hours more to march through an open country over good, level roads, and through hard, dry open woods, a distance of less than five miles. So much for "the bad, narrow country roads." The "resistance offered by the enemy's cavalry" is the only factor not eliminated. And in the face of the unquestioned fact that General Bragg's whole plan of attack and battle for September 18, 1863, is admitted by himself, to have been a failure and been brought to naught, I here and now declare, that even where there is no evidence that Minty's brigade ever fired a shot or drew a saber on that day, the conclusion must be irresistible to all military tacticians, that the presence, movements, and tactics of that command on that day saved Rosecrans' army from a most crushing blow—a blow, too, about to fall when it was totally unprepared and when its constituent parts were so dislocated as to be physically impossible of being united in time to succor each other.

Vale's analysis was right on point and clearly showed that Bragg's blaming of the roads for the delay of his advance on September 18 was nothing but a red herring and demonstrated that the sole reason for the frustration of Bragg's battle plan for that day was the determined stand by Minty's 973 officers and men and the two guns of the Chicago Board of Trade Battery that fought at Reed's Bridge. This was no small feat.[11]

Vale's well-respected history of the Saber Brigade addressed these events in detail. "From all which it will be seen that the minutes of fighting were worth hours, and each individual casualty in Minty's and Wilder's brigades worth hundreds of men to Rosecrans' army, that 18th of September, 1863," he declared. "Yet in the histories of the campaign and battle, the whole matter is ignored as though it had never occurred; in order that the willful blindness of a favorite corps commander may not be made manifest."[12]

Vale also quoted from an anonymous letter to Minty written by an unidentified but high-ranking officer of the Army of the Cumberland. That officer's analysis of the impact of Minty's stand is worth repeating here as it cogently puts the Saber Brigade's fight that day in its true context. "It will, I think, be seen that you held on that day, September 18th, the key of the position, the left of the army, and so successfully that the rebels' plan was frustrated," wrote the unidentified officer. "It cost General Thomas thousands of men to maintain it, persistently fought for on two days. Had the rebels succeeded early on the morning of the 18th, in taking Reed's bridge, not only Colonel Wilder, but the whole army, would have been seriously compromised. I am sure, had General Rosecrans known all the facts, he would have added the 18th to the number of days, 'the army could not have dispensed' with the cavalry."[13]

Rev. Thomas B. Van Horne penned an early history of the Army of the Cumberland at the request of George H. Thomas, the army's final commander. "In preparing for battle on the 18th, he [Bragg] had overlooked causes of detention, and this mistake gave General Rosecrans time to throw his army to the left, between him and Chattanooga," wrote Van Horne. "At nightfall on the 18th Bragg was by no means ready for

11 Vale, "Address of Captain Joseph G. Vale," 306-7.

12 Vale, *Minty and the Cavalry*, 232-33.

13 Ibid., 241-42.

battle, having entirely failed to deliver it on the 18th, as he had planned. Minty and Wilder were on the watch at Reed's and Alexander's Bridges. These two brigades resisted so persistently that General Bragg mentioned their actions as one cause of delay."[14]

Some point to the low levels of casualties in the fights for Reed's Bridge and Alexander's Bridge as evidence they were insignificant actions. Viewing these actions in terms of casualties does not do them justice. The object of both Minty's and Wilder's actions was to delay Bragg's advance and buy time, not to inflict heavy losses on the enemy. Inflicting casualties on the enemy was a bonus, not the primary objective. When viewed in that light, Minty and Wilder were even more successful, suffering light losses as a result of the sound planning and execution of their delaying maneuvers.[15]

In many ways, the stands at Reed's Bridge and Alexander's Bridge were even more remarkable than the much-better known delaying action fought by Brig. Gen. John Buford's two brigades at Gettysburg ten weeks earlier. Buford, with 2,900 troopers and the 6-gun battery of Lt. John H. Calef, held off Maj. Gen. Henry Heth's 10,000-man Confederate

14 Thomas B. Van Horne, *History of the Army of the Cumberland; Its Organization, Campaigns and Battles*, 2 vols. (Cincinnati: Robert Clarke & Co., 1875), vol. 1, 330-31. Van Horne also wrote a biography of Thomas.

15 For example, the October 6, 1863 issue of the *Pottsville Miner's Journal* newspaper reported the following casualties for Company F of the 7th Pennsylvania (which was raised in Pottsville) for the entire campaign: "Lieut. [Bernard] Reilly who was wounded in the [hand at the] battle of Chickamauga, reports to us the following list of casualties in his company, as far as he learned them before leaving the field:
Killed
John Ward, of Fishbach.
Owen Brennan, of Donaldson, killed by a round shot.
Wounded
John Reilly, of Pottsville; leg amputated.
Corporal [John] Williams, of St. Clair.
[John] Lynch, of Pottsville.
Geo. M. Boyer, of Schuylkill Haven.
Danl. King, of this County, lost his leg.
In addition he states that Capt. [David G.] May [Company K] of Cumberland County, Pa. was killed [September 21, 1863, on Missionary Ridge]; and that Capt. [Cyrus] Newlin of Philadelphia, and Capt. [James] Andress of West Chester, were wounded in skirmishing before the battle, the Seventh having the advance." Charles E. Bates of Company E of the 4th U.S. Cavalry claimed that the Saber Brigade lost 198 men on September 18. See Bates to his parents, November 5, 1863, "Bates Letters—November 5, 1863," Regular Cavalry in the Civil War, June 9, 2008, https://regularcavalryincivilwar.wordpress.com/category/bates-letters/.

infantry division of Lt. Gen. A. P. Hill's 3rd Corps for several hours on the morning of July 1, 1863. In addition to holding against Heth, Buford's two brigades then had to stand against the Confederate infantry of Lt. Gen. Richard S. Ewell's 2nd Corps until sufficient infantry from the 1st and 11th Corps arrived in time to relieve his hard-pressed troopers, who were on the verge of running out of ammunition. The covering force action designed and implemented by Buford was intended to trade space for time. Buford's men bought sufficient time to permit Union infantry to arrive on the battlefield.[16]

Minty and Wilder did not have the luxury of knowing the Army of the Cumberland's infantry was coming to relieve them. Their delaying action was not designed or intended to trade space for time in the traditional sense—no Union forces were expected to arrive.

Minty's stand is particularly notable. With a mere 973 officers and men and two pieces of artillery, the Saber Brigade held off about 6,000 veteran Confederate infantry for the better part of 12 hours that dry, dusty September day. By contrast, Buford had three times as many men available to him to hinder the advance of the grayclad infantry at Gettysburg on July 1, 1863. Minty not only conducted a longer delaying action by taking excellent advantage of the terrain, including Pea Vine Ridge and the steep, muddy banks of West Chickamauga Creek, but he also created a choke point that forced Bushrod Johnson to either shove the determined Saber Brigade aside or to seek another crossing point. The impassability of West Chickamauga Creek acted as a force multiplier, since it funneled the Confederates through a single choke point, Reed's Bridge, instead of being able to fan out as the Army of Northern Virginia did at Gettysburg. The time Minty's stand gained proved to be absolutely invaluable to William Starke Rosecrans and the Army of the Cumberland and, in fact, may have directly saved the army from destruction as well as hundreds of lives that day.

Similarly, Wilder's men used the combination of the depth of Chickamauga Creek at Alexander's Bridge and the steep, muddy banks to hold off Walker's corps for two hours that afternoon. More important, and unlike Minty's men, the soldiers of the 72nd Indiana wisely removed the planking from Alexander's Bridge to build a lunette in the middle

16 For a detailed discussion of these events, see Wittenberg, *The Devil's to Pay*.

of the road, rendering the bridge impassable to Shot-Pouch Walker's Confederates. That, in turn, forced Walker to disengage at Alexander's Bridge and to search for another ford where his men could cross and flank Wilder out of his position at Alexander's Bridge.

The combination of delays achieved at both bridges, of course, completely frustrated Bragg's plans for September 18 while giving Rosecrans an opportunity to take the steps he did to shift his army into a position where Bragg was no longer an imminent threat. While historians and veterans of the battle have long failed to count September 18, 1863, as the first day of the battle of Chickamauga, it was indeed the opening of the great fight and made the second and third day's events possible. Failing to include September 18 as the true opening of the battle of Chickamauga does an injustice to the men who fought and died that day, including the 207 Confederate dead who suffered at the hands of Minty and Wilder.

In short, the stands by Wilder and Minty and the critical intelligence reports they generated finally jolted Rosecrans into recognizing the dire situation facing his army. He moved his advance troops up about four miles to the Snodgrass farm-Reed's Bridge area to avoid being flanked by Bragg. The Confederate commander not only did not know this, but he shifted his own advance four miles downstream to the area between Thedford's Ford and Lee and Gordon's Mills so that Rosecrans would not outflank him. Rosecrans did not know about Bragg's shift of positions either. Thus Rosecrans moved to where he thought Bragg would be, and Bragg moved to where he believed Rosecrans was, passing like ships in the night. It set the stage for a confused and chaotic day of heavy fighting the next day, September 19.

After guarding wagon trains for most of September 19, Minty received orders to take possession of the Rossville and Ringgold Road. He sent patrols as far north as Red House Bridge. His patrol ran into Col. John Scott's cavalry on the west side of the Chickamauga, which Minty "considered an encroachment on our territory, and at once attacked and drove him across the bridge to the east side of the creek." By the time Minty secured the bridge, it was dark. He fell back to McAfee's Church, formerly Granger's headquarters, and then moved well to the right to link up with Union infantry, but he failed to find the foot soldiers in the darkness. "We remained in position all night, sitting on the ground, holding our horses, and procuring but little rest," he recalled. "We were pretty well worn out with our three days' fighting and want of food and rest, and the feeling that the battle was going against us. The night was cold and we were thoroughly chilled."[17]

After falling back toward Chattanooga from Horseshoe Ridge, Thomas took a position on Missionary Ridge near Rossville. Thomas ordered Minty to buy as much time as possible for his troops to prepare their defenses. Minty's Saber Brigade held a position three miles in front of the army until 10:15 a.m. on September 21, when Forrest's command attacked with three times Minty's numbers. Minty's troopers stubbornly held on as long as they could before retiring to Rossville Gap. They then fought with desperation on Missionary Ridge, where the beleaguered cavalrymen made a determined last stand, all the while taking fire from three batteries of Confederate horse artillery. Barnett's battery of Granger's Reserve Corps came to Minty's assistance and engaged the Confederate gunners in counterbattery fire. Once again, as the great battle of Chickamauga came to a close, the fate of the Army of the Cumberland rested in Robert H. G. Minty's capable hands.

Providing the army's rearguard defense, Minty said, "By 7 o'clock we were again in our saddles, showing a bold front on every possible occasion and checking the enemy as much as possible." He added, "We passed inside our lines in front of Chattanooga at about 1 p.m. It took the rebels six hours to drive us the four miles between Rossville and our advanced works at Chattanooga."[18] The 7th Pennsylvania Cavalry lost heavily that day. Captain David G. May, commander of Company K, was killed, as was Pvt. Andrew Lavale of Company E. Several others were wounded. While moving to the rear of the Army of the Cumberland's position at Rossville, Lt. Bernard Reilly Jr. of Company F was wounded.

From Rossville the Saber Brigade moved to the left of the army, taking a position on Missionary Ridge. It remained there until it was withdrawn to a position near Rossville on the morning of September 22, where it skirmished for most of the morning. Toward evening, the brigade was ordered to report to Chattanooga. The 7th Pennsylvania

17 Minty, "Minty's Saber Brigade," *National Tribune*, March 3, 1892.

18 Ibid.

was chosen to perform rearguard duty and did not arrive at Chattanooga until about 7:00 that evening.[19] An hour later, the 4th Michigan and the 7th Pennsylvania were ordered to work in the trenches, which they did until sunrise on the morning of September 23. Hence "the Seventh Pennsylvania Cavalry opened and closed the battle of Chickamauga and was engaged and under fire five days, from seven A. M., Friday, September 18, to Thursday evening, September 22. . . . To Pennsylvania belongs the honor of opening and closing the battle," claimed George Steahlin, the regimental adjutant.[20]

Similarly, the artillerists of Lt. Trumbull D. Griffin's 2nd Section of the Chicago Board of Trade Battery claimed the honor of firing the first artillery shots of the battle of Chickamauga. Minty correctly pointed out that Griffin's gunners also fired the last shots near Chattanooga at about noon on September 22. They rightfully and proudly bragged about their important role in the battle for years after the fact.[21]

Minty accurately and proudly declared: "The battle of Chickamauga, as told of in history, lasted two days, the 19th and 20th of September, 1863. For the 'Saber Brigade' it lasted five days, on every one of which, except the 19th, when it was protecting the trains on the Dry Village road, it had its full share of fighting."[22] His men opened the great battle with his effective delaying action at Reed's Bridge, and he then closed it with another equally effective delaying action near Rossville, intended to buy time for Thomas to prepare his defenses. His brigade's service on both days was exemplary and demonstrated beyond a shadow of a doubt that not only were his men proficient with the blade, but they were equally effective with their carbines.

19 Charles Bates of Company E of the 4th U.S. Cavalry claimed "my Regiment was the last to enter Chattanooga, being on the rear guard" in a November 1863 letter to his parents, but it appears this claim was incorrect. See Bates to his parents, November 5, 1863, "Bates Letters—November 5, 1863," Regular Cavalry in the Civil War, June 9, 2008, https://regularcavalryincivilwar.wordpress.com/category/bates-letters/.

20 Steahlin, "Address and Historical Sketch," 311. There were only seven Pennsylvania units in the Army of the Cumberland in September 1863: three regiments of infantry, three regiments of cavalry (including the 7th Pennsylvania Cavalry), and one battery of artillery.

21 Chicago Board of Trade Battery, *Historical Sketch of the Chicago Board of Trade Battery*, 43, 89.

22 Minty, "Minty's Saber Brigade," *National Tribune*, March 3, 1892.

The Lightning Brigade was seemingly everywhere on the battlefield during the two days of brutal fighting that occurred on September 19 and 20. For two days and two nights the lines of the Lightning Brigade held, including holding their position at the Widow Glenn farm property on the afternoon of September 20 while Rosecrans's position on the southern end of the battlefield melted away under the force of a sledgehammer attack by Longstreet's troops. After repulsing determined attack after attack until the action shifted north toward Horseshoe Ridge, Wilder's troops leisurely withdrew, claiming the honor of being the only portion of the Army of the Cumberland's forces not to give way at any time during the battle of Chickamauga. Their performance there was extraordinary, proving beyond doubt that Wilder's experiment of using mounted infantry armed with rapid-firing Spencer rifles could be extremely effective on the battlefield.[23]

The Army of the Cumberland's commander, Maj. Gen. William S. Rosecrans, in praising "the brilliant part" Wilder's Lightning Brigade played during the campaign, wrote: "His bold and successful advance on Dalton and reconnaissance thence by Leet's Tanyard to Gordon's Mills unquestionably checked a very serious movement on Crittenden's corps, at a time when it would have been very dangerous to us. His command also merits the thanks of the country for its noble stand at the crossing of the Chickamauga, where his and Minty's cavalry brigade resisted the enemy so obstinately on the afternoon of the 18th." The Ohioan concluded, "I trust Colonel Wilder will be promoted for his many gallant services."[24]

A former Confederate officer twice wounded at Chickamauga, Tomlinson Fort Jr., who later served as mayor of Chattanooga, declared, "There were no better fighters in the Federal Army" than the Lightning Brigade. He also said that Wilder "always got the 'mostest' men to the place before the other fellow, and that, Forrest said, was war. There was not another brigade in the Federal Army that made such a reputation for fighting so far as we were concerned." The Lightning Brigade proved the truth of that statement beyond any doubt during the three days of fighting at Chickamauga.[25]

23 For a detailed monograph devoted to the role of the Lightning Brigade during the entire battle of Chickamauga, see Baumgartner, *Blue Lightning*.

24 *OR* 30, pt.1, 79.

25 Quoted in the *Chattanooga Times*, September 21, 1899.

"The fame of Wilder's Brigade cannot perish from the memories of men so long as mankind shall reverence true bravery and undaunted courage," declared Indiana governor Claude Matthews at the dedication of the Chickamauga and Chattanooga National Military Park in 1895. "To Indiana is due the credit of the fame of the brigade, for the 17th Indiana Regiment furnished the leader, Colonel John T. Wilder."[26] Major General George H. Thomas, recognizing the critical service performed by the Lightning Brigade on the night of September 18, recommended Wilder for promotion to brigadier general, declaring, "For his ingenuity and fertility of resource in occupying the attention of an entire corps while our army was getting around its flank."[27] Wilder instead received a brevet to brigadier general of volunteers for his extraordinary service at Chickamauga.

He never got to wear the stars of a full-rank general, however, even though both Rosecrans and Thomas recommended him for promotion several times. On September 22, just two days after the end of the battle of Chickamauga, Wilder reported that he was too unwell for further duty and turned over command of the Lightning Brigade to Col. Abram O. Miller of the 17th Indiana. On September 25 he took a leave of absence. Although he returned to duty in October, Wilder's health remained precarious for the balance of his service with the Army of the Cumberland.[28] After participating in the Atlanta campaign, he went to Nashville, where his always delicate health failed as a lingering result of the typhoid fever that laid him low after the battle of Corinth in 1862. In the fall of 1864 Wilder's continued poor health finally forced him to resign his commission. Colonel Miller was a competent soldier who had demonstrated his value on numerous battlefields, including Chickamauga, and he commanded the Lightning Brigade for the rest of the war.[29]

After the war, Wilder recognized that East Tennessee offered him many opportunities for commercial success. In 1867 he organized the

26 Henry V. Boynton, comp., *Dedication of the Chickamauga and Chattanooga National Military Park, September 18-20, 1895* (Washington, DC: Government Printing Office, 1896), 262.

27 Quoted in Samuel C. Williams, "General John T. Wilder," *Indiana Magazine of History* 31, no. 3 (1935): 190.

28 *OR* 30, pt. 3, 779.

29 Williams, "General John T. Wilder," 195.

Roane Iron Works and operated the first two modern iron-blast furnaces in the South at Rockwood, Tennessee. In 1870 he built a rail mill in Chattanooga and became very wealthy in the iron and coal businesses. He was the general manager of the Roane Iron Company, president and proprietor of the Wilder Machine Works, vice president of the Cleveland, Columbus and Cincinnati Railroad, president of the Roane Mountain Hotel Company, and general manager of the Fentress Coal and Coke Company during his long and successful postwar career. Sadly, he lost much of his fortune during the panic of 1893, but he remained in the business until 1911, when he finally retired from his remaining ventures.

Wilder married Martha Jane Stewart of Greensburg, Indiana, in 1858, and they raised five daughters and one son. She "was a devout member of the Methodist Church" and "possessed many fine qualities of heart and mind, and was most devoted to the welfare of her husband and children." Martha Wilder died on February 29, 1892. In 1904, Wilder married Dora E. Lee, the daughter of a Confederate officer and a relative of Robert E. Lee. Dora was an accomplished woman in her own right; she was the first woman to pass the medical licensing examination in Tennessee. They lived together happily for the remainder of his life.[30]

"It would be difficult to include in one brief sketch the many varied civic and industrial activities of General Wilder," declared one who tried. "He has built railroads, turnpike roads and hotels, has founded and extended great industrial plants, and in every position has been a leader. He represented the state of Tennessee as commissioner to the World's Fair at Vienna. He was one of the organizers of the Republican Party in the middle fifties, and has always been loyal to its principles. [In 1896], he was nominated by his party for congressman in the Chattanooga district, and cut the normal majority from three thousand to four hundred. At Knoxville he served as pension agent for eight years, and is one of the commissioners of the Chickamauga Battlefield Park. He was once elected mayor of Chattanooga [in 1871], though he served only eight months, when he resigned. During that time, however, he established the free school system of the city." In 1877 he was appointed postmaster of Chattanooga and held that position until 1882. In 1897 he moved

30 Hale and Merritt, *A History of Tennessee and Tennesseans*, vol. 6, 1608-12.

to Knoxville after receiving an appointment from President William McKinley as federal pension agent.[31]

"Perhaps no incident in Wilder's post-war career so marks the man as his intervention to prevent the arrest and prosecution of General Nathan Bedford Forrest when the latter was charged with breaking the terms of his parole on surrender in 1865 by taking part in the operations of the original Ku Klux Klan. On learning of the steps being taken against Forrest, Wilder visited Forrest in Memphis to get from him his own statement as to his motives and attitude," wrote an early biographer of Wilder. "Convinced that Forrest had sincerely headed the Klan for the protection and betterment of his people, Wilder went to Washington and prevailed upon President Grant to see that no arrest should be made of the great Southern leader. There can be little doubt that Grant was easily persuaded, though Wilder had enlisted the aid of Senators Oliver P. Morton and John A. Logan and Richard J. Oglesby. General and Mrs. Forrest paid a return visit of a week to the Wilders in their home on the terrace in Chattanooga. Many a story of the war must then have been told!"[32]

The appointment as a commissioner of the Chickamauga and Chattanooga National Military Park particularly suited the old soldier, who took great pleasure in taking veterans of both sides to the Chickamauga battlefield and reliving their exploits with them. As demonstrated by the episode with Forrest above, Wilder seemed to have a special affinity for old foes that came back to see the battlefield and to relive their memories with the former commander of the Lightning Brigade. He was a familiar sight on that old hallowed ground.

Despite the harm done to his health by his 1862 bout with typhoid fever, John T. Wilder nevertheless reached old age. He died in Jacksonville, Florida, on October 20, 1917, at the ripe old age of 87. He and Dora were in Florida, enjoying their annual winter vacation, when he died suddenly. His remains were returned to Chattanooga, and Wilder was buried alongside his first wife, Martha, in Forest Hills Cemetery. "We feel that an edition, the chief object of which is to celebrate the growth of Chattanooga, would be incomplete if it omitted to fittingly acknowledge the services

31 Ibid., vol. 6, 1608-13.

32 Williams, "General John T. Wilder," 202.

A post-war view of Minty as a Brevet Brigadier General. *Judith Minty*

of General John T. Wilder in the days of the town's small things," wrote publisher Adolph Ochs in an editorial that ran in a special edition of the *Chattanooga Times* on December 8, 1892, describing the Hoosier's entire life and contributions. "He has been the true-tried, never-flinching friend of Chattanooga in sunshine, stormy adversity and prosperity. He cannot be forgotten or neglected but by the ungrateful."[33] Brevet Brigadier General John T. Wilder lived a long and productive life, earning great success in every field of endeavor that he tried, be they military, industrial, or political. Wilder was that rare sort of self-made genius who did so much to make the United States the world leader that it became after the Civil War. But nowhere did he contribute more than on the battlefield at Chickamauga.

Unlike his comrade in arms, Col. Robert H. G. Minty served throughout the war. In the fall of 1863, however, shortly after the action at Chickamauga, he was arrested and court-martialed for "disobedience to orders and conduct subversive of good order and military discipline" on charges brought by his new division commander, Brig. Gen. George Crook, after his brigade unexpectedly arrived late for an on October 7 encounter with Wheeler's troopers at Farmington, Tennessee. While Crook remained in the field, the unresolved charges prevented Minty from commanding his brigade for the next four months, which rankled him immensely. "There is no foundation for the charges," he declared, feeling like he had been "cast aside like a piece of useless furniture."[34]

33 Special edition, *Chattanooga Times*, December 8, 1892.

34 Robert H. G. Minty to John Robertson, January 13, 1864, RG 59-14, Records of the Michigan Military Establishment, National Archives and Records Administration, Washington, DC.

The trial lasted for several days in February 1864. Crook testified that he gave Minty verbal orders to march at daylight on the day in question, but when asked whether he had specified the time, the road, and the direction Minty was to take, Crook admitted that he could not remember. The court-martial board found that Crook's orders were vague and quickly acquitted Minty of the charges. The colonel then returned to his command after four long, unwelcome months away from his beloved Saber Brigade.[35]

Although he was acquitted, the court martial undoubtedly played a role on preventing Minty from ever receiving a well-deserved promotion to brigadier general. In August 1864, in a letter to the adjutant general of Michigan, Minty complained that when his command returned from Brig. Gen. Judson Kilpatrick's ill-fated cavalry raid into Georgia that summer, "We found that Colonel [Eli] Long [who formerly commanded a regiment in Minty's brigade] had been appointed a Brigadier. At Stones River he was a Captain and I a Brigade Commander. Since then he has repeatedly acted under my orders. Next time we go out together I will have to act under his. I am the *oldest Brigade Commander* in the cavalry of this Army and I am now the Junior Brigade Commander in my own Division."[36] The requested promotion never came through, although Minty did receive a brevet to brigadier general and then a second brevet to major general for his distinguished service in the war.

After his acquittal, Minty ably and effectively commanded his brigade throughout the campaigns of 1864, prompting the Michigan adjutant general to write, "During Sherman's last campaign, Minty with his brigade was always where hard work and desperate fighting were to be performed," including a desperate saber charge, "literally cutting his way through the rebel army and saving Kilpatrick's command."[37] During the winter of 1864-65, Minty's brigade was transferred to the cavalry corps of Maj. Gen. James H. Wilson, which was preparing to

35 Bitter, *Minty and His Cavalry*, 157-71. Bitter provides a detailed discussion of the court-martial charges and proceedings that the reader should investigate if these events are of interest.

36 Ibid., 279.

37 Quoted in R. H. G. Minty, "Picketing and Scouting: Incidents in the History of the Saber Brigade, Army of the Cumberland," *National Tribune*, April 4, 1895.

campaign through the Deep South. On April 2, 1865, Wilson's command steamrolled a smaller scratch force commanded by Forrest, now a lieutenant general. At Selma, Alabama, Minty personally led a determined saber charge upon the rebel earthworks that resembled his greatest moment at Shelbyville in June 1863.

During this long raid through Alabama, Minty assumed command of a division, the highest command he would achieve during his military service, but he did so as a colonel. After the surrender of Confederate forces in Virginia and North Carolina, Minty's troopers led the pursuit of President Jefferson Davis, who was then fleeing for his life. A detachment of Minty's own 4th Michigan Cavalry men captured Davis on May 10, 1865, much to the delight of their old commander. General Wilson made one last effort to obtain a promotion for the diminutive Englishman, hoping that it would enable the army to retain Minty in the service. But it was too late. He and the men of the 4th Michigan Cavalry were on their way home.

Of his own military career, Minty said, "I was four years, less 15 days, in the service and never lost a flag, a guidon or a gun." He added, "with his usual luck," he survived the war "without a scratch" and was "personally engaged in 109 battles and skirmishes in which blood flowed, he had five horses shot under him . . . and thirteen bullets pierced his clothing." The Saber Brigade distinguished itself in most of those engagements, earning eternal glory for the troopers that followed Minty's guidon. His war and his military career, however, were now over.[38]

After the war, Minty returned to Detroit to resume his life with his wife and family. When he mustered out of the volunteer service, he was offered a commission as a major in the newly formed 8th U.S. Cavalry, but he turned down the offer immediately, a decision that he later regretted.[39] Instead, he resumed his career in railroading. He took a job as an agent with the Michigan Central Railroad Company in Detroit. Soon the family relocated to Jackson, Michigan, about 75 miles west of Detroit. He then helped to build the Grand River Valley Railroad, a new line that opened in 1869, acting as its general construction superintendent. For the next

38 Quoted in Bitter, *Minty and His Cavalry*, 391.

39 Ibid., 442.

several years Minty worked for a variety of different railroads around the country.

After one of their children died, Minty and his wife, Grace, began to drift apart. Grace's younger sister, Laura, had stayed with the family until 1871, when she announced she wanted to earn a living on her own. This was a ruse. Laura instead took up with Minty, her brother-in-law, while he was working in New Albany, Indiana, for a few years. The couple had a child in southern Indiana at about the same time that Grace gave birth to another daughter in Michigan. Although he and Grace did not divorce, for years Minty lived with Laura as if they were married instead of living with his wife, raising several children concurrently with those that Grace was rearing. When this web of deceit finally came to light and fell apart, it cost Minty the most lucrative job of his life. Minty begged Grace to lie for him in order to save his job, but the faithful woman refused to participate in the subterfuge and would not agree to a divorce. Minty was forced to resign in disgrace. In 1884 Minty and Laura were married after Minty hired a crooked lawyer to obtain a sham divorce from Grace. While technically not bigamy due to the fraudulent divorce, it was quite unsavory and also dangerously close to bigamy, which was illegal in all states.[40]

In 1886 Robert and Laura Minty relocated to Ogden, Utah, to take a position with a new line being built, the Utah and Northern Railroad, and then a position with the Union Pacific Railroad. While he resided in Utah, Minty began to write articles for a popular newspaper for Union veterans of the Civil War called the *National Tribune*, which was published in Washington, DC.[41] He spent many years composing a series of articles that, when compiled together, were a detailed memoir of his Civil War service as well as a history of the Saber Brigade. Minty published dozens of these articles, which were largely lost to history until author Rand Bitter compiled them in a single volume, which

40 The foregoing information was distilled from Bitter, *Minty and His Cavalry*, 379-438.

41 Founded in 1877, the *National Tribune* claimed a circulation of 250,000 at the height of its popularity. The last paper published under the banner of the *National Tribune* was in 1917. The paper's name was then changed to *Stars and Stripes* to cover the First World War. *Stars and Stripes* is still published today.

was published in 2006.[42] Beginning in 1901, Minty wrote a number of articles on the Civil War that were published in the *Los Angeles Times*. He participated in various veterans' activities, including heading a post of the Grand Army of the Republic—a veterans organization much like today's American Legion—doing all he could to preserve the memory of the sacrifices of the soldiers who followed his guidon. He held such posts in Odgen, Utah, and Tucson, Arizona.

After spending years in Utah, with many intervening summers in Butte, Montana, and following a failed bid for an appointment as U.S. marshal for Utah, Minty moved in 1896 to the small copper-mining town of Jerome, Arizona, where he managed the mine's railroad operations. After several years, he commuted hundreds of miles south to Tucson, where he spent three years organizing and funding a future road between Phoenix and southern Mexico, but the venture came to naught. He returned broke to Jerome and ran a small lumber yard in his old age, but only for a short time.[43]

Minty died on August 24, 1906, at the age of 74. The feisty little Englishman was buried in Ogden, Utah, where he had spent much of his postwar life. Both Grace and Laura survived him, and both filed claims for his pension. Even in death, their bitter fight over him continued. Grace was ultimately awarded the widow's military pension after a lengthy proceeding to determine which woman was rightfully entitled to it.[44]

John T. Wilder and Robert H. G. Minty both played significant roles in the ultimate Union victory in the Civil War, but nowhere was their influence more felt or more critical than at two obscure, otherwise anonymous crossings on West Chickamauga Creek—Reed's Bridge and Alexander's Bridge—on September 18, 1863. Their stands that day saved the Army of the Cumberland from an even worse defeat than it suffered at the battle of Chickamauga and gave it a chance to live on and fight another day and achieve the battlefield glory found in 1864 and 1865.

42 Unfortunately this book was privately published by Bitter in 2006 and had very short print runs. It can be very difficult and expensive to purchase, if a copy can even be located. Seriously interested parties should seek to contact him directly.

43 Detailed in Bitter, *Minty and His Cavalry*.

44 Ibid., 492-500.

I hope this volume has given the reader an appreciation of the long odds these men faced that pivotal day and of the extraordinary job they did in carrying out the very difficult mission given them by William S. Rosecrans on that occasion.

Epilogue

In 1888 the U.S. War Department began taking steps to develop the Chickamauga battlefield into "a western Gettysburg—a Chickamauga memorial."[1] By that time numerous monuments had already been erected at Gettysburg, and Bvt. Brig. Gen. Henry V. Boynton, who had been lieutenant colonel of the 35th Ohio Volunteer Infantry at Chickamauga, was determined to create a similar commemoration. With John T. Wilder elected as its first president, the Chickamauga Memorial Association was formed in 1889. Major General Joseph Wheeler, former Confederate cavalry corps commander, was elected vice president in a show of postwar unity.

After drafting the authorizing legislation, Boynton presented his case to Congress, which passed the necessary enabling act and authorized the creation of the Chickamauga and Chattanooga National Military Park, comprising nearly 8,000 acres and two major battlefields, to be placed under the jurisdiction of the War Department. After going through the legislative process and undergoing amendments, the bill authorizing the formation of the park and appropriating funds for the acquisition of land finally passed. President Benjamin Harrison signed the bill on

1 Quoted in Timothy B. Smith, *A Chickamauga Memorial: The Establishment of America's First Civil War National Military Park* (Knoxville: University of Tennessee Press, 2009), 13. Smith has written a fascinating book that describes the hurdles faced as well as the steps taken to commemorate the battlefield at Chickamauga.

Veterans of the 7th Pennsylvania Cavalry at their monument. *Pennsylvania at Chickamauga and Chattanooga*

August 20, 1890. The first national military park commemorating the Civil War had been formed.[2]

Boynton was appointed the new park's official historian, and steps were taken to build roads, lay out the park itself, and then mark it with memorials. Each regiment was permitted to place a monument at the point where it played its most significant role in the battle, as well as additional location markers anywhere else those units fought on the battlefield. Finally, Wilder's Lightning Brigade, which has markers scattered all over the Chickamauga battlefield, was also given permission to construct a brigade monument on the Widow Glenn farm where Wilder's men made their epic stand on September 20, 1863. By 1895 the pieces were in place.

The new park was dedicated on August 18-20, 1895, on the 32nd anniversary of the great battle. The first day, September 18, was set aside for various states to dedicate their monuments on the battlefield. Thus it was most appropriate the monuments to Minty's and Wilder's brigades were dedicated on the anniversary of their stands at Reed's and Alexander's Bridges. The Michigan and Missouri commissions dedicated their monuments that morning while Ohio and Wisconsin

2 Ibid., 13-36. The bulk of the Chickamauga battlefield proper lies within the park boundaries, whereas only small sections of the Chattanooga battlefield are included. The Chattanooga unit was developed using the so-called Antietam Plan, whereby only sufficient land to build roads and have a place to erect monuments was purchased.

dedicated theirs at noon, with Illinois, Indiana, and Minnesota at 2:00, and Massachusetts dedicating its units at 4:00 that afternoon. Tens of thousands attended, and so did Governor William McKinley of Ohio, a prominent Civil War veteran and a future U.S. president. Reunions for the veterans were held on the nights of September 19 and 20, with former Confederate general and then U.S. Senator Edward C. Walthall presiding at the Confederate reunion.[3]

All of the official proceedings were compiled by Boynton into a single 374-page book titled *Dedication of the Chickamauga and Chattanooga National Military Park, September 18-20, 1895: Report of the Joint Committee to Represent the Congress at the Dedication of the Chickamauga and Chattanooga National Military Park.*[4] Most of the states that dedicated monuments also published their own books to commemorate the dedication ceremonies, including Pennsylvania, Michigan, and Indiana.

The monuments to the three regiments of the Saber Brigade are on the site of Jay's Sawmill, where Minty's troopers made their last stand in the fight to defend Reed's Bridge. Originally, the battlefield park was going to include the ground around Reed's Bridge where Minty's troopers made their stand on September 18, but that land was not purchased. Thus the monuments were erected at the sawmill site. Some of that land has since been acquired by the Civil War Trust and will soon be incorporated into the national park.

The monument to the 7th Pennsylvania Cavalry features a handsome bas-relief of a mounted trooper, while a bronze plaque affixed to the monument to the 4th Michigan Cavalry shows the fighting at Reed's Bridge in some detail. The monument to the 4th U.S. Cavalry was also placed there. A few hundred yards to the west along the Reed's Bridge Road are position markers for the brigades of Daniel McCook Jr. and Mitchell, situated where they spent that long, cold night.

Robert H. G. Minty, 63 years old at the time, delivered the keynote speech at the dedication of the monument to his old regiment, the 4th Michigan Cavalry. After reviewing the history of the Tullahoma campaign

3 Ibid., 57-59.

4 Boynton also published a touring guide to the Chickamauga battlefield that is still useful. See Henry V. Boynton, *The National Military Park: Chickamauga-Chattanooga, An Historical Guide, With Maps and Illustrations* (Cincinnati: Robert Clarke Co., 1895).

and the events preceding Chickamauga, Minty delved into a detailed description of the fighting at Reed's Bridge on September 18, 1863, as well as the activities that occurred that night. He then addressed his brigade's role in the rest of the battle of Chickamauga.

He concluded his valediction in a grand style: "We, my comrades, hold a proper and enviable pride in the brilliant record made by our regiments and our brigade; and we will leave that record as a treasured inheritance to our children, with the pleasing consciousness that not many years hence, when we, old white headed men, have answered our last roll call on earth, and have joined the Grand Army beyond, they will take a personal and honorable pride in the treasured heirloom, and in having the right to say, 'Our fathers were members of the Saber Brigade of the Army of the Cumberland.'"[5]

Minty then arranged for the dedication speech to be published in a pamphlet. Most but not all of the speech was also included in a book published by the state of Michigan that included all of the dedication speeches for the Michigan units that fought at both Chickamauga and Chattanooga.

Minty's former staff officer, Capt. Joseph G. Vale, delivered the primary speech at the dedication of the monument to the 7th Pennsylvania Cavalry, which occurred on November 15, 1897. After covering the Saber Regiment's role in the campaign, Vale concluded: "The casualties are a matter of public record and need not be specifically adverted to here. Our dead we mourned as we had honored and respected them in life. Our wounded and disabled we have succored and sustained. And here, on this historic field, we place this monument, with its inscriptions and tablets, as a reminder to posterity of some part of Pennsylvania's contribution to the peace and prosperity the nation today enjoys."[6]

A number of 7th Pennsylvania officers also addressed the regiment's veterans that day, including adjutant Lt. George F. Steahlin, Capt. Heber S. Thompson (whose detachment opened the ball at Reed's Bridge), Lt. Col. Charles L. Greeno, and Medal of Honor recipient Maj. Charles C. Davis. "We are proud of the record of the old Seventh, not only

5 Charles E. Belknap, comp., *History of the Michigan Organizations at Chickamauga, Chattanooga and Missionary Ridge 1863* (Lansing: Robert Smith Printing Co., 1899), 280; Minty, *Remarks of Brevet Major General R. H. G. Minty*, 10.

6 Vale, "Address of Capt. Joseph G. Vale," 308.

in the battle of Chickamauga, but in the more than one hundred other engagements in which we had a part," declared a proud Greeno. "We never failed to meet the expectations of our superior officers in the performance of any duty assigned to us. We are here, a goodly number, I am glad to say, just for a few hours; many of us meeting for the first time since we were mustered out at Harrisburg at the close of the war."[7]

Colonel Abram Miller of the 72nd Indiana, who succeeded Wilder in command of the Lightning Brigade, suggested erecting a monument to the entire Lightning Brigade. He proposed each regiment's veterans donate $1,000 and the veterans of Lilly's battery donate $500. Wilder agreed to match whatever amount the veterans raised. In 1892 Wilder received a contract to build the monument, a tower, but it was nearly abandoned due to the financial panic of 1893. The yet-unfinished edifice, along with the individual memorial markers to the various units of the Lightning Brigade and Lilly's battery in West Viniard field, was dedicated with the rest of the battlefield park on September 19, 1895. The brigade monument was finally completed in 1899. It stands nearly 90 feet tall and greatly resembles a rook, such as one would find on a chessboard. It stands atop a slight rise on the Widow Glenn farm property, dominating that portion of the battlefield, just as the Lightning Bridge itself did on September 20, 1863. Those who climb to its summit are afforded a spectacular view of much of the battlefield.

The reunion of the veterans of the Lightning Brigade was held on the Chickamauga battlefield, where the veterans of Chattanooga's N. B. Forrest Camp of the United Confederate Veterans joined them in a show of unity. Major James Connolly of the 123rd Illinois gave the dedication speech and was followed by seven other speakers, including Brig. Gen. Smith D. Atkins of the 92nd Illinois, Illinois governor John Riley Tanner (who had served in the 98th Illinois), and finally by the former commander of the Lightning Brigade, John T. Wilder himself.

A visibly emotional Wilder turned the monument over to the national park and proudly declared:

> This monument to steadfast patriotism and unyielding courage was built by contributions from the gallant men who composed the Brigade. It stands on

7 Greeno, "Address of Lieut.-Col. Charles L. Greeno," in *Pennsylvania at Chickamauga*, 313.

> the spot where General Rosecrans' headquarters were on the 19th and forenoon of the 20th. It is erected in no vainglorious mood. It marks the line where the bravest of brave Americans met in headlong conflict, each determined to win, and where the best armament proved successful. On this grand battlefield thousands died in defense of those principles that they had been trained to believe in, and which they thoroughly believed were right; where else on God's earth could such a conflict be carried to a close and find such results? These men were honorable Americans, and when the war was fought to a finish all agreed to live in peace, and have honestly kept their compact. No other people could have done this in good faith.
>
> I am as proud of the memory of those who died under one flag as I am of those who fell under the other; both believed that they were right; both died for the right as they saw it. We who fought for the stars and stripes give the hand of friendly fellowship to those who fought for the stars and bars. The sons of both sides have proved their readiness to march shoulder to shoulder to any part of the world where their common country calls and prove that their chief pride is in showing how the sons of the men of the great Civil War can best imitate the actions of their fathers. I have the honor of turning over the custody of this monument. May it stand for ages to show the coming generations how their ancestors fought for their principles. It stands as a monument to the valor of those who fought on both sides. May its lessons be learned by all our descendants.[8]

The proceedings from the dedication of the Wilder Brigade Monument were published for posterity, preserving Wilder's sentiments for future generations.

Thus the regiments of both the Saber Brigade and the Lightning Brigade have all been properly commemorated on the Chickamauga battlefield. Their valor and their sacrifice stand in silent witness to the severe fighting that took place on September 18, 1863. Even though that dry, dusty Friday has traditionally not been considered part of the main battle of Chickamauga, the exploits of the 3,200 Union soldiers of those two brigades held off nearly 20,000 Confederates for most of that day, thwarted Bragg's best-laid battle plans, and saved the Army of the Cumberland from almost certain destruction.

8 Kilborn, *Dedication of the Wilder Brigade Monument*, 19.

Appendix A

Order of Battle, Reed's Bridge, September 18, 1863

UNION FORCES
ARMY OF THE CUMBERLAND
Major General William S. Rosecrans

CAVALRY CORPS
Brigadier General Robert B. Mitchell

2ND DIVISION
Brigadier General George Crook

1ST BRIGADE
Colonel Robert H. G. Minty
4th Michigan Cavalry (Maj. Horace Gray)
4th U. S. Cavalry (Capt. James B. McIntyre)
7th Pennsylvania Cavalry (Lt. Col. James B. Seibert)

HORSE ARTILLERY
CHICAGO BOARD OF TRADE BATTERY
Second Section (two guns) (Lt. Trumbull D. Griffin)

14TH CORPS
Major General George H. Thomas

4TH DIVISION
Major General Joseph J. Reynolds

1ST BRIGADE
Colonel John T. Wilder
Detachment: 72nd Indiana Mounted Infantry (Col. Abram O. Miller)
123rd Illinois Mounted Infantry (Col. James Monroe)

CONFEDERATE FORCES
ARMY OF TENNESSEE
General Braxton Bragg

LONGSTREET'S CORPS
Brigadier General Bushrod R. Johnson
Major General John B. Hood

JOHNSON'S PROVISIONAL DIVISION
Brigadier General Bushrod R. Johnson

JOHNSON'S BRIGADE
Colonel John S. Fulton
17th Tennessee Infantry (Lt. Col. Watt W. Floyd)
23rd Tennessee Infantry (Col. R. H. Keeble)
25th Tennessee Infantry (Lt. Col. R. B. Snowdon)
44th Tennessee Infantry (Lt. Col. John L. McEwen, Jr.)
Battery E, 9th Georgia Artillery Battalion (Lt. William S. Everett)

GREGG'S BRIGADE
Brigadier General John Gregg
3rd Tennessee Infantry (Col. Calvin H. Walker)
10th Tennessee Infantry (Col. William Grace)
30th Tennessee Infantry (Lt. Col. James J. Walker)
41st Tennessee Infantry (Lt. Col. James D. Tillman)
50th Tennessee Infantry (Col. Cyrus A. Sugg)
1st Tennessee Infantry Battalion (Maj. Stephen H. Colms)
7th Texas Infantry (Col. Hiram B. Granbury)
Bledsoe's (Missouri) Battery (Lt. R. L. Wood)

HOOD'S DIVISION
Brigadier General Evander M. Law

ROBERTSON'S BRIGADE
Brigadier General Jerome B. Robertson
3rd Arkansas Infantry (Co. Van H. Manning)
1st Texas Infantry (Capt. R. J. Harding)
4th Texas Infantry (Lt. Col. John P. Bane)
5th Texas Infantry (Maj. J. C. Rogers)

FORREST'S CAVALRY CORPS
Brigadier General Nathan Bedford Forrest

Escort Company: Jackson's Tennessee Cavalry (Capt. J. C. Jackson)

PEGRAM'S DIVISION

Brigadier General John Pegram

SCOTT'S BRIGADE

Colonel John S. Scott

Detachment of John Hunt Morgan's Command (Lt. Col. R. M. Martin)

Appendix B

Order of Battle, Alexander's Bridge, September 18, 1863

UNION FORCES
ARMY OF THE CUMBERLAND
Major General William S. Rosecrans

14TH CORPS
Major General George H. Thomas

4TH DIVISION
Major General Joseph J. Reynolds

1ST BRIGADE
Colonel John T. Wilder
17th Indiana Mounted Infantry (Maj. William T. Jones)
Detachment: 72nd Indiana Mounted Infantry (Col. Abram O. Miller)
18th Battery, Indiana Light Artillery (Capt. Eli Lilly)

CONFEDERATE FORCES
ARMY OF TENNESSEE
General Braxton Bragg

RESERVE CORPS
Major General William H. T. Walker

LIDDELL'S DIVISION
Brigadier General St. John R. Liddell

LIDDELL'S BRIGADE
Colonel Daniel C. Govan
2nd–15th Arkansas Infantry (Lt. Col. Reuben F. Harvey)
5th–13th Arkansas Infantry (Col. L. Featherston)

6th–7th Arkansas Infantry (Col. D. A. Gillespie)
8th Arkansas Infantry (Lt. Col. George F. Baucum)

WALTHALL'S BRIGADE

Brigadier General Edward C. Walthall
24th Mississippi Infantry (Lt. Col. R. P. McKelvaine)
27th Mississippi Infantry (Col. James A. Campbell)
29th Mississippi Infantry (Col. William F. Brantley)
30th Mississippi Infantry (Col. Junius I. Scales)
34th Mississippi Infantry (Maj. William G. Pegram)

ARTILLERY BATTALION

Captain Charles Swett
Fowler's (Alabama) Battery (Capt. William H. Fowler)
Warren Light Artillery (Mississippi) (Lt. H. Shannon)

Appendix C

Vidette and Outpost Duty Defined

Major General Antoine Fortuné De Brack was a French cavalry officer and the leading theorist of light cavalry operations of the nineteenth century. His writings on the subject remained the primary treatise for about a century until horse cavalry finally became obsolete with the development of tanks and other modern armored vehicles.

De Brack was born in 1789 as the son of a royal tax collector. On December 30, 1805, the 16-year-old boy was admitted to the Fontainebleau military school before he transferred to the French Military Academy of Saint Cyr in 1806. After graduating on March 5, 1807, he was assigned to the 7th Hussars in Silesia in Germany. He participated in the French Grand Army's campaigns in Prussia, Poland, Germany, and Russia during the Napoleonic Wars. He received the Legion of Honor for his valor at the July 5–6, 1809 battle of Wagram, wherein Napoleon's Grand Army defeated the Austrian Army of the Archduke Charles. After the Napoleonic Wars, De Brack spent a number of years as an aide-de-camp to the Emperor of Brazil, Dom Pedro. In 1830, he transferred to the 3rd Chasseurs with the rank of lieutenant colonel and was then promoted to colonel of the 4th Hussar Regiment in 1832. He was eventually promoted to major general on August 24, 1838, and commanded the School of Cavalry at Saumur until 1840. "Independently of his chivalrous courage proven numerous times on the fields of battle, General Brack was gifted with a robust natural spirit and originality which caused the world to seek him out, and he possessed a perfect knowledge in matters of arms (military strategy)." He was placed on leave during the revolution of February 1848, and died on January 21, 1850.[1]

1 Charles Mullié, *Biographie des célébrités militaires des armées de terre et de mer de 1789 à 1850*, 2 vols (Paris: Poignavant et Compagnie, 1852), vol. 1, 227-228. The author is grateful to Daniel Mallock and Christopher Carson for translating the pertinent passages for him.

He wrote the first edition of his book *Outposts of the Light Cavalry* in 1831. The critical little volume was reprinted numerous times, and remained a standard reference for French Army officers until the Second World War. It was translated into German and was used by the German Army until First World War. In 1893, Maj. Camillo C. C. Carr of the 8th U. S. Cavalry translated the 1863 edition of the book into English and published it in the United States. Carr's translation remained a standard reference for the United States Army's horse cavalry until the last units were dismounted in 1932.[2] West Point instructor Dennis Hart Mahan, who drafted most of the U. S. Army's field manuals during the first half of the nineteenth century and who was a keen student of Napoleonic tactics, incorporated most of De Brack's theories into his works, including his seminal 1861 outposting treatise and the 1863 outposting manual mentioned in Chapter 3 of this book.

De Brack's book provides the best description of how nineteenth century light cavalry performed the sort of vidette, patrol and outpost duty that is featured in this book, which is why it is presented here verbatim, including the original spellings of words.[3] To assist the reader in gaining a better understanding of how Civil War-era light cavalry performed these duties, I have decided to include Carr's translation of the entire chapter of De Brack's book that deals with vidette, patrol and outpost duty verbatim in this appendix. Even though De Brack's work spells out Napoleonic tactics, those tactics remained in widespread use for another century, meaning that De Brack's work remained a valid and appropriate treatise in 1863. Hopefully, the reader will find it an interesting and educational reference. The chapter was written in a question and answer format.

GRAND GUARDS, PICKETS, SMALL POSTS, VEDETTES, AND PATROLS

Q. *What is a grand guard?*

A. An advance guard placed between the main body and one of its detachments, to relieve or support the vedettes in case of an attack by the enemy, in order to give the necessary time to the detachment or cantonment which is cover, to prepare for defense or retreat.

Q. *Where is the grand guard posted?*

A. Upon the route by which it is presumed the enemy will advance to attack the bivouac.

Q. *Why?*

A. To delay the attack and give the bivouac time to prepare to meet it in good shape. As nearly as possible at the center of the line of vedettes.

2 Antoine Fortuné De Brack, *Cavalry Outpost Duties*, Maj. Camillo C. C. Carr, trans. (New York: John Wiley & Sons, 1893).

3 There are two spellings of the word "vidette" that are both proper, the other being "vedette." While I have chosen to use the spelling "vidette" in the main body of this book, I have maintained Carr's translation here, including his use of the spelling "vedette."

Q. *Why?*

A. So that the vedettes attacked will, in retreating upon it, be at the same time approaching their supports. Therefore the junction of several roads or paths is a favorable place for posting a grand guard. The latter should bear to the vedettes the same relation that the hinged end of a fan does to the upper ends of its spread sticks.

Q. *Who posts the grand guard?*

A. The commanding officer himself, unless he has with him an experienced officer worthy of his entire confidence.

Q. *When does he post it?*

A. After having reconnoitered the ground thoroughly, and obtained the best possible information concerning it.

Q. *How is the strength of the grand guard determined?*

A. By the number of vedettes required, allowing for four men for each vedette posted.

Q. *How is a grand guard formed?*

A. Upon reaching the ground where it is to be posted, the advance guard being mounted, the men detailed for the grand guard move out of ranks, and place themselves in front of the line, facing the enemy. The officers designated to command them cause them to break into columns and march under the direction of the commander of the advance guard, who has already reconnoitered the ground. On arriving at the place where the grand guard is to take post, they form line and halt. Then the men who are to form the small posts are designated, and they move out of ranks to the front and face toward the enemy. The corporals, or old soldiers, who are to command the small posts of four mean each, move out of ranks and recognize the men who are to be placed under their command. This preparatory work having been completed, the small post detachments are reunited and marched off under the orders of the commander of the grand guard, and under the direction of the commander of the advance guard, or the office detailed to perform this duty; this officer moves toward the center of the line of small posts about to be established, and halts. The central post is first placed, as well as the vedette which it is to furnish, then the posts which are to occupy the line upon one of the flanks move out together, and are posted successively, as well as their vedettes. This duty performed, the commander of the advance guard, always accompanied by that of the grand guard, returns to the central point, inspecting on his way the line of vedettes he has just traced, and rectifying it if necessary; then he completes the line by doing for the second part of his small post detachments what he did for the first.

Q. *Has he no duty to perform in regard to the posting of the vedettes?*

A. Yes; to give to the commander of the grand guard all the topographical information he possesses in regard to the ground, and to communicate to him his ideas as to the probable operations of the enemy, so that he may be fully advised as to the point he must specially watch. To these details he adds such orders as he thinks should be executed under such or such circumstances.

Q. *What does the commander of the grand guard do upon returning to his post?*

A. He dismounts his command and prescribes the duties of the rounds. He orders the officers and non-commissioned officers who will have command of them to reconnoiter the line of small posts and vedettes. Next he accompanies the commander of advance guard, who indicates to him the line to be occupied by the grand guard at night, and gives him directions as to his line of retreat in certain cases. He accompanies this officer as far as the picket and informs himself in regard to its position. On returning to his guard he thoroughly re-examines the ground passed over, so that if the grand guard should be attacked at night, no matter from what side, he could withdraw as well as by day, by taking advantage of his knowledge of the ground to avoid the obstacles which might obstruct the retreat of one uninformed in regard to them.

Q. *What does the commander of the grand guard do on reaching his post again?*

A. He gives out the countersign, which is communicated to the small posts; inspects the arms; receives the forage sent to him from the picket, or the regiment; directs one-half of his horses to be unbridled and fed, but not unpacked, while the men remain near them. He visits his small posts and vedettes frequently, and often he goes outside of his line so as to judge better of the opportunity offered to the enemy to make an unexpected attack. He requires his vedettes to recognize him whenever he comes in view; then he questions them to assure himself that they understand their orders, and inspects their arms to make certain that they will not misfire. He makes his tours with greater frequency if the enemy is near, if his men are not well trained, are much fatigued, or if the weather is very bad. He allows the grand guard and vedettes to put on their cloaks, but not to turn up their collars, as that would prevent their hearing distinctly. In very bad weather he reduces the number of hours which a vedette has to remain on post.

If the enemy is seen to execute any movements, he warns his commander; if the movement is an important one, he sends an officer or intelligent non-commissioned officer to explain it clearly. If the vedettes discharge their pieces, he causes his command to bridle and mount, and goes in person to the point whence the sound of firing seems to come. If attacked, he will withdraw in good order, skirmishing, and execute what is prescribed for rear guards. If rounds visit him he will receive them himself. He sends out patrols which keep up constant communication between the small posts. These patrols, taken from the half of the command whose horses are kept bridled, are sent out more frequently when the small posts and vedettes are unusually distant. Whenever he leaves the grand guard he temporarily transfers the command to the senior officer present, to whom he gives detailed instructions as to his duties.

Q. *Should a grand guard be allowed to have a fire?*

A. Sometimes; but it must not light up very much space, and the place for it must be chosen so that the enemy can see as little of it as possible.

Q. *What is a small post?*

A. A grand guard of the grand guard.

Q. *What are the duties of a commander of a small post?*

A. He posts a vedette, gives him the countersign and his instructions, and makes known to him certain signals to be used. Then he thoroughly reconnoiters the surrounding ground for a view to discovering what advantages or obstacles it would present in case of an attack upon the line compelling a retreat of the whole upon the advanced guard. He must keep his vedettes constantly in sight as well as those on each side of him, and closely observe the country in advance of the line he is charged with guarding. Whenever his vedette makes a signal which he does not understand clearly he mounts his horse and goes to discover the meaning of it. If it proves to be serious, he mounts the men of the small post and sends to warn the grand guard. Should it prove to be of no importance, he reassures and reprimands the vedette, and signals to the small post to dismount, in order that this movement, indicating no cause for alarm, may reassure the grand guard.

If the vedette discharges his piece, the small post mounts instantly. Whenever the commander of a small post leaves it, he must keep within view of his men, and mount or dismount them by means of signals agreed upon beforehand.

If, in looking over the ground in front of his vedettes, he discovers any movements which have escaped the notice of the vedette, he must call his attention to them either by signals or by going to him and telling him of them, and reprimand him sharply for his inattention. He must frequently inspect the arms in the hands of his men, and especially those of the men posted as vedettes.

Sleep and are both forbidden to the commander of a grand guard or a small post.

At daybreak and at nightfall their vigilance must be redoubled, for these are the hours chosen for making attacks. They must see everything with their own eyes, and prevent their men being seized by panics, which spread easily, call a whole army to arms, and bring discredit upon the officer commanding the post where they originate.

During the whole time that reconnaissances are out the horses of the large posts are kept bridled.

Q. *May a small post have a fire?*

A. Not without special permission.

Q. *May the horses be unbridled?*

A. Never.

Q. *What is a vedette?*

A. A mounted sentinel posted in the vicinity of the enemy.

Q. *What are his duties?*

A. To watch with the greatest attention the movements of the enemy, if he is within sight; to let no noise escape his notice; to watch carefully everything which may be of interest to the guard of the detachment to which he belongs; to signal to his small post notice of everything which may appear threatening, and to give warning of an attack by discharging his piece.

Q. *Which is the best place to choose for placing a vedette?*

A. One from which he can see everything without being seen; thus, a long piece of wall, a clump of trees, a hedge, a shallow ditch, are all favorable for masking a vedette; he should never fail to employ them for concealing his presence.

Q. *If the point from which a vedette can get the best view should be a bare hill, what should he do?*

A. Place himself a little in rear of the crest so that the line of the crest will cover him as much as possible, without preventing his seeing beyond it.

Q. *If a lancer is posted as a vedette and can, with a little care, conceal himself, what should he do?*

A. Lower his lance, or remove his pennon, so that it may not betray his position.

Q. *If the ground upon which the chain of vedettes is placed is undulating, should vedettes also be placed in the depressions?*

A. Vedettes must be posted wherever the approach of the enemy is to be feared: thus, one vedette is placed upon a height to observe a plain, another at the foot of a mountain to observe a gorge, a wood, or a sunken road, and to protect the vedettes who, on the hill-tops, might, if not warned, be surrounded before they know it.

Q. *What further precautions are to be observed in choosing posts for vedettes?*

A. To take care that the vedette placed in a depression is able to see, as well as possible, one or two of those on the same line with him, in order that he may be warned by them of any danger threatening him, in case of a movement by the enemy.

Q. *What orders apply to all vedettes?*

A. Never dismount unless by special permission of the commander of the grand guard, and always have the carbine or pistol in readiness to fire.

Q. *In posting a vedette what orders are given him?*

A. First, point out to him the ground he is to observe. Indicate all the points of special importance which he is to watch; direct him to look frequently toward the other vedettes who, with him, form the chain; next give him a signal by which he warns, and is warned by, the other vedettes that it is necessary to re-double vigilance, and be prepared for coming events. Then give him another signal with which to warn the commander of his own small post who, on seeing it, immediately comes out to reconnoiter.

Q. *Can the distance at which the enemy is seen to be estimated?*

A. At 2,000 meters, men and horses are seen as mere points; at 1,200, infantry can be distinguished from cavalry; at 800 individual movements may be distinguished; at 700, the heads of the men may be distinguished from their bodies; at 400, the head of a man can be clearly seen.

Q. *Is a vedette permitted to leave or change his post?*

A. Never, under any pretext, without special permission, given in advance.

Q. *Is he required to observe anything besides the enemy?*

A. It is his duty to see everything that takes place: for instance, if he should see a peasant come out of a wood, enter it again, go out of it and approach the chain of vedettes, it is probable that he is a spy, and the small post should be signaled. If a dust is seen to rise regularly along the horizon, it is probably made by a marching column, and warning should be given; if a signal is made by another vedette, it must be repeated as a warning to his own small post.

Q. *When danger threatens, what should be done?*

A. The vedettes are doubled. In this case one of them may be sent back to warn the small post, if necessary, while the other remains in observation of the enemy; if the vedettes have special orders to leave their posts to reconnoiter in front of their line, to arrest suspicious characters found prowling about, etc., one of them will perform that duty while the other remains on post. In the case of double vedettes are numerous enough to form a strong line of resistance, and skirmish, while retreating, if not pushed back too briskly.

Q. *What should a vedette do when he sees himself about to be attacked?*

A. Turn his horse to the left, bringing his right flank toward the enemy, so that he can more quickly complete his left about, and when the movement of the enemy is decided, discharge his carbine.

Q. *How often are the vedettes relieved?*

A. Ordinarily, each one will be relieved after one hour's duty, so that the whole post will be relieved every four hours.

Q. *Are the vedettes posted at night in the places occupied during the day?*

A. At night the vedettes are brought nearer to the small posts, these nearer to the grand guards, and these nearer to the detachment. In daytime the horizon of vedette cannot be too extended; but at night it is quite different, and, in order that the vedette may be able to see, especially when the night is dark, the line of the horizon must be brought closer to him. For that reason the vedette who, in the daytime, was placed upon a height, must be posted in a hollow at night, and his eyes must be fixed attentively and at a suitable distance, upon the line of the neighboring ground which cuts the line of the sky. Should the enemy present himself, not matter how dark the night may be, the vedette will be able to see him outlined against the horizon and, if on challenging him no answer is made, the vedette will fire. A position for the night should be taken only after it has become too dark for the enemy to perceive the retrograde movement. The positions for the day should be taken up by the vedettes just at dawn, so as to prevent the enemy's guessing at the positions occupied at night, and from which the vedettes are moved forward. In making this forward movement care should be taken to scout well to the front to avoid falling into ambuscades.

Q. *What is a picket?*

A. Troops placed between the detachment and the grand guard.

Q. *Where is it posted?*

A. Should troops be bivouacked in rear of a village, the picket would be posted at the opposite side, toward the enemy, and a few hundred yards in rear of the grand guard.

Q. *Will the men be permitted to occupy houses?*

A. The horses may be assembled and placed in open barns; the men will bivouac.

Q. *And the horses kept bridled?*

A. Only half of them.

Q. *what is generally the numerical force of the picket?*

A. It should equal that of the grand guard.

Q. *What is its duty?*

A. It posts 1 sentinel 25 paces in its front, with orders to listen for any suspicious noises coming from the direction of the grand guard, and to prevent men passing, without permission, from the bivouac to the outposts.

Q. *Does it not also keep a sentinel over the arms of the command?*

A. No; for the arms remain upon the horses, and the sentinel, spoken of above, is not far away. The picket assures the safety of the rear of the grand guard, and furnishes patrols which scout in front and on the flanks. If the grand guard is attacked, the picket warns the main body, supports the outposts, and retires only when they do so. The officers of the picket are permitted to take turns in sleeping.

Q. *If it always necessary to have a picket in rear of the grand guard?*

A. No, a grand guard needs the support of a picket only when very near the enemy, or when the latter is likely to make an attack. When these conditions do not exist, it is useless to double the duty; but in such a case the main body in bivouac will have to exercise increased vigilance.

Q. *What is a patrol?*

A. A detachment of flying vedettes.

Q. *Of what are patrols usually comprised?*

A. Ordinarily of two troopers commanded by a corporal, or an old soldier. They are much more useful than vedettes and may sometimes entirely replace them. In that case their duty is continuous, and their observation constant.

Q. *Under what circumstances would that be the case?*

A. If infantry and cavalry bivouac together, the former would furnish the sentinels, the latter the patrols.

If a partisan, harassed and in danger, has retreated, and barricaded himself at a farm, from the tops of whose buildings he can see to a great distance, he posts no vedettes, but patrols the surrounding county. Good patrols, conducted intelligently, are generally much more efficient than vedettes.

Q. *Why?*

A. Because the nature of that duty admits of no sleeping; it compels men to display all their resources of intelligence and courage; and the exploration of the country is made more thoroughly and to a greater distance.

Q. *How should men conduct themselves when on patrol?*

A. March without noise of any kind; carry on no conversation; fasten the sabre so that the scabbard will strike against neither the spur nor the stirrup; carry the carbine in one hand, so that it will make no noise by striking against the swivel, or fastenings of the sling-belt. Keep the horses on dirt roads, so that no noise will be made by their shoes striking the stones of paved road. In daytime the men must move along under cover of hedges, walls, sunken roads, and ravines; they must lower their lances, so that their pennons will not betray them; they must conceal themselves in woods, and make their observations through the openings.

At night they must endeavor to see even in the darkness; halt frequently, follow sunken roads, and refrain from smoking, so as not to light up their faces. If the enemy is encountered they must not fire, but conceal themselves, and one of the patrol must be sent, if possible without risk of discovery, to warn the grand guard. The men of a cavalry patrol must not march side by side, but one behind the other, and far enough part to enable them to see well, to afford protection to one another, and, in case of falling into an ambuscade, to prevent the whole patrol being cut off and captured at once.

The routes which patrols travel may be relative to our chain of vedettes, either interior or exterior; in the latter case, greater vigilance must be exercised, because the danger is greater. The exterior patrols should consider themselves flying vedettes who have the advantage over fixed ones of being able to reconnoiter everything which arouses their suspicions; of marching, halting, and concealing themselves as long as they may think necessary. It is often useful to send patrols of one or two men to distant points, where they may remain in observation for several hours at a time.

A patrol which has ventured too far, and which a hostile post challenges, must be careful not to reply, if they do not speak the enemy's language, or if, before going out, they have not learned a few words of the language which, spoken in answer to the challenge, may suspend the examination, and give them time to turn about without danger, and, gain some ground to the rear.

If the enemy is advancing on our posts and is likely to arrive there before they are warned of his coming, the patrol should discharge their carbines and return, skirmishing, by the road on which they went out.

I have been told that in the campaign of Portugal our cavalry, being obliged to march over rocky and sonorous ground, put pieces of sheepskin on their horses' feet (the wool inside), and tied them about the fetlocks, so that our patrols approached very close to the English vedettes without the latter hearing them. This would be a good thing to try again under similar circumstances.

A trooper on patrol may sometimes be surprised in spite of the greatest vigilance, especially if he has to traverse a wooded and broken country. He should halt frequently, and carefully watch his horse's ears. The direction in which they point may give him valuable information. It is an indication he cannot afford to despise, as it is instinctive; and if the horse persists in his action, especially to the point of being frightened, the cause of it should be discovered, if possible. Two patrols, meeting outside the chain of outposts, should recognize each other, if possible, without challenging, especially if the enemy is known to be in the vicinity. When patrols are sent out, the outposts should be informed in regard to their numbers, uniforms, etc., so that there may be no doubt or hesitation about admitting them whey the return to their own lines.

Q. *Are the grand guards and pickets allowed to go out foraging?*

A. No; if the enemy is near or a surprise is feared, the supplies for men and horses are sent out from the main body.

Q. *How are the horses of a grand guard watered?*

A. A small number at a time. Those already sent to water must return before others are allowed to go out.

Driving Tour

The following is a driving tour of the sites associated with the narrative in this book. All told, you will cover approximately 40 miles and see nearly all of the important sites referenced in this book. The format is as follows: You will get driving directions with some narrative. There will also be a reference to a GPS benchmark. Those GPS benchmarks are listed at the end of the tour. If you program them into your GPS unit, it will take you from place to place and you will not have to worry about measuring out the distances prescribed in the tour. The tour begins and ends at the Chickamauga battlefield visitor center.

There are places on this route that are private property. Please respect that and do not trespass. Also, be careful as you make stops along the roads outside the national park, as traffic can be brisk.

There are some unique features of the marking of the battlefield at Chickamauga. Each regiment or battery that fought there was permitted to erect a main monument on the spot where that particular unit did the bulk of its fighting. The rules established when the park was created, however, also permit each unit to have a smaller position marker anywhere where it fought. Consequently, Wilder's units have multiple markers on the battlefield along with each regiment's (and Lilly's battery's) main monument in Viniard field. This can make interpreting the battle confusing at times.

Most of all: Please enjoy the tour! Let's begin.

Begin at the Visitor Center. (Benchmark 1)

Leave the parking lot and turn left onto LaFayette Road. (Benchmark 2)

Travel north 1.6 miles and turn right onto Cloud Springs Road, which is also known as State Route 146. (Benchmark 3)

Proceed for 5 miles and then turn right onto Ringgold Road (U.S. Route 41). (Benchmark 4)

Proceed 7.1 miles through the town of Ringgold. Your approach follows the route of Brig. Gen. Horatio Van Cleve's infantry brigade as it advanced on the

Ringgold Station. *Author*

railroad depot. Stop at the old Atlantic and Western Depot, which was built in 1849 and was the last building passed by *The General* during the 1862 Great Locomotive Chase. Wilder's men advanced on the town of Ringgold from the north, marching along the railroad tracks. Spend a few minutes reading the markers and visiting the depot, because it played a significant role in the Chickamauga campaign. (Benchmark 5)

Leave the depot and proceed straight on U.S. Route 41. Travel .4 mile and you will find the first of a number of Atlanta campaign pavilions constructed in the 1930s to mark the route of Maj. Gen. William T. Sherman's 1864 Atlanta campaign. Here, you will find a handsome monument to Maj. Gen. Patrick Cleburne, which was dedicated in 2009. This monument commemorates Cleburne's role in the November 1863 battle of Ringgold Gap and is not associated with the Chickamauga campaign. It is nevertheless worth a stop since you will pass right by it. (Benchmark 6)

Continue on U.S. Route 41 for 1.7 miles until you reach the Joseph T. McConnell Park. Park your car there and get out. Bathroom facilities are available here. Across the road you will see a large electrical substation that was the site of Catoosa Platform, where Lt. Gen. James Longstreet's corps debarked from the trains bringing them north from Atlanta. The platform was a temporary structure, and it was destroyed shortly after the battle. On the other side of the pavilion for the McConnell Park is the circa 1849 Old Stone Church, which still has its original pews and altar

Patrick Cleburne monument at Ringgold Gap. *Author*

Site of Catoosa Platform, from Old Stone Church. *Author*

Old Stone Church. *Author*

and was used as a Confederate hospital during the battle of Chickamauga. The restored church also houses a Civil War museum. (Benchmark 7)

Leave the parking lot at Joseph T. McConnell Park and turn right onto U.S. Route 41 and head back toward Ringgold. After 2.9 miles turn right onto GA Route 51. (Benchmark 8)

Proceed on GA Route 51 for 2.6 miles and then turn right onto Mount Pisgah Road. (Benchmark 9)

Proceed on Mount Pisgah Road for 3.8 miles. You are following the route of Col. John T. Wilder's Lightning Brigade as it marched toward Leet's Tanyard. There will be a pull-off to the right at the site of Leet's Spring and Tanyard and a Chickamauga campaign wayside marker. Stop and get out of your car. Read the marker and observe the terrain. Pegram's Confederate cavalry held the high ground behind the large house across the road during the fighting for Leet's Tanyard on September 13, 1863. (Benchmark 10)

Get back in your car and continue west along the Mount Pisgah Road for 1.9 miles. The name of the road then changes to Peavine Road. (Benchmark 11)

Continue west on Peavine Road. The name of the road will change again, this time to Longhollow. Proceed for .6 mile and turn right on Longhollow Road, which is a different road than Longhollow, even though the names are almost identical. This is confusing, so be careful. (Benchmark 12)

The Leet's Tanyard battlefield. *Author*

Proceed on Longhollow Road for 1.1 miles and turn left onto Red Belt Road. (Benchmark 13)

Proceed on Red Belt Road for 2.5 miles until you reach Lee and Gordon's Mills. Turn right at the gate and proceed to the restored mill. Here, you will get your first good look at West Chickamauga Creek. The mills were the headquarters of Maj. Gen. Thomas Crittenden, commander of the Army of the Cumberland's 20th Corps. Colonel Robert H. G. Minty reported to Crittenden here. (Benchmark 14)

Turn right onto Red Belt Road and proceed for .1 mile. Turn left on Lee-Gordon Mill Circle. You will see numerous markers for various Georgia cavalry units of Maj. Gen. Joseph Wheeler's corps who fought here on September 20, 1863, along this road. The markers are shaped like tents. (Benchmark 15)

Proceed for .2 mile and go straight at the traffic light. (Benchmark 16)

Proceed for .6 mile and turn left onto Crittenden Avenue. You are now entering the town of Chickamauga. This was not an incorporated town in September 1863. (Benchmark 17)

Proceed for .8 mile and turn left onto West 10th Street. (Benchmark 18)

Proceed for .3 mile and turn left on Cove Road. (Benchmark 19)

Proceed for .1 mile until you reach the site of the Gordon-Lee Mansion, which was the home of James Gordon in 1863. Find a parking space and enjoy the beautiful grounds of the mansion, which is now owned by the town of Chickamauga. This was Maj. Gen. William S. Rosecrans's headquarters for a time during the

Modern view of Lee and Gordon's Mill. *Author*

Gordon-Lee Mansion. *Author*

Monuments to McCook's Brigade near Jay's Sawmill. *Author*

days before the opening of the battle of Chickamauga. Across the road is Crawfish Springs, which was the primary water source for this area. This large and active spring provided cold, clear water in large quantities. You will note a number of Georgia unit markers along the street there. (Benchmark 20)

Get back in your car and retrace your route. Proceed along Cove Road for .1 mile and then turn right onto West 10th Street. (Benchmark 21)

Proceed on West 10th Street for .3 mile and turn left onto Crittenden Avenue. (Benchmark 22)

Proceed on Crittenden Avenue for .75 miles and turn right onto Lee-Gordon Mill Road. (Benchmark 23)

Proceed on Lee-Gordon Mill Road for .6 mile and turn left onto Lafayette Road (U.S. Route 27). (Benchmark 24)

Proceed on Lafayette Road for .4 mile and turn right onto Old Lafayette Road, which is the historic road that cuts through the heart of the Chickamauga battlefield. (Benchmark 25)

Proceed north on Old Lafayette Road for 3.72 miles. You will pass through sites of some of the heaviest fighting of the Civil War. Turn right onto Reed's Bridge Road at the traffic light. (Benchmark 26)

Proceed east on Reed's Bridge Road for 1.7 miles. You will come to the monuments for Col. Daniel McCook's brigade and Col. Ferdinand Van Derveer's

Detail of the 69th Ohio Infantry monument. *Author*

brigade, which engaged the Confederates around Reed's Bridge during the early morning hours of September 19, 1863. This stop is out of chronological sequence, but logistics require stopping now as it would be too difficult to backtrack here later. (Benchmark 27)

Continue east on Reed's Bridge Road. The name of the road will change to Boynton Ridge Road. (Benchmark 28)

Continue on Boynton Ridge Road for 1.3 miles and continue straight at the stop sign. (Benchmark 29)

Proceed 1.1 miles to the intersection of Boynton Ridge Road and Three Notch Road. Three Notch Road represents the line of Minty's vidette posts. These vidette posts provided an early warning system for the approach of Confederate infantry. (Benchmark 30)

Turn left onto Three Notch Road and proceed .1 mile and turn left onto Old Mill Road. (Benchmark 31)

Proceed on Old Mill Road for .4 mile and then left onto Old Mill Lane. (Benchmark 32)

Proceed on Old Mill Lane for .1 mile and then stop at the bridge over Pea Vine Creek. Be careful where you stop your car. If you stand on the bridge and look to the south, this was the site of Peeler's Mill. In the winter, when the foliage is down, you should be able to see some concrete pillars. While those pillars are postwar, they mark the site of the original mill until it was moved in the 1930s. Minty's troopers

Pea Vine Creek. *Author*

camped in this area on the night of September 17, 1863. (Benchmark 33)

Get back in your car and proceed east on Old Mill Lane for .4 mile. Turn right onto Boynton Road. (Benchmark 34)

Continue on Boynton Road for .9 mile to the Boynton United Methodist Church parking lot. This is an optional stop. If you choose to stop there, you will find the graves of Jimmy and Jemimah Reed, the owners of the Reed farm. Both are buried there, side by side. Jimmy rests under a Confederate marker. (Benchmark 35)

Pull out of the church parking lot and turn right onto Boynton Road. Proceed for .1 mile and turn right onto Pine Grove Road. (Benchmark 36)

Proceed on Pine Grove Road for .5 mile and then turn left onto Monroe. (Benchmark 37).

Proceed on Monroe for .2 mile and then stop your car. You are on the eastern slope of Pea Vine Ridge here, which was the site of Minty's first line of battle. His dismounted troopers made a stand on this ridge for approximately 45 minutes before the sheer weight of Confederate numbers drove his troopers off. (Benchmark 38)

Get back in your car and turn around. Proceed .2 mile back down the hill and then turn right onto Pine Grove Road. (Benchmark 39)

Proceed on Pine Grove Road for .5 mile to Boynton Road. Turn right on Boynton Road. (Benchmark 40)

Boynton Church. *Author*

Jemima Reed grave at Boynton Church. *Author*

Chickamauga Creek at Reed's Bridge. *Author*

Continue on Boynton Road for 1.2 miles to the stop sign. Continue straight after the stop sign. Note the name of the road changes to Reed's Bridge Road here. (Benchmark 41)

Continue west on Reed's Bridge Road for .3 mile until you come to the pull-off at Reed's Bridge itself. Stop and get out of your car. Walk down to the banks of West Chickamauga Creek. Note the sharp bend in the creek on the other side of the modern bridge and also note the original bridge abutments just to the north of the modern bridge. Those bridge abutments mark the site of Reed's Bridge on September 18, 1863. (Benchmark 42)

Get back in your car and proceed west along Reed's Bridge Road for .7 mile to Jay's Mill Road. Note the terrain as you proceed west along Reed's Bridge Road, particularly to the north of the road. This is the ground where Minty's brigade made its primary stand. The two guns of the Chicago Board of Trade Battery were positioned along the edge of the wood line at the crest of the ridge. You will soon reenter Chickamauga National Military Park. Turn left onto Jay's Mill Road and stop in the parking area. Here, you will find the monuments to Minty's brigade. This is also where the sharp skirmish between McCook's men and Confederate soldiers took place during the night of September 18-19 and where Maj. Gen. Nathan B. Forrest launched the opening attacks of the main battle early on the morning of September 19. (Benchmark 43)

Monument to the 4th Michigan Cavalry. *Author*

Monument to the 7th Pennsylvania Cavalry. *Author*

Detail of the 7th Pennsylvania Cavalry monument. *Author*

Monument to the 4th U.S. Cavalry. *Author*

The modern view of Alexander's Bridge. *Author*

Turn right out of the parking lot and continue south on Jay's Mill Road for 1 mile. Turn left onto Alexander's Bridge Road. (Benchmark 44)

Proceed east on Alexander's Bridge Road for .6 mile and pull over just before you get to Alexander's Bridge. Park your car and get out. You will see Indiana regimental position markers for the 17th and 72nd Indiana regiments of Wilder's Lightning Brigade. The lunette constructed by the men of Company A of the 72nd Indiana would have been in the middle of the road just before the bridge. Feel free to walk across the bridge and see the Confederate perspective. Note the sharp bend in the road. Confederate infantry would have been deployed on either side of the road. (Benchmark 45)

Return to your vehicle and turn around. Head west on Alexander's Bridge Road for .25 mile to the parking area to the right. Park your car there and carefully cross the road to the site of the Alexander farm buildings. This is where the guns of Capt. Eli Lilly's 18th Indiana Battery were deployed, and it was also held by some of Wilder's men. The wooden Alexander farmhouse was set ablaze by Confederate artillery fire and burned to the ground. Return to your car. (Benchmark 46)

At the intersection take the left fork onto Viniard-Alexander Road and proceed for 1.3 miles to the pullover area on the left. Pull over there and park. This is the site of Wilder's line of battle during the night fighting with Hood's infantry. Note the position markers there and the close proximity to the Confederate positions. This was a blind fight at close quarters. (Benchmark 47)

Monument to Wilder's Brigade. *Author*

Proceed along Viniard-Alexander Road for .2 mile to the eastern edge of the Viniard farm, site of more fighting during the night of September 18 and early morning hours of September 19. Again, note the Indiana position markers for the 17th and 72nd Indiana of Wilder's brigade. (Benchmark 48)

Proceed west along Viniard-Alexander Road to the intersection of Lafayette Road. Stop at the pullover and park there. If you wish to visit the main line of monuments for all of the units of Wilder's Lightning Brigade, carefully cross Lafayette Road and head for the line of monuments on the low ridge line in front of you. It's a walk of approximately .24 mile to reach this line of monuments. There you will find monuments to the 17th Indiana, 72nd Indiana, 98th Illinois, and the 123rd Illinois as well as Lilly's 18th Indiana Battery. The monument to the 92nd Illinois is near the Brotherton cabin, as the 92nd Illinois was not engaged with the rest of the brigade. (Benchmark 49)

Turn left on Lafayette Road and continue south for .1 mile. Turn right onto Glenn-Viniard Road. (Benchmark 50)

Proceed on Glenn-Viniard Road for .7 mile and pull into the parking area on your right. Park and visit the Wilder's Brigade Monument, which is the large structure that looks like a rook. Sometimes the tower is open and you can walk to the top. Be aware the tower is often infested with wasps, and you run the risk of having a losing encounter with those wasps. When the wasps are at their worst, the gate to the tower will be locked. This 65-foot-tall structure recognizes the many contributions of the Lightning Brigade at Chickamauga and stands on the site of their determined stand on September 20. (Benchmark 51)

Get back in your car and turn right onto Glenn-Viniard Road and proceed for 1.1 miles. Here, the name of the road changes to Glenn-Kelly Road. (Benchmark 52)

Proceed on Glenn-Kelly Road for 1.3 miles to the intersection with Lafayette Road and turn left onto Lafayette Road. (Benchmark 53)

Proceed north on Lafayette Road for .5 mile and turn left into the parking area of the Chickamauga National Military Park's visitor center, which is the place where you began your tour. (Benchmark 54)

You have now completed the tour of sites associated with the actions described in this book. I hope you have enjoyed the tour and have learned something along the way.

GPS BENCHMARKS

Benchmark 1: N 34° 56.407″
W 85° 15.576″
Benchmark 2: N 34° 56.395″
W 85° 15.543″
Benchmark 3: N 34° 57.797″
W 85° 15.555″
Benchmark 4: N 34° 58.587″
W 85° 11.315″
Benchmark 5: N 34° 54.951″
W 85° 06.477″
Benchmark 6: N 34° 54.5586″
W 85° 06.166″
Benchmark 7: N 34° 54.390″
W 85° 04.646″
Benchmark 8: N 34° 55.060″
W 85° 07.404″
Benchmark 9: N 34° 52.259″
W 85° 08.553″
Benchmark 10: N 34° 50.269″
W 85° 11.512″
Benchmark 11: N 34° 50.832″
W 85° 13.369″
Benchmark 12: N 34° 51.248″
W 85° 13.725″
Benchmark 13: N 34° 52.224″
W 85° 13.729″
Benchmark 14: N 34° 52.990″
W 85° 16.052″
Benchmark 15: N 34° 53.046″
W 85° 16.078″
Benchmark 16: N 34° 52.985″
W 85° 16.192″
Benchmark 17: N 34° 52.969″
W 85° 16.396″
Benchmark 18: N 34° 52.296″
W 85° 17.118″
Benchmark 19: N 34° 52.332″
W 85° 17.484″
Benchmark 20: N 34° 52.253
W 85° 17.581″
Benchmark 21: N 34° 52.331″
W 85° 17.492″

Benchmark 22: N 34° 52.296″
W 85° 17.118″
Benchmark 23: N 34° 52.963″
W 85° 16.955″
Benchmark 24: N 34° 52.986″
W 85° 16.219″
Benchmark 25: N 34° 53.338″
W 85° 16.048″
Benchmark 26: N 34° 56.508″
W 85° 15.526″
Benchmark 27: N 34° 55.926″
W 85° 12.899″
Benchmark 28: N 34° 55.703″
W 85° 12.660″
Benchmark 29: N 34° 55.410″
W 85° 11.402″
Benchmark 30: N 34° 55.544″
W 85° 10.357″
Benchmark 31: N 34° 55.592″
W 85° 10.361″
Benchmark 32: N 34° 55.772″
W 85° 10.681″
Benchmark 33: N 34° 55.724″
W 85° 10.675″
Benchmark 34: N 34° 55.491″
W 85° 10.512″
Benchmark 35: N 34° 55.411″
W 85° 11.411″
Benchmark 36: N 34° 55.428″
W 85° 11.458″
Benchmark 37: N 34° 55.794″
W 85° 11.567″
Benchmark 38: N 34° 55.808″
W 85° 11.654″
Benchmark 39: N 34° 55.424″
W 85° 11.458″
Benchmark 40: N 34° 55.702″
W 85° 12.655″
Benchmark 41: N 34° 55.787″
W 85° 12.995″
Benchmark 42: N 34° 55.835″
W 85° 13.738″
Benchmark 43: N 34° 54.952″
W 85° 14. 046″

Benchmark 44: N 34° 54.446″
W 85° 13.794″
Benchmark 45: N 34° 54.679″
W 85° 13.918″
Benchmark 46: N 34° 54.090″
W 85° 15.093″
Benchmark 47: N 34° 54.162″
W 85° 15.353″
Benchmark 48: N 34° 54.213″
W 85° 15.668″
Benchmark 49: N 34° 54.068″
W 85° 15.690″
Benchmark 50: N 34° 54.309″
W 85° 16.256″
Benchmark 51: N 34° 55.047″
W 85° 15.941″
Benchmark 52: N 34° 56.165″
W 85° 15.571″
Benchmark 53: N 34° 56.407″
W 85° 15.576″
Benchmark 54: N 34° 56.407″
W 85° 15.576″

Bibliography

PRIMARY SOURCES:

Newspapers:

Atlanta Daily Appeal

Chattanooga Times

The Columbus Dispatch

The Daily Courier (Lafayette, Indiana)

Dayton Herald (Dayton, Tennessee)

Evansville Daily Journal

Houston Weekly Telegraph (Houston, Texas)

Indianapolis Daily Journal

Lafayette Journal and Courier (Lafayette, Indiana)

Lagrange Standard (Lagrange, Indiana)

The National Tribune

New York Times

Pottsville Miner's Journal

Semi-Weekly Wisconsin (Milwaukee, Wisconsin)

The Sunny South

Wabash Weekly Express

Manuscript Materials:

Special Collections, Ball State University, Muncie, Indiana:

George W. Kemper papers

Center for Archival Collections, Bowling Green State University, Bowling Green, Ohio:

Brigham family papers

Dumond family papers

Archives, Chickamauga/Chattanooga National Military Park, Ft. Oglethorpe, Georgia:

George A. Grammer diary

Theodore Petzoldt reminiscences

Charles Frederick Terrill letter of September 22, 1863

John T. Wilder, "Revised Report for the Battle of Chickamauga," November 26, 1888

Unit files:

"Capsule History of Battery M, 1st Illinois Light Artillery, 8/12/62-7/26/65"

69th Ohio Volunteer Infantry file: L. E. Hicks, "The Capture of Reed's Bridge. A Check to Bragg's Flank Movement at Chickamauga."

86th Illinois Infantry file

Post-war report of Col. J. J. Turner, 30th Tennessee Infantry

Undated letter by Sylvanus H. Stevens to Edgar D. Swain

Special Collections, Detroit Public Library, Detroit, Michigan:

James Vernor letters

Special Collections, Duke University, Durham, North Carolina:

Benjamin Nourse diary

Confederate Veteran papers

W. F. Shropshire reminiscences

Special Collections, Robert W. Woodruff Library, Emory University, Atlanta, Georgia:

Honnoll family papers

Georgia Department of Archives and History, Atlanta, Georgia:

Frank T. Ryan Reminiscences

Sallie B. Veal collection

Illinois State Historical Library, Springfield, Illinois:

Edward Kitchell diary

Manuscripts Section, Indiana State Library, Indianapolis, Indiana:

Alva G. Greist journal

William Records memoir

John T. Wilder papers

Smith Library, Indiana Historical Society, Indianapolis, Indiana:

John M. Bernard letters

Diary of unidentified member of the 72nd Indiana Infantry

Joseph A. Scott reminiscences

Archives, State Historical Society of Iowa, Des Moines, Iowa:

John C. McLain diary

Michigan State Archives, Lansing, Michigan:

4th Cavalry Regimental Files

Special Collections, Michigan State University, East Lansing, Michigan:

Othniel Gooding letters

Archives, Minnesota Historical Society, St. Paul, Minnesota:

Robert Burns letters

Mississippi Department of Archives and History, Jackson, Mississippi:

"History of Company H, 1st Arkansas Mounted Rifles"

National Archives and Records Administration, Washington, DC:

Army of the Cumberland Brigade Returns, RG 94, Entry 65, Boxes 28 and 64

Bushrod R. Johnson diary for 1863

Quarterly Statements of Ordnance in Cavalry, 1862-1864, Statement for September 30, 1863,

RG 59-14, Records of the Michigan Military Establishment

RG 94, Consolidated Service Records

RG 156, Records of the Chief of Ordnance

Archives, Ohio Historical Society, Columbus, Ohio:

Richard T. Foster diary

John D. Inskeep diary

William H. Kemper papers

Pennsylvania State Archives, Harrisburg, Pennsylvania:

Charles C. McCormick Family Papers

Tennessee State Library and Archives, Nashville, Tennessee:

Civil War Collection:

Col. James L. Cooper memoirs

John H. Freeman diary

William Gibbs Allen memoirs

William E. Sloan diary

James Franklin Witherspoon file

Special Collections, Tippecanoe County Historical Society, Lafayette, Indiana:

W. D. Crouse journal

Archives, United States Army Command and General Staff College, Fort Leavenworth, Kansas:

Reminiscences of Captain William Henry Harder, Co. D, 23d Tennessee Infantry Regiment

Special Collections, University of Arkansas, Fayetteville, Arkansas:

Daniel Harris Reynolds diary for 1863

Bentley Historical Library, University of Michigan, Ann Arbor, Michigan:

D. H. Haines, "Record of Fourth Michigan Cavalry"

Henry Potter diary for 1863

Richard B. Robbins account of the Battle of Chickamauga

Special Collections, University of Tennessee at Chattanooga, Chattanooga, Tennessee:

John T. Wilder papers

Southern Historical Collections, Wilson Library, University of North Carolina, Chapel Hill, North Carolina:

Leroy Moncure Nutt papers

John P. and Sallie Ecklin Thurman papers

Special Collections, Vigo County Public Library, Terre Haute, Indiana:

John H. Rippetoe letters

Special Collections, Virginia Polytechnic Institute, Blacksburg, Virginia:

Thomas M. Burns letters

Robert T. Ramsay Archival Center, Wabash College, Crawfordsville, Indiana:

Henry Campbell, "Three Years in the Saddle," unpublished manuscript

Archives, Western Reserve Historical Society, Cleveland, Ohio:

Braxton Bragg papers

Published Sources:

Abbott, J. N. "Opening of Chickamauga Fight," *The National Tribune*, April 9, 1914.

Allen, William G. "Lieutenant W. G. Allen Fights Gen. J. T. Wilder's Infantry Twelve Days," *Dayton Herald*, May 18, 1911.

—. *Reminiscences of William G. Allen, McKenzie's 5th Tennessee Regiment*. Dayton, TN: Rhea County Historical and Genealogical Society, 2000.

Annual Report of the Adjutant General of the State of Michigan, for the Year 1863. Lansing: John A. Kerr & Co., 1864.

Belknap, Charles E., comp. *History of the Michigan Organizations at Chickamauga, Chattanooga and Missionary Ridge 1863*. Lansing: Robert Smith Printing Co., 1899.

Bell, C. W. R. "Reminiscences of Chickamauga," *Confederate Veteran* 12 (1904): 71.

Berry, Thomas F. *Four Years with Morgan and Forrest*. Oklahoma City, OK: The Harlow-Ratcliff Co., 1914.

Blackburn. Theodore W. *Letters from the Front, A Union "Preacher" Regiment (74th Ohio) in the Civil War*. Dayton, OH: Morningside Bookshop, 1981.

Boynton, Henry V., comp. *Dedication of the Chickamauga and Chattanooga National Military Park, September 18-20, 1895*. Washington, DC: Government Printing Office, 1896.

—. *The National Military Park: Chickamauga-Chattanooga. An Historical Guide. With Maps and Illustrations*. Cincinnati: Robert Clarke Co., 1895.

Bradner, J. W. "Reed's Bridge: It was Never Burned at All," *The National Tribune*, November 15, 1914.

Campbell, Henry. "The 18th Ind. Battery," *The National Tribune*, November 1, 1906.

Carter, Howell. *A Cavalryman's Reminiscences*. New Orleans: The American Printing Co., 1900.

Clay, H. B. "On the Right at Chickamauga," *Confederate Veteran* 21 (1913): 439-440.

Connolly, James A. *Three Years in the Army of the Cumberland*. Bloomington, IN: Indiana University Press, 1987.

Cullum, George W. *Biographical Register of the Officers and Graduates of the U.S. Military Academy at West Point, N.Y., from Its Establishment, March 16, 1802 to the Army Reorganization of 1866*-1867. 2 vols. New York: D. Van Nostrand, 1868.

Cunningham, Sumner A. *Reminiscences of the 41st Tennessee: The Civil War in the West*. Ed. by John A. Simpson. Shippensburg, PA: White Mane, 2000.

Davis, Charles C. "Address of Major Charles C. Davis," *Pennsylvania at Chickamauga and Chattanooga. Ceremonies at the Dedication of the Monuments Erected by the Commonwealth of Pennsylvania*. Harrisburg: W.S. Ray, 1901: 313-315.

De Brack, Antoine Fortuné. *Cavalry Outpost Duties*. Trans. By Maj. Camillo C. C. Carr. New York: John Wiley & Sons, 1893.

Dedication of the Wilder Brigade Monument on Chickamauga Battlefield on the Thirty-Sixth Anniversary of the Battle, September 20, 1899. Marshall, IL: The Herald Press, 1900.

Dornblaser, Thomas F. *My Life-Story For Young and Old*. Philadelphia: privately published, 1930.

—. *Sabre Strokes of the Pennsylvania Dragoons in the War of 1861-1865*. Philadelphia: Lutheran Publication Society, 1884.

Doyle, Julia A., John David Smith and Richard M. McMurry, eds. *This Wilderness of War: The Civil War Letters of George W. Squier, Hoosier Volunteer*. Knoxville: University of Tennessee Press, 1998.

Doyle, William E. "Chickamauga. Wilder's Brigade at the Glenn House, and Previous Work," *The National Tribune*, June 6, 1901.

Duke, Basil W. *History of Morgan's Cavalry*. Cincinnati: Miami Printing & Publishing Co., 1867.

Emerson, Samuel Henry. *History of the War of the Confederacy '61 to '65*. Malvern, AR: n.p., 1913.

Field Manual 34-35, *Armored Cavalry Regiment and Separate Brigade Intelligence and Electronic Warfare Operations*. Washington, DC: Department of the Army, 1990.

"First Shot at Chickamauga," *The National Tribune*, February 26, 1914.

Fitch, John. *Annals of the Army of the Cumberland: Biographies, Descriptions of Departments, Accounts of Expeditions, Skirmishes, and Battles*. Philadelphia: J. B. Lippincott, 1864.

Floyd, David B. *History of the Seventy-Fifth Regiment of Indiana Volunteers, Its Organization, Campaigns, and Battles (1862-1865)*. Philadelphia: Lutheran Publication Society, 1893.

"Fourth Texas Infantry at Chattanooga," *Houston Weekly Telegraph*, November 12, 1863.

Gammage, W L. *The Camp, the Bivouac, and the Battlefield. Being a History of the Fourth Arkansas Regiment, for its First Organization Down to the Present Date*. Selma, AL: privately published, 1864.

"General Burnside's East Tennessee Campaign," *Semi-Weekly Wisconsin*, September 18, 1863.

Goodrich, John T. "Gregg's Brigade in the Battle of Chickamauga," *Confederate Veteran* 22 (1914): 264-265.

Gray, Alonzo. *Cavalry Tactics as Illustrated by the War of the Rebellion together with Many Interesting Facts Important for Cavalry to Know*. In 2 parts. Ft. Leavenworth: U. S. Cavalry Association, 1910.

Green, Curtis. "Sixth Georgia Cavalry at Chickamauga," *Confederate Veteran* 8 (1900): 324.

Greeno, Charles L. "Address of Lieut.-Col. Charles L. Greeno," *Pennsylvania at Chickamauga and Chattanooga. Ceremonies at the Dedication of the Monuments Erected by the Commonwealth of Pennsylvania.* Harrisburg: W.S. Ray, 1901: 311-313.

Handerson, Henry E. *Yankee in Gray: The Civil War Memoirs of Henry E. Handerson.* Cleveland, OH: Press of Case Western Reserve University, 1962.

"Harry", "Letter from the 17th Indiana Regiment," *Weekly Wabash Express*, July 22, 1863.

Heitman, Francis B. *Historical Register of the United States Army, From Its Organization, September 29, 1789, to September 29, 1889.* 2 vols. Washington, DC: U.S. Government Printing Office, 1890.

Hill, D. H. "Chickamauga—The Great Battle of the West," included in Robert U. Johnson and Clarence C. Buel, eds. *Battles and Leaders of the Civil War.* 4 vols. New York: The Century Co., 1884-1887. 3:638-662.

Historical Sketch of the Chicago Board of Trade Battery, Horse Artillery Illinois Volunteers. Chicago: The Henneberry Co., 1902.

Hood, John Bell. *Advance and Retreat: Personal Experiences in the United States and Confederate States Armies.* New Orleans: G. T. Beauregard, 1880.

Hughes, Nathaniel Cheairs, Jr., ed. *The Civil War Memoir of Philip Dangerfield Stephenson, D.D.* Baton Rouge: Louisiana State University Press, 1995.

Ikard, Robert W., ed. "Lieutenant Thompson Reports on Chickamauga: A Comparison of Immediate and Historical Perspectives of the Battle," *Tennessee Historical Quarterly* (1985): 417-438.

Indiana at Chickamauga 1863-1900: Report of the Indiana Commissioners Chickamauga National Military Park. Indianapolis: William D. Burford, 1901.

Instructions for Officers and Non-Commissioned Officers on Outpost and Patrol Duty, and Troops in Campaign, in two parts. Washington, DC: U.S. Government Printing Office, 1863.

"J. C. M." "A Story of the War," *The Sunny South*, August 15, 1896.

"J. E. R." "The Battle of Chickamauga, *The Daily Courier*, October 4, 1863.

Jordan, Thomas and J. P. Pryor. *The Campaigns of Lieut.-Gen. N. B. Forrest and of Forrest's Cavalry.* New Orleans: Blelock & Co., 1868.

Jordan, William C. *Some Events and Incidents During the Civil War.* Montgomery, AL: The Paragon Press, 1909.

King, C. B. "The Saber Brigade," *The National Tribune*, June 1, 1893.

Larson, James. *Sergeant Larson, 4th Cav.* San Antonio, TX: Southern Literary Institute, 1935.

Linville, Dale Edward. *Battles, Skirmishes, Events and Scenes: The Letters and Memorandum of Ambrose Remley.* Crawfordsville, IN: Montgomery County Historical Society, 1997.

Magee, Benjamin F. *History of the 72nd Indiana Volunteer Infantry of the Mounted Lighting Brigade*. Lafayette, IN: S. Vater and Co., 1882.

Mahan, Dennis Hart. *An Elementary Treatise on Advanced-Guard, Out-Post, and Detachment Service of Troops, and the Manner of Posting and Handling Them in Presence of an Enemy.* New Orleans: Bloomfield & Steel, 1861.

McManus, Christopher, Thomas H. Inglis and Otho James Hicks, eds. *Morning to Midnight in the Saddle: Civil War Letters of a Soldier in Wilder's Lightning Brigade*. Bloomington, IN: Xlibris, 2012.

McTeer, Will A. "Smith's Raid," *The National Tribune*, May 28, 1891.

"Military Record of Robert H. G. Minty, in the United States Volunteer Army of the Civil War, 1861-1865," included in the Proposed Volunteer Retired List, *Senate Documents* vol. 8, 59th Congress, 1st Session. Washington, D.C.: Government Printing Office, 1906.

Minnich, John W. "Unique Experiences in the Chickamauga Campaign," *Confederate Veteran* 35 (1927): 381.

Minty, Robert H. G. "Minty's Saber Brigade—The Part They Took in the Chattanooga Campaign. Preliminary Maneuvers—Chasing Dibrell's Cavalry All Over the Country. Minty's Close Call," *The National Tribune*, February 25, 1892.

—. "Minty's Saber Brigade—The Part They Took in the Chattanooga Campaign. Chickamauga—Holding the Creek Against Overwhelming Numbers. Left in the Lurch—The Saber Brigade the Last Troops to Enter Chattanooga," *The National Tribune*, March 3, 1892.

—. "Picketing and Scouting. Incidents in the History of the Saber Brigade, Army of the Cumberland," *The National Tribune*, April 4, 1895.

—. *Remarks of Brevet Major General R. H. G. Minty, Made September 18, 1895, at the Dedication of the Monument Erected to the Fourth Michigan Cavalry at Reed's Bridge, Chickamauga National Park*. Ogden, UT: Brantley Paper Co., 1896.

Morton, John Watson. *The Artillery of Nathan Bedford Forrest's Cavalry*. Nashville: Church, Smith and Lamar, 1909.

Mullié, Charles. *Biographie des célébrités militaires des armées de terre et de mer de 1789 à 1850*. 2 vols Paris: Poignavant et Compagnie, 1852.

Murray, W. J. *History of the Twentieth Tennessee Regiment Volunteer Infantry, C.S.A.* Nashville, TN: The Publication Committee, 1904.

Ninety-Second Illinois Volunteers. Freeport, IL: Journal Steam Publishing House and Bookbindery, 1875.

Oates, William C. *The War Between the Union and the Confederacy and Its Lost Opportunities with a History of the 15th Alabama Regiment and the Forty-Eight Battles in Which it was Engaged.* New York: Neale Publishing Co., 1905.

Pickrell, William N. *History of the Third Indiana Cavalry*. Indianapolis: Aetna Printing Co., 1906.

Polk, J. M. *The Confederate Soldier and Ten Years in South America*. Austin, TX: Von Boeckmann-Jones Co., 1910.

Rea, William P. "Roasted Bacon at the Bridge. 69th Ohio Man Helped Set the Bridge on Fire," *The National Tribune*, October 15, 1914.

Remarks of Brevet Major General R. H. G. Minty Made September 18, 1895 at the Dedication of the Monument Erected to the Fourth Michigan Cavalry at Reed's Bridge, Chickamauga National Park. Ogden, UT: Brantley Paper Co., 1896.

Robbins, Edward M. *Civil War Experiences 1862-1865*. Carthage, IL: privately published, 1919.

Robbins, R. B. "At Reed's Bridge: Splendid Work Done by the Cavalry on the Left at Chickamauga," *The National Tribune*, November 14, 1895.

Rogers, Robert M. *The 125th Regiment Illinois Volunteer Infantry. Attention Battalion!* Champaign, IL: Gazette Steam Print, 1882.

Salt, W. C. "Among the First," *The National Tribune*, November 29, 1917.

Shuster, James H. "Holding Reed's Bridge," *The National Tribune*, August 11, 1910.

Sipes, William B. *The Seventh Pennsylvania Veteran Volunteer Cavalry: Its Record, Reminiscences and Roster*. Pottsville, PA: Pottsville Miner's Journal, 1905.

Smith, Carolyn D., ed. "Reminiscences of J. W, Minnick, 6th Georgia Cavalry," *Northwest Georgia Historical & Genealogical Society Quarterly*, Vol. 29, No. 3 (Summer 1997): 19-28.

Smith, E. A. *Records of Walthall's Brigade of Mississippians*. Brewton, AL: n.p., 1904.

Smith, J. D. "Walthall's Brigade at Chickamauga," *Confederate Veteran* 11 (1904): 483-484.

Souvenir of the Seventeenth Indiana Regiment. A History from Its Organization to the End of the War Giving Description of Battles, etc. Elwood, IN: Model Printing & Litho. Co., 1913.

Stanley, David Sloan. *An American General: The Memoirs of David Sloan Stanley*. Ed. by Samuel W. Fordyce, IV. Santa Barbara, CA: The Narrative Press, 2003.

Steahlin, George F. "Address and Historical Sketch," *Pennsylvania at Chickamauga and Chattanooga. Ceremonies at the Dedication of the Monuments Erected by the Commonwealth of Pennsylvania*. Harrisburg: W.S. Ray, 1901: 308-311.

Stewart, Nixon B. *Dan McCook's Regiment, 52nd O. V. I. A History of the Regiment, Its Campaigns and Battles. From 1862-1865*. Alliance Ohio: Review Print, 1900.

Swan, Joseph. "At Chickamauga. A Few Observations and Criticisms Regarding that Battle," *The National Tribune*, November 30, 1893.

Thatcher, Marshall P. *A Hundred Battles in the West. St. Louis to Atlanta, 1861-1865. The Second Michigan Cavalry with the Armies of the Mississippi, Ohio, Kentucky and Cumberland, under Generals Halleck, Sherman, Pope, Rosecrans, Thomas and Others; With Mention of a Few of the Famous Regiments and Brigades of the West*. Detroit: L. F. Kilroy, 1884.

The War of the Rebellion: A Compilation of the Official Records of the Union and Confederate Armies.128 volumes in 3 series. Washington, D.C.: United States Government Printing Office, 1889.

Vale, Joseph G. "Address of Captain Joseph G. Vale," *Pennsylvania at Chickamauga and Chattanooga. Ceremonies at the Dedication of the Monuments Erected by the Commonwealth of Pennsylvania*. Harrisburg: W.S. Ray, 1901: 300-308.

—. *Minty and the Cavalry: A History of Cavalry Campaigns in the Western Armies*. Harrisburg, PA.: Edwin K. Meyers, 1886.

Van Horne, Thomas B. *History of the Army of the Cumberland. Its Organization, Campaigns and Battles*. 2 vols. Cincinnati: Robert Clarke & Co., 1875.

West, John Camden. *A Texan in Search of a Fight: Being the Diary and Letters of a Private Soldier in Hood's Texas Brigade*. Waco, TX: Press of J. S. Hill & Co., 1901.

Wilder, John T. "The Battle of Hoover's Gap," *Sketches of War History, 1861-1865*, vol. 6, Ohio Commandery, Military Order of the Loyal Legion of the United States. Cincinnati: Monfort, 1908: 168-173.

—. "Preliminary Movements of the Army of the Cumberland before the Battle of Chickamauga," *Sketches of War History, 1861-1865*, vol. 9, Ohio Commandery, Military Order of the Loyal Legion of the United States. Cincinnati: Monfort, 1911: 263-272.

Wilson, George S. "Wilder's Brigade of Mounted Infantry in the Tullahoma-Chickamauga Campaigns," *The National Tribune*, October 12 and 26, 1893.

Wilson, James H. *Under the old Flag: Recollections of Military Operations in the War for the Union, the Spanish War, the Boxer Rebellion, etc.* 2 vols. New York: D. Appleton and Co., 1912.

Secondary Sources:

Allardice, Bruce S. *Confederate Colonels: A Biographical Register*. Columbia: University of Missouri Press, 2008.

Arace, Michael. "OSU, USC Roots Lie with Ohio Brothers," *The Columbus Dispatch*, September 12, 2008.

Barnhill, Floyd R., Sr. *The Fighting Fifth. Pat Cleburne's Cutting Edge: The Fifth Arkansas Infantry Regiment, C.S.A.* Jonesboro, AR: privately published, 1990.

Bass, Ronald R. *History of the Thirty-first Arkansas Confederate Infantry*. Conway, AR: Arkansas Research, n.d.

Bauman, Ken. *Arming the Suckers, 1861-1865: A Compilation of Illinois Civil War Weapons*. Dayton, OH: Morningside, 1989.

Baumgartner, Richard A. *Blue Lightning: Wilder's Mounted Infantry Brigade in the Battle of Chickamauga*. Huntington, WV: Blue Acorn Press, 2007.

Bilby, Joseph G. *A Revolution in Arms: A History of the First Repeating Rifles*. Yardley, PA: Westholme Publishing, 2005.

Bitter, Rand K. *Minty and His Cavalry: A History of the Saber Brigade and Its Commander*. Privately published, 2006.

Bonds, Russell S. *Stealing the General: The Great Locomotive Chase and the First Medal of Honor.* Yardley, PA: Westholme Publishing, 2006.

Booth, Louise. *The Beleaguered Forty-First Tennessee*. Villa Park, CA: D. R. Booth Associates, 1996.

Bradley, Michael R. *Tullahoma: The 1863 Campaign for the Control of Middle Tennessee*. Shippensburg, PA: White Mane, 1999.

Broome, Doyle D., Jr. "Daring Rear-Guard Defense." *America's Civil War* 6 (November 1993): 34–40.

Brown, Russell K. *To the Manor Born: The Life of General William H. T. Walker*. Athens, GA: University of Georgia Press, 1994.

Collier, Calvin L. *First In—Last Out. The Capitol Guards, Ark. Brigade*. Little Rock, AR: Pioneer Press, 1961.

"Colonel Josiah B. Park," *Illinois Central Magazine*, Vol. 4, No. 12 (June 1916): 11-22.

Cummings, Charles M. *Yankee Quaker Confederate General: The Curious Career of Bushrod Rust Johnson*. Columbus, OH: The General's Books, 1993.

Davis, William C. and Julie Hoffman, eds. *The Confederate General*. 6 vols. Harrisburg, PA: National Historical Society, 1991.

Eldik, James Van. *From the Flame of Battle to the Fiery Cross*. Las Cruces, NM: Yucca Tree Press, 2001.

Evans, David. *Sherman's Horsemen: Union Cavalry Operations in the Atlanta Campaign*. Bloomington: Indiana University Press, 1996.

Green, Curtis. "Sixth Georgia Cavalry at Chickamauga," *Confederate Veteran* 8 (1900): 324.

Green, Francis A. *The Witness of a House*. Chickamauga, GA: Gordon-Lee House, 1984.

Gremillion, Nelson. *Company G 1st Regiment Louisiana Cavalry CSA*. Privately published, 1986.

Hale, Will T. and Dixon L. Merritt. *A History of Tennessee and Tennesseans: The Leaders and Representative Men in Commerce, Industry and Modern Activities*. 8 vols. Chicago: The Lewis Publishing Co., 1913.

Hazlett, James C., Edwin Olmstead, and M. Hume Parks. *Field Artillery Weapons of the Civil War*. 2nd ed. Bloomington: University of Illinois Press, 2004.

Herberich, John L. *Masters of the Field: The Fourth United States Cavalry in the Civil War*. Atglen, PA: Schiffer Publishing, 2015.

Hunt, Roger D. *Colonels in Blue: Indiana, Kentucky and Tennessee*. Jefferson, NC: McFarland & Co., 2014.

—. *Colonels in Blue: Union Army Colonels of the Civil War. The Mid-Atlantic States*. Mechanicsburg, PA: Stackpole, 2007.

Hunt, Roger D. and Jack R. Brown. *Brevet Brigadier Generals in Blue*. Gaithersburg, MD: Olde Soldier Books, 1997.

Lamers, William M. *The Edge of Glory: A Biography of General William S. Rosecrans, U.S.A.* Baton Rouge, Louisiana: Louisiana State University Press, 1961.

McElroy, Joseph C. *Chickamauga: Record of the Ohio Chickamauga and Chattanooga National Park Commission*. Cincinnati: Earhart & Richardson, 1896.

Merrill, James M. *Spurs to Glory: The Story of the United States Cavalry*. Chicago: Rand, McNally & Co., 1966.

Mowery, David L. *Morgan's Great Raid: The Remarkable Expedition from Kentucky to Ohio*. Charleston, SC: The History Press, 2013.

Peacock, Jane Bonner, ed. "A Wartime Story: The Davidson Letters, 1862-1865," *The Atlanta Historical Bulletin*, Vol. XIX, No. 1 (1975), 8-__.

Polk, William M. *Leonidas Polk: Bishop and General*. 2 vols. New York: Longmans, Green & Co., 1915.

Powell, David A. *Failure in the Saddle: Nathan Bedford Forrest, Joe Wheeler, and the Confederate Cavalry in the Chickamauga Campaign*. El Dorado Hills, CA: Savas-Beatie, 2010.

—. *The Chickamauga Campaign: A Mad Irregular Battle. From the Crossing of Tennessee River Through the Second Day, August 22-September 19, 1863*. El Dorado Hills, CA: Savas-Beatie, 2014.

Powell, William H., ed. *Officers of the Army and Navy (Volunteer) Who Served in the Civil War*. Philadelphia: L. R. Hamersly & Co., 1893.

Reid, Whitelaw. *Ohio in the War. Her Statesmen, Generals and Soldiers*. 2 vols. Cincinnati: The Robert Clarke Co., 1895.

Robertson, William Glenn. "The Chickamauga Campaign: The Armies Collide," *Blue and Gray* Magazine, Vol. 24, Issue 3 (Fall 2007): 6-29, 40-50.

Rowell, John W. *Yankee Artillerymen: Through the Civil War with Eli Lilly's Indiana Battery*. Knoxville: University of Tennessee Press, 1975.

Sartain, James. *History of Walker County Georgia*. Dalton, GA: The A. J. Showalter Co., 1932.

Schiller, Laurence D. "A Taste of Northern Steel," *North & South*, Vol. 2, No. 2 (1999): 30-46.

——. *Of Sabres and Carbines: The Emergence of the Federal Dragoon*. Danville, VA: Blue & Gray Education Society, 2001.

Schuylkill County Pennsylvania Genealogy—Family History—Biography Containing Historical Sketches of Old Families and of Representative and Prominent Citizens Past and Present. 2 vols. Chicago: J. H. Beers & Co., 1916.

Smith, Timothy B. *A Chickamauga Memorial: The Establishment of America's First Civil War National Military Park*. Knoxville: University of Tennessee Press, 2009.

Starr, Stephen Z. *The Union Cavalry in the Civil War*. 3 vols. Baton Rouge: Louisiana State University Press, 1979-1985.

Sunderland, Glenn W. *Lightning at Hoover's Gap: Wilder's Brigade in the Civil War*. New York: Thomas Yoseloff, 1969.

——. *Wilder's Lightning Brigade and Its Spencer Repeaters*. Washington, IL: The Book Works, 1984.

Thomas, Dean S. *Round Ball to Rimfire: A History of Civil War Small Arms Ammunition. Part Two: Federal Breechloading Carbines & Rifles*. Gettysburg, PA: Thomas Publications, 2002.

Trauschweizer, Ingo. *The Cold War U.S. Army: Building Deterrence for Limited War*. Lawrence: University Press of Kansas, 2008.

Warner, Ezra J. *Generals in Blue: Lives of the Union Commanders*. Baton Rouge: Louisiana State University Press, 1964.

——. *Generals in Gray: Lives of the Confederate Commanders*. Baton Rouge: Louisiana State University Press, 1959.

Weaver, Jeffrey C. *The 5th and 7th Battalions North Carolina Cavalry and the 6th North Carolina Cavalry (65th North Carolina State Troops)*. Privately published, 1995.

Welsh, Jack D., M.D. *Medical Histories of Confederate Generals*. Kent, OH: Kent State University Press, 1995.

Whalen, Charles and Barbara Whalen. *The Fighting McCooks-America's Famous Fighting Family*. Bethesda, MD: Westmoreland Press, 2006.

Williams, Samuel C. "General John T. Wilder," *Indiana Magazine of History*, Vol. 31, Issue 3 (1935): 169-203.

Wittenberg, Eric J. *The Devil's to Pay: John Buford at Gettysburg. A History and Walking Tour*. El Dorado Hills, CA: Savas-Beatie, 2014.

Wittenberg, Eric J. and Scott Mingus. *The Second Battle of Winchester: The Confederate Victory that Opened the Door to Gettysburg*. El Dorado Hills, CA: Savas-Beatie, 2015.

Wyeth, John Allan. *Life of Lieutenant-General Nathan Bedford Forrest*. New York: Harper & Bros., 1908.

Websites:

Caughey, Don. "Bates Letters—November 5, 1863," https://regularcavalryincivilwar.wordpress.com/category/bates-letters/.

——. "Fiddler's Green: Joseph Rendlebock," https://regularcavalryincivilwar.wordpress.com/2009/02/06/fiddlers-green-joseph-rendlebock/.

——. "Fiddler's Green: James B. McIntyre," http://regularcavalryincivilwar.wordpress.com/2014/12/17/fiddlers-green-james-b-mcintyre/.

——. "Fiddler's Green: Thomas Hood McCormick," https://regularcavalryincivilwar.wordpress.com/2015/02/03/fiddlers-green-thomas-hood-mccormick/.

Find-a-Grave entry for Col. James Monroe, http://www.findagrave.com/cgi-bin/fg.cgi?page=gr&GRid=70110968.

History of the City of Ringgold, Georgia. http://www.cityofringgold.com/OurHistory.aspx.

Reed family genealogy. http://www.angelfire.com/ga4/jholc/Reed.html.

Trumbull Durrance Griffin, www.wc.rootsweb.ancestry.com/cgi-bin/igm.cgi?&db=mbwheeler&id=1040772.

Index

Author

About the Author

Eric J. Wittenberg is an attorney, accomplished American Civil War cavalry historian, and an award-winning author.

In addition to penning articles for a variety of different magazines, Eric is also the author, co-author, or editor of more than twenty books on Civil War cavalry subjects, including *The Battle of Monroe's Crossroads: The Civil War's Final Campaign* (Savas Beatie, 2006), *Plenty of Blame to Go Around: Jeb Stuart's Controversial Ride to Gettysburg* (Savas Beatie, 2006), *One Continuous Fight: The Retreat from Gettysburg and the Pursuit of Lee's Army of Northern Virginia, July 4-14, 1863* (Savas Beatie, 2008), and *"The Devil's to Pay": John Buford at Gettysburg. A History and Walking Tour* (Savas Beatie, 2014), which won the Gettysburg CWRT's 2015 Book Award. His *Gettysburg's Forgotten Cavalry Actions: Farnsworth's Charge, South Cavalry Field, and the Battle of Fairfield, July 3, 1863* (Thomas, 1998; revised and expanded by Savas Beatie, 2011) was the recipient of the prestigious Bachelder-Coddington Literary Award. His latest bestseller, with Scott L. Mingus, Sr., is *The Second Battle of Winchester: The Confederate Victory That Opened the Door to Gettysburg* (Savas Beatie, 2016).

Eric, who regularly leads battlefield tours and speaks widely on the war, lives and works in Columbus, Ohio, with his wife Susan.